Recognition and Enforcement
of Annulled Foreign Arbitral Awards

VÖLKERRECHT EUROPARECHT UND INTERNATIONALES WIRTSCHAFTSRECHT

Herausgegeben von Peter Hilpold und August Reinisch

Band 12

PETER LANG

Frankfurt am Main · Berlin · Bern · Bruxelles · New York · Oxford · Wien

Claudia Alfons

Recognition and Enforcement of Annulled Foreign Arbitral Awards

An Analysis of the Legal Framework and its Interpretation in Case Law and Literature

PETER LANG
Internationaler Verlag der Wissenschaften

Bibliographic Information published by the Deutsche Nationalbibliothek
The Deutsche Nationalbibliothek lists this publication in the Deutsche Nationalbibliografie; detailed bibliographic data is available in the internet at http://dnb.d-nb.de.

ISSN 1862-457-X
ISBN 978-3-631-60378-9

www.peterlang.de

Foreword

This thesis on the question of enforcement of annulled awards would not have been possible without the dedication of Prof. Verschraegen. Happily, Prof. Verschraegen was willing to supervise my work and always kindly provided extensive support regarding discussion as well as questions. She gave shape to my thesis and helped me to focus on the subject despite many matters surrounding it. For allher commitment I am deeply indebted to Prof. Verschraegen.

In this context, I would also like to thank Prof. Reinisch, who readily agreed to take over the second appraisal and generously offered his assistance with technical questions.

I would have never addressed this topic if I had not joined the Dispute Resolution Group of Freshfields Bruckhaus Deringer LLP, where I received the opportunity of discovering the exciting world of international arbitration. In a way I had not experienced before, my work at Freshfields was challenging and encouraging at the same time. It aroused my enthusiasm for international arbitration and provided the true joy of practicing law.

My sincere thanks go to Dr. Horavth for his generosity and for integrating me into his outstanding DR-Group. Notwithstanding his extraordinary responsibilities, Dr. Horvath was always open for concerns and interested in my professional development.

In addition, without Dr. Konrad's daily commitment I would have never gained so many insights into the various facets of commercial and investment arbitration. The tasks I was assigned were manifold, exciting and always enriching. He was the one who convinced me to write a dissertation on international arbitration and assured me his full support. He kept his word and I am much obliged.

The greatest part, not only regarding this work, is owed to my dear parents. They always encouraged me to go ahead and gave me their unconditional support. I am deeply grateful for what they gave to me. To them I dedicate this thesis.

Table of Contents

List of Abbreviations

Am. Rev. Int. Arb.	American Review of International Arbitration
Arb. Int.	Arbitration International Quarterly
BB	Betriebs-Berater
BGH	Bundesgerichtshof
Ch.	Chapter
Disp. Resol. J.	Dispute Resolution Journal
doc.	Document
ed	Editor
e.g.	Example given
EGV	Vertrag zur Gründung der Europäischen Gemeinschaft
E. S. P.	Empresa de Servicios Publicos
et al.	Et alii
et seq.	Et sequens
EvBl	Evidenzblatt
fn.	Footnote
HK	Hongkong
i. a.	Inter alia
ICC	International Chamber of Commerce
ICC Bull.	ICC International Court of Arbitration Bulletin
ICLQ	International Comparative Law Quarterly
ICSID	International Centre for Settlement of Dispute Resolution
i.e.	Id est
Int. Arb. L. Rev.	International Arbitration Law Review
IPRax	Praxis des Internationalen Privat- und Verfahrensrechts
J. D. I.	Journal du Droit International
J. Int'l Arb.	Journal of International Arbitration
L.L.C.	Limited Liability Company
Ltd.	Limited
Mealey's Int. Arb. Rep.	Mealey's International Arbitration Report

MüKo	Münchener Kommentar zur Zivilprozeßordnung
Nig.	Nigeria
No.	Number
OGH	Oberster Gerichtshof
OLG	Oberlandesgericht
para.	Paragraph
RCADI	Recueil des Cours de l'Academie de Droit International
RCDIP	Revue Critique de Droit International Privé
RDAI	Revue du Droit des Affaires Internationales
RDI	Revue de Droit International
RdW	Recht der Wirtschaft
Rev. Arb.	Revue de l'Arbitrage
Rev. Crit. DIP	Revue Critique de Droit International Privé
RIS	Rechtsinformationssystem
RTD com.	Revue Trimestrielle de Droit Commercial
S. A.	Société Anonyme
Sec.	Section
S. P.	Société Privé
SZ	Zeitschrift der Savigny-Stiftung .
Tul. L. Rev.	Tulane Law Review
U. N.	United Nations
UNCITRAL	United Nations Commission on International Trade Law
U. S.	United States of America
WBl	Wirtschaftsrechtliche Blätter
Y. B. Com. Arb.	Yearbook of Commercial Arbitration
v.	Versus
Vol.	Volume
ZfRV	Zeitschrift für Rechtsvergleichung
ZPO	Zivilprozessordnung

A. Introduction

I. International Arbitration Today

Today's growing inter-connectedness of the global economy frequently involves business transactions with different legal cultures, which usually entail unfamiliarity and disproportions when at least one party is reliant on foreign legal and court systems. In the course of the last few decades, international arbitration has increasingly developed from a remedy for only "the happy few" to an ordinary means of adequate dispute resolution for such complex contractual relations. International arbitration provides parties with a neutral forum, a specialised and independent panel, and the opportunity to conduct proceedings in an agreed language and little court intervention. International arbitration also provides for them easy and efficient enforcement of the resulting award.

Another particularity of international arbitration is that distinct subject matters may be governed by different systems of law. However, the determination of the applicable law, as will be demonstrated, is a fairly debated issue among arbitration practitioners and scholars. Generally speaking, the term "applicable law" may refer to the following legal matters: (i) the main contract; (ii) the arbitration agreement; (iii) the parties' capacity to lawfully enter into an arbitration agreement; (iii) the arbitration proceedings, including the capacity and jurisdiction of the arbitrators, time limits, interim judicial assistance and the form, validity and finality of the award; and (v) the enforcement of the resulting award.

Achieving quick, easy and broad satisfaction of the awarded claims is actually the "overarching goal" of parties entering into international arbitration.[1] In the event the losing party fails to comply with the award, the prevailing party must be able to resort to an effective regime and support of state authorities in order to obtain satisfaction from the awarded claims. With enforcement usually being targeted at the losing party's assets, detecting such assets is essential at the outset because the parties are frequently "global players", with assets most likely spread

1 Lew, Proof of the Applicable Law in International Commercial Arbitration, in Festschrift für Otto Sandrock zum 70. Geburtstag, Berger/Ebke/Elsing/Großfeld/Kühne (eds.) (2000), 585.

over different states, and most likely states other than the forum state. Therefore, the arbitral award must be recognised and enforced abroad, particularly in the state where the assets are located.

II. Need for Free Circulation of Arbitral Awards

It is essential that the award be brought forward from the legal jurisdiction in which it was issued ("forum state") and enforced in another legal jurisdiction where the losing party's assets are located ("addressee state", "enforcing state"). Such portability is deemed to be "one of the most important features"[2] of an award rendered in international arbitration and is, beyond the scope of national legislation, predominantly governed by bi- and multilateral treaties aiming to connect national legal orders for creation of an intertwining effective arbitration regime. In view of the variety of such treaties, and the particular impact of the 1958 *New York Convention on the Recognition and Enforcement of Foreign Arbitral Awards* (discussed in detail below), arbitral awards are widely enforceable.[3]

1. Substance of Recognition and Enforcement

In the context of free portability of awards rendered in international arbitration, it is of basic importance to differentiate between recognition and enforcement, as do the majority of international treaties and national legal systems.[4] Even though both recognition and enforcement are involved in giving effect to the award, recognition may be carried out without enforcement, while enforcement at the same time essentially involves recognition of the award by the court rendering the leave for enforcement.[5] Thus it seems appropriate to distinguish between "recognition" from "recognition and enforcement".[6]

---

2 See Redfern/Hunter, Law and Practice of International Commercial Arbitration (2004), para. 10-20.

3 Schütze, Rechtsverfolgung im Ausland (1998), paras. 247 et seq.; Öhlberger, Vollstreckung ausländischer Schiedssprüche in Österreich und deren Formvoraussetzungen nach dem New Yorker Übereinkommen, SchiedsVZ 2007, 77.

4 Haas, Convention on the Recognition and Enforcement of Foreign Arbitral Awards, New York, June 10 1958, in Weigand (ed.), Practioner's Handbook on International Arbitration (2002), Article III para. 2.

5 Redfern/Hunter (2004), op. cit., para. 10-09 et seq.

6 Ibid., para. 10-10. In the following treatise the term "enforcement" refers to 'recognition and enforcement' unless otherwise verbalised.

a) Scope of Recognition

Recognition implies the integration of the award into the legal system of the country whose court is recognising the award, and the extension of the *res judicata* effect to the concluded dispute.[7] *Res judicata* refers to the finality of the present decision, precluding a novel reconsideration of the very subject matter between the identical parties.[8]

Generally speaking, the mere recognition of an arbitral award is a defensive measure, which is essentially carried out when the prevailing party in arbitration proceedings intends to retain the outcome and to prevent legal remedies against the award by requesting a court to identify the award as "valid and binding" on the parties.[9]

b) Scope of Enforcement

Enforcement, in contrast, is a rather offensive action also identified as "the battle to turn that award into money"[10] – providing not merely for the recognition of the legal force and effect of the award, but also ensuring its performance through the available legal channels.[11] A court considering an award as suitable for enforcement implicitly recognises the award as valid and binding upon the parties (*res judicata*) giving rise to the approval of enforcement. In this context, the concepts of recognition and enforcement interact as mutual parts, giving ample legal effect to foreign awards.[12]

---

7 Haas (2002), op. cit., Article III para. 3.; Söderlund, Lis Pendens, Res Judicata and the Issue of Parallel Judicial Proceedings, 22 J Int'l Arb (2005), 303, noting that "most legislations in continental Europe explicitly provides that 'the arbitral award is res judicata in relation to the dispute it resolves'" (e.g. Articles 1476 and 1500 of the French New Code of Civil Procedure, Article 1703 of the Belgian Judicial Code, Article 1059(1) of the Netherlands Code of Civil Procedure, Article 1055 of the German Code of Civil Procedure, whereas jurisdictions with common law tradition are rather "silent on the matter (as is, e.g. the case in Swedish law)."

8 For more detailed information on res judicata see Söderlund (2005), op. cit., 301-322.

9 See Redfern/Hunter (2004), op. cit., paras. 10-11; Haas (2002), op. cit., Article III para. 5.

10 Tannock, Judging the Effectiveness of Arbitration through the Assessment of Compliance with Enforcement of International Arbitration Awards, 21 Arb Int (2005), 83 with reference to Kaplan speech to the Franco-British Law Society in Paris in 2001, reproduced in 19 J Int'l Arb (2002), 170.

11 See Redfern/Hunter (2004), op. cit., paras. 10-11–10-12.

12 Ibid., paras. 10-11–10-12; Fouchard/Gaillard/Goldmann On International Commercial Arbitration, Gaillard/Goldmann (eds.) (1999), para. 1667.

Recognition and enforcement of arbitral awards beyond the jurisdiction of the relevant home state is predominantly governed by regional and international bi- and multilateral treaties, which contribute to a fairly wide scope and progressive development of free circulation of international arbitral awards. Therefore the international recognition and enforcement of arbitral awards is more likely, compared to national judgements,[13] whose international enforceability is not similarly promoted by an internationally effective regime, – with the exception of the European Council Regulation 44/2001, which provides for the enforceability of national court decisions in civil and commercial matters within Europe.[14] Thus, the high likelihood of worldwide recognition and enforcement of foreign arbitral awards is in fact a major advantage of arbitration as a dispute resolution mechanism in international trade.[15]

Among the multitude of treaties, the June 10 1958 New York Convention on the Recognition and Enforcement of Foreign Arbitral Awards is of enormous importance.[16] Another significant, though regional treaty is the European Convention on Commercial Arbitration of April 21 1961.[17] In addition, several bilateral treaties have been concluded between states in order to grant mutual promotion and protection of the recognition and enforcement of their corresponding arbitral awards. The concurrence of all such treaties contributed to a remarkable standardisation of recognition and enforcement of arbitral awards by the early 1960s.[18]

13 Ibid.,para. 10-17;Plaßmeier,Vollstreckungnicht„endgültiger" Schiedssprüche – Zugleich eine Anmerkung zum Beschluss des BayObLG vom 22 .11. 2002 (SchiedsVZ 2003, 142), SchiedsVZ (2004), 234-237.

14 Schütze (1998) op. cit., paras. 247 et seq.; Horvath, What weight should be given to the Annulment of an Award under the Lex Arbitri? – The Austrian and German Perspectives, 26 J. Int'l Arb (2009), 251; Redfern/Hunter (2004), op. cit., para. 10-17 at fn. 30.

15 See ibid., paras. 10-17.

16 The text of the New York Convention is available on *http://www.uncitral.org/uncitral/en/uncitral_texts/arbitration/NYConvention.html*

17 The text of the European Convention is available on *http://www.jurisint.org/en/ins/153.html*

18 Horvath (2009), op. cit., 252.

3. Moot Case

Despite the multitude – or maybe due to the multitude – of national and international legislation on enforcement of foreign awards, curious situations may occur. For example:

An award rendered in an international arbitration proceeding in Vienna is subsequently challenged in the Austrian courts, and successfully set aside based on a violation of Austrian public policy. While such a result is as equally satisfying for the defending party, as disappointing for the initially prevailing party, the tides are turning when it comes to enforcement: While English courts may give credence to the Austrian annulment decision by deciding to reject the request for enforcement of the nullified award; German courts, in contrast, may grant enforcement to the nullified award and hence give effect to something that was once called a legal *nullum*.

But it may get even worse: A second arbitration proceeding on the same matter may be initiated in Austria, and this time the underlying party of the first arbitration may obtain an award in his favour – contradictory to the original award. Subsequently the party may try to have the second award enforced in Germany. However, German courts now would have to deny enforcement of the second, though effective award, simply because the original, though nullified award, was recognised before and hence became a *res judicata* capable of precluding any further adjudications on the very subject matter. Notwithstanding, the battle is not yet lost for the second award: the English court that previously refused to enforce the first award – and thus has no res judicata in the present matter – may now readily grant enforcement of the second contradictory award.

Accordingly, both parties of the arbitration were not only able to obtain an award in their favour, but were also granted enforcement of the merits. At first glance, this might appear as an exemplary win-win situation. But the opposite is true: Both parties lost in subsequent arbitration and underwent the related enforcement proceedings – their own achievements were thus swept away.

Such an outcome contravenes the common sense of justice. Parties calling for any kind of dispute resolution have a fair interest and need for a lawful and effective decision, only open for a review by a higher level of jurisdiction, but not for contradictory findings on a parallel level, that is furthermore equally enforceable. Obviously, recognition and enforcement of arbitral awards notwithstanding their previous annulment by a foreign court is a complex issue.

As for the introductory moot case it is, in fact, improbable that an award violating Austrian public policy will "pass muster" in Germany due to several similarities between the German and the Austrian legal orders. But the illustrated constellation may as well involve states whose legal systems and concepts of public policy are significantly different and therefore more difficult to reconcile.

4. *Purpose of the Subsequent Examination*

The demonstrated feasibility to enforce arbitral awards notwithstanding a previous annulment by competent courts in the forum state has been identified as "one of the most hotly debated subjects" in international arbitration.[19]

The purpose of the subsequent thesis is to trace the origins of such remarkable outcomes in enforcement decisions. The examination therefore begins with the leading international treaties affecting recognition and enforcement of foreign arbitral awards, continuing with their complex interplay on the highly controversial phenomenon of recognition and enforcement of set aside awards.

Since the USA and West-Europe rank among the major venues for international arbitration,[20] the examination is subsequently aimed at the distinctive case law of predominantly French, U.S. American, Austrian and German courts entailing a study of the underlying conflicting concepts of the role of the arbitral seat as to the validity of arbitral awards. At the end it is attempted to point out feasible improvements towards harmonisation of the presently inconsistent case law.

19 Gaillard, The Representation of International Arbitration, 238 New York Law Journal, 4 October 2007.

20 Webster, Evolving Principles in Enforcing Awards Subject to Annulment Proceedings, 23 J Int'l Arb (2006), 205.

B. International Jurisdiction on Recognition and Enforcement

As indicated, the most significant treaties in the field of recognition and enforcement of awards rendered in an international arbitration procedure will be reviewed in the following treatise. The relevant regime governing recognition and enforcement in the individual case is affected by the features and applicable laws of both the state that issued the award as well as the state that is asked to enforce the award. There are still pivotal questions left open and they are heavily disputed.

I. First Conventions on International Arbitration

The very first multilateral treaty specifically on recognition and enforcement of arbitral awards was the Montevideo Convention of 1889 concluded by several Latin American states and thus a treaty with mere regional range.[21] More than three decades later in 1923 the first truly international treaty on arbitration matters, the Geneva Protocol came into force, followed in 1927 by the Geneva Convention, collectively the Geneva Treaties. Since the Geneva Convention refers to the Geneva Protocol and merely Signatories to the Geneva Protocol could accede to the Geneva Convention, both treaties form a kind of unit.[22]

Even though the Geneva Treaties were later displaced within the range of the New York Convention, they represent the first treaties that stayed abreast of the increasing development of international trade, which resulted in a growing significance of international arbitration. The Geneva Treaties were both drawn up under the auspices of the United Nations' predecessor, the League of Nations, and established fundamental principles in international arbitration that were adopted not only by the New York Convention, but also by conventions relying on it and the UNICTRAL Model Law.[23]

21 Redfern/Hunter (2004), op. cit., paras. 1-144 with reference to The Register of Texts of Conventions and other Instruments concerning International Trade Law, Volume II (1973), United Nations, 5.

22 Mezger (1965), op. cit., 232.

23 Redfern/Hunter (2004), op. cit., paras. 10-20.

1. Geneva Protocol (1923)

In the course of the brisk development of international trade after the First World War, international commercial arbitration was progressively used as an adequate mechanism of dispute resolution giving rise to the first truly international Convention on the field of commercial arbitration: the Geneva Protocol on Arbitration Clauses in Commercial Matters of September 24, 1923, initiated by the International Chamber of Commerce (hereinafter "ICC"), and drawn up under the auspices of the League of Nations.[24]

The Geneva Protocol consists of only four articles aimed at the enforcement of the arbitration agreement and the resulting award.[25] The Protocol provides for validity and effectiveness of arbitration agreements, a free determination of the arbitral procedure by the parties, and an obligation for the courts to grant enforcement within their territory in accordance with domestic legislation.[26] The Protocol's application is restricted to arbitration clauses concluded between parties stemming from distinct signatory states, unless the signatories availed themselves of the Protocol's optional reservation to arbitration clauses for pure commercial matters.[27] The Geneva Protocol's most serious obstacle is that its promotion of enforcements restricted to the award's forum state,[28] rather demonstrates, therefore, a rather limited scope and impact, even though its significance as to the establishment of an international standard on recognition and enforcement of international arbitration agreements and awards should not be minimised.[29]

2. Geneva Convention (1927)

The Geneva Convention on the Execution of Foreign Arbitral Awards was concluded on 26 September 1927 under the auspices of the League of Nations.[30] Its primary aim was to revise the territorial restrictions of the Geneva Protocol and enable enforcement in all states affiliated with the Convention. However, the

24 See full text list of contracting states, their dates of ratification/accession and optional reservations on Register of Texts of Conventions and other Instruments concerning International Trade Law, Vol. II, 8, van den Berg, The New York Arbitration Convention of 1958: Towards a Uniform Judicial Interpretation (1981), 6.

25 Redfern/Hunter (2004), op. cit., para. 1-145; van den Berg (1981), op. cit., 6.

26 Gaillard/Goldmann (eds.) (1999), op. cit., para. 242.

27 Geneva Protocol, Article 1

28 See Redfern/Hunter (2004), op. cit., paras. 10-22.

29 Ibid., paras. 10-21.

30 Register of Texts of Conventions and other Instruments concerning International Trade Law, Vol. II, 13.

application was still limited to awards rendered in, and to parties being subject to, a signatory.

Pursuant to the Geneva Convention both the constitution of the arbitral tribunal and the course of the arbitral procedure need to comply with the law governing the arbitration process, which is, in the majority of cases, the law of the forum state. The party seeking enforcement is obliged to prove such compliance as well as the finality of the award, documented by a corresponding declaration by a court of the forum.[31] This is perceived as a "leave for enforcement" granted by the forum state and is additional to the obligatory permission for enforcement by the court in the addressee state. Both requirements amount to the onerous *double exequatur.* Nevertheless, the Geneva Convention promoted the effectiveness of arbitral awards by precluding any review on their merits, and therefore is still entrenched in international arbitration as the principle interdiction of the *révision au fond.*[32]

Despite the limited range of the Geneva Treaties, they proved to be pivotal in the establishment of international arbitration, particularly with regard to enforcement, which was only available after protracted proceedings in national courts under applicable domestic laws before the implementation of the Geneva Treaties.[33]

II. New York Convention on the Recognition and Enforcement of Foreign Arbitral Awards (1958)

1. Historical Development

Even though the Geneva Treaties were a milestone on the way to established international arbitration, during the emergence of global markets and increasingly complex international economy after the Second World War, the Treaties' restrictions became increasingly apparent and motivated the ICC to draft another international convention, this time on the enforcement of *international* arbitral

31 Paulsson, The Case of Disregarding LSAS (Local Standard Annulments) under the New York Convention, 7 Am Rev Int'l Arb (1996), 105.

32 See Redfern/Hunter (2004), op. cit., para. 1-146; Gaillard/Goldmann (eds.) (1999), op. cit., para. 244-246; van den Berg (1981), op. cit., 6 et seq; Haas, (2002), op. cit.; Smit/Pechota, New York Convention on the Recognition and Enforcement of Foreign Arbitral Awards, in International Arbitration Treaties (2005), 35; Freyer/Gharavi, Finality and Enforceability of Foreign Arbitral Awards: From "Double Exequatur" to the Enforcement of Annulled Awards: A Suggested Path of Uniformity Amidst Diversity, 13 ICSID Review – Foreign Investment Law Journal (1998), 102; Abascal, Effects of Annulment, Dis Res Int (2008), 172; Mourre/di Brozolo, Towards Finality of Arbitral Awards: Two Steps Forward and One Step Back, 23 J Int'l Arb (2006), 186.

33 See Redfern/Hunter (2004), op. cit., paras. 10-21.

awards. The ICC saw the major shortcoming of the Geneva Convention in the restricted enforceability of only those awards that profoundly comply with the procedural domestic law of the forum state.[34] Therefore, the ICC's draft was rather aimed at awards detracted from national law, exclusively based on the arbitration agreement between the parties. The main purpose was the establishment of a *"truly international arbitration"*, by providing for uniform, fair and effective international standards on the recognition and enforcement of the arbitration agreement and the emerging award.[35]

In 1953 the ICC's drafted treaty was submitted to the United Nations Economic and Social Council (ECOSOC), whose panel of experts, however, came up with its own draft, which, though adopting some of the ICC's proposals, was more evocative of the tradition of the Geneva Treaties. The drafted Convention's name emphasised the diverging purposes: unlike the ICC draft's reference to *international* awards, the ECOSOC's Convention was directed at the recognition and enforcement of *foreign* arbitral awards[36], even though the ECOSOC identified the immanent risk of defeated enforcement notwithstanding the award's compliance with the parties' agreement, simply based on a deviation from local law.[37] The ECOSOC recognised the imminent risk that enforcement could be defeated, if the addressee's court is obliged to refuse the enforcement of an award, which indeed complies with the parties' agreement as to the nomination of the arbitral tribunal and the course of the arbitration, but does not entirely comply with the requirements of the forum state's procedural law.[38]

The ECOSOC draft was finally submitted to the Conference, which convened in the United Nations' Headquarter in New York from May 20th to June 10th 1958. Notwithstanding some restrictive amendments, the agreed main objective was to issue a new international treaty providing for recognition and enforcement of arbitration agreements and awards in order to replace the Geneva Treaties in an advanced way. On June 10th 1958 the Conference finally concluded the adoption of what is now known as the New York Convention on the Recognition and Enforcement of Foreign Arbitral Awards.[39] Even though the internationalists' draft was not adopted, it contributed to essential improvements of the New York

34 Van den Berg, New York Convention of 1958: Refusals of Enforcement, 18 ICC Bull. (2007), 25.
35 Paulsson (1996), op. cit., 104; van den Berg (1981), op. cit., 7; Smit/Pechota (2005), op. cit., 35 et seq.
36 Van den Berg (2007), op. cit., 25.
37 Ibid., 25.
38 Ibid., 25.
39 Redfern/Hunter (2004), op. cit., para. 1-147; Gaillard/Goldmann (eds.) (1999), op. cit., para. 247, 254, van den Berg (1981), op. cit., 6 et seq.

Convention like the abolition of the onerous double exequatur and the increased significance of the parties' agreements.[40]

2. Core Characteristics

The New York Convention was *ab initio* of extraordinary importance and had a great impact on the autonomy and integrity of international arbitration. With its wide range – the number of its signatories meanwhile adds up to 148 – and its innovative system facilitating recognition and enforcement of arbitral awards and promoting the validity of arbitration agreements, the New York Convention was appreciated as "the single most important pillar on which the edifice of international arbitration rests" and "perhaps could lay claim to be the most effective instance of international legislation in the entire history of commercial law".[41] On the occasion of the 50th anniversary of the New York Convention in 2008, the UN-Secretary General Ban Ki-Moon noted: "At the time this document was signed, commercial arbitration was not in wide use as an alternative to solving commercial disputes in national courts. Fifty years on, arbitration has emerged as a fundamental mechanism for solving disputes in international commerce, and the Convention is celebrated as a cornerstone of the rule of law in international trade relations."[42]

The main, though not the sole target of the New York Convention is a more simplified and effective procedure for obtaining recognition and enforcement of foreign arbitral awards and – despite its narrow naming – also of arbitration agreements.[43] Therefore, the Convention provides for unified substantive preconditions, which are, however, to be properly distinguished from requirements set out by national procedural law.[44] In order to make the Convention as autonomous

---

40 New York Convention, Articles III and IV require enforcement without a prior proof of finality in the forum state, while New York Convention, Article V(1)(d) provides for validity of the composition of the arbitral tribunal and the arbitral procedure if it was only in accordance with the parties' agreement. See also Paulsson (1996), op. cit., 105 et seq.

41 Redfern/Hunter (2004), op. cit., para. 10-23 with reference to Wetter, The Present Status of the International Court of Arbitration of the ICC: An Appraisal, American Review of International Arbitration (1990), 91; Mustill, Arbitration: History and Background, 6 J Int'l Arb (1989), 43; Schwebel, A celebration of the United Nations' New York Convention, 12 Arbitration International (1996), 823; see also Haas (2002), op. cit., para. 3.

42 http://www.un.org/News/Press/docs/2008/sgsm11397.doc.htm

43 See Redfern/Hunter (2004), op. cit., paras. 10-24; Gaillard/Goldmann (eds.) (1999), op. cit., para. 1670; Smit/Pechota (2005), op. cit., 40.

44 Gaillard/Goldmann (eds.) (1999), op. cit.,para. 1671.

as possible, its interpretations should be guided by the Convention's wording, meaning, purpose and history and by universal and comparative law principles.[45]

A particular purpose and advantage of the New York Convention is the removal of the *double exequatur*, and the reversion of the burden of proof for enforcement, which were both required by the Geneva Convention.[46] As the New York Convention, unlike its predecessor, does not require the parties to the arbitration to be subject to distinct contracting states, its range is wider and its applicability considerably improved.[47] Due to these several advancements, the New York Convention aims to replace both the Geneva Protocol and the Geneva Convention, in relation to parties being signatories to either of the Geneva Treaties and the New York Convention. Consequently, Article VII(2) provides:

> *"(t)he Geneva Protocol on Arbitration Clauses of 1923 [2] and the Geneva Convention on the Execution of Foreign Arbitral Awards of 1927 [3] shall cease to have effect between Contracting States on their becoming bound and to the extent that they become bound, by this Convention."*[48]

The 1958 New York Convention may (depending on each Signatory's date of accession) nevertheless take precedence over the 1923 and 1927 Geneva Treaties in accordance with the principle of *lex posterior derogat lex priori*.

However, the New York Convention is not a self-executing treaty in many states and its effectiveness is dependent on implementation within the signatories' national law.[49] Even the wide range of the New York Convention may be limited, if a signatory avails itself of one of the optional reservations to awards rendered in another Contracting State and/or to awards related to commercial arbitration, as permitted by Article I(3) of the New York Convention.

A controversial issue left unanswered by the New York Convention is whether the competent jurisdiction for the review of arbitral awards is the forum state or the state of enforcement.[50] Even though the ECOSOC Draft Convention specifically provides for sanctions or consequences in the case of non-compliance, the New York Convention contains no such provision.[51]

---

45 Haas (2002), op. cit., para. 8.
46 Smit/Pechota (2005), op. cit., 40; Gaillard/Goldmann (eds.) (1999), op. cit., para. 1677.
47 Smit/Pechota (2005), op. cit., 37.
48 All signatories of both the Geneva Protocol and the Geneva Convention, except for Iraq, became parties to the New York Convention.
49 Hamlin, Contractual Alteration of the Scope of Judicial Review: The U.S. Experience, 15 J Int'l Arb (1998), 61.
50 Haas, (2002), op. cit., para. 1.
51 Haas (2002), op. cit., Article III, para. 7.

3. General Applicability

Basically, the nationality of the parties is not of relevance for the applicability of the New York Convention, instead it is essential that the forum state and the state of enforcement are different.[52] However, contracting states may avail themselves of one of the reservations set out by the Convention:[53] the so-called *reciprocity reservation* provides for a limitation of the Convention's applicability merely to awards made in another contracting state, though with regard to the ever-growing range of the Convention the reciprocity reservation seems to be abstract, and increasingly obsolete.[54] The other reservation provided by the Convention is the so-called *commercial reservation* limiting the Convention's scope to awards rendered in disputes "arising out of legal relationships, whether contractual or not, which are considered as commercial under the national law of the State making such declaration".[55] This reference to national law, and the need to identify what is to be considered as commercial, caused some uncertainties, as the perception of 'commercial matters' may differ from state to state and thus does not contribute to a consistent application.[56]

The New York Convention makes several references to local laws, involving a remarkable dependency on national legislation,[57] as evidenced in Article III:

"Each Contracting State shall recognize arbitral awards as binding and enforce them in accordance with the rules of procedure of the territory where the award is relied upon, under the conditions laid down in the following articles. There shall not be imposed substantially more onerous conditions or higher fees or charges on the recognition or enforcement of arbitral awards to which this Convention applies than are imposed on the recognition or enforcement of domestic arbitral awards."

While the Convention sets forth general preconditions for recognition and enforcement, it does not provide a specific course for the recognition and enforcement procedure, but leaves it to the corresponding regulations of the enforcing state's procedural law. If the national law of the state, where enforcement is sought, fails to define distinct enforcement procedure for foreign awards, the Convention al-

52 Freyer, The Enforcement of Awards Affected by Judicial Orders of Annulment at the Place of Arbitration, in Enforcement of Arbitration Agreements and International Arbitral Awards the New York Convention in Practice, Gaillard/di Piedro (eds), (2008), 757.
53 See New York Convention, Article I(3).
54 Redfern/Hunter (2004), op. cit., paras. 10-27.
55 New York Convention, Article I(3).
56 Redfern/Hunter (2004), op. cit., para. 10-28.
57 Freyer (2008), op. cit., 757.

ternatively provides for application of the regular procedure for domestic awards. Another reference to national law was made in Article V(1)(e), which allows for observance of annulment decisions of forum states assumably based on national law. The arbitration procedure, in contrast, may be autonomously defined by the parties, while national law applies only in absence of a complete and detailed party agreement.[58]

4. Arbitration Agreement

Article II of the New York Convention obliges its signatory states to recognise parties' arbitration agreements involving present as well as future disputes arising from contractual and non-contractual legal relations. The requirements set out for the arbitration agreements are similar to those of Article I of the Geneva Protocol. Each signatory warrants recognition to any agreement in which the parties declare to submit a dispute to arbitration – provided the arbitrability of the disputed matter and the written form of the agreement. According to the Convention, written agreements involve arbitration clauses contained in a contract, as well as separate arbitration agreements, which must all be signed by each party. Due to these specifications it is acknowledged that the question as to whether the formal requirements to the arbitration agreement are met, is not governed by national procedural law, but by the New York Convention.

5. Arbitral Award

Although the New York Convention contains several provisions for arbitration agreements, its major purpose is to facilitate recognition and enforcement of arbitral awards. Principally, the Convention covers any foreign arbitral award rendered to settle a dispute between individuals or legal entities. The basic benchmarks set out by the Convention suffice to determine what constitutes a relevant arbitral award; accordingly no reference to national procedural law is made.[59]

As mentioned above, the New York Convention – unlike the ECOSOC draft covering *international* awards – refers merely to *foreign* awards. This is specified in Article 1(1):

"This Convention shall apply to the recognition and enforcement of arbitral awards made in the territory of a State other than the State where the recognition and enforcement of such

58 Paulsson (1996), op. cit., 106; Gaillard/Goldmann (eds.) (1999), op. cit., para. 1671.
59 See also Smit/Pechota (2005), op. cit., 37.

awards are sought, and arising out of differences between persons, whether physical or legal. It shall also apply to arbitral awards not considered as domestic awards in the State where their recognition and enforcement are sought."

Accordingly, an award is to be considered as *foreign*, if it is made within the territory of any state other than the contracting state in which enforcement is sought. Though Article I(1) favours a territorial approach to determine an arbitral award as foreign, the Convention does not specify what determines the location where the award is deemed to be *made*. Thus, the award may either be considered made at the place of the arbitration proceeding – which is the country where the arbitration actually took place, or the stipulated seat – or the place where the award was perfected. Whilst the majority of scholars and international arbitration practitioners concordantly favour the stipulated seat of the arbitration proceeding (the *situs arbitri*), British courts take an objective approach referring to the place of perfection of the award.[60]

Intending to embrace the majority of awards, the New York Convention's scope is extended to awards *not* being considered as *domestic* in accordance with the relevant domestic arbitration law in the country where recognition and enforcement is sought[61], as well as to awards resulting from both institutional and *ad hoc* proceedings.[62] Generally, the Convention applies to any award rendered in any state (or in accordance with any law) other than the signatory state in which enforcement is sought. Each contracting state is bound under public international law to recognise arbitral awards as 'binding' and grant enforcement in accordance with its domestic laws, which, however, may not impose more onerous penalties, such as higher fees, on foreign awards than for enforcement of domestic awards.[63]

a) Identification of Arbitral Awards

As the New York Convention does not provide further specifications, it remains the task of domestic arbitration law of the forum state to identify what qualifies an arbitral award as capable of enforcement due to the New York Convention.[64] Preconditions may set out the due manner of delivery, signatures requirements, or that the award may not just be an interim award.

60 "A document is made when and where it is perfected. An award is perfected when it is signed." Cited by Haas (2002), op. cit., Article I para. 8 with reference to House of Lords July 24, 1991, 1992 XVII YCA, 599, 603 et seq.

61 See New York Convention, Article I(1) second phrase.

62 See New York Convention. Article I(2).

63 See New York Convention, Article III.

64 Van den Berg (2007), op. cit., 39; Schwab/Walter, Schiedsgerichtsbarkeit (2005), Ch. 57 para. 20.

In this context another precondition is highly disputed, namely whether an award has to be merely binding or already final. The distinction between a final and a binding award is particularly relevant for the related distinct legal consequences.

A *binding* award – similar to an effective court decision – constitutes a complete and final disposition of the issues in dispute. As the term indicates, such an award is legally binding (*obligatoire*, *verbindlich*). A binding award is no longer subject to ordinary legal remedies to the arbitral tribunal or national courts, but extraordinary remedies, such as the application for or pendency of annulment proceedings do not impair the binding nature of an award.[65]

A *final* award also signifies a definite and final determination of all the issues submitted to arbitration so "that the rights and obligations of the two parties, with respect to the issues submitted, do not stand in need of further adjudication".[66] It concludes the arbitration and terminates the authority of the arbitrators to produce further findings.

An award may not be considered as final (*définitive*, *endgültig*) if it is still open for opposition, appeal or defeasance (opposition, appel, pouvoir en cassation). Accordingly, a *final* award is more than *binding*. It requires that the arbitral award is, besides ordinary legal remedies, also no longer open for extraordinary relief.[67]

(ii) Under the Geneva Convention, the party seeking enforcement was required to prove the award's finality under the laws of its country of origin. Therefore the award could no longer be capable of legal remedies and thus ready to obtain a leave for enforcement by domestic courts, which, in turn, is essential for enforcement abroad.[68] As indicated above, this regime requiring the pursuing party to obtain two distinct rulings on enforcement in both the forum state and the addressee state, became known as *double exequatur*.[69] The double exequatur was deemed to be "cumbersome" and one of the Geneva Convention's most significant obstacles, which the drafters of the New York Convention sought to remove and therefore debated extensively at the Conference of Plenipotentiaries at the United Nations' Headquarters. As indicated before, there were two contradictory drafts in existence. The ICC Draft on the Enforcement of International Awards simply intended

65 Ibid., Ch. 57 para. 20.

66 Rocket Jewelry Box, Inc. v. Noble Gift Packaging, Inc., 157 F.3d 174, 176 (2d Cir. 1998); ConnTech Dev. Co. v. Univ. of Conn. Educ. Props., Inc., 102 F.3d 677, 686 (2d Cir. 1996); Local 63, Textile Workers Union of Am., C.I.O. v. Cheney Bros., 141 Conn. 606, 617 (1954).

67 Schwab/Walter (2005), op. cit., Ch. 57 para. 30

68 Sampliner, Enforcement of Foreign Arbitral Awards after Annulment in their Country of Origin, 11 Mealey's Int Arb Rep (1996), 23.

69 Ibid., 23.

the requirement that the award had not been set aside instead of requiring finality[70], whereas the Report of the Committee on the Enforcement of International Arbitral Awards[71] favoured the existing double exequatur and even reinforced the notion that the award be "final and operative" in its country of origin in order to obtain enforcement abroad.[72]

(iii) Presumably the present version of the New York Convention attempted to balance the two conflicting approaches by requiring foreign awards to be 'binding' rather than 'final' as expressed in Articles III and V(1)(e).[73] While Article III sets out the general obligation for contracting states to recognise capable awards as 'binding', Article V(1)(e) provides for a reason to refuse enforcement if the losing party can prove that the award "has not become binding" on the parties.

b) Determination of the Binding Nature

Notwithstanding the expedient abrogation of the burdensome double exequatur, a new issue arose.

Article I(d) of the Geneva Convention provided for a definition of 'final'[74] awards:

"To obtain such recognition or enforcement, it shall, further, be necessary: (d) That the award has become final in the country in which it has been made, in the sense that it will not be considered as such if it is open to opposition, appeal or pourvoi en cassation (in the countries where such forms of procedure exist) or if it is proved that any proceedings for the purpose of contesting the validity of the award are pending."

70 Freyer/Gharavi (1998), op. cit., 103 with reference to the ICC Brochure No. 174 (Paris 1953).

71 Ibid., 103: "The Committee was established on April 6, 1954, by resolution of the United Nation's Economic and Social Council 'to study the matter raised by the International Chamber of Commerce... and to report its conclusions to the Council, submitting such proposal as it may deem appropriate, including if it seems fit, a draft convention.' The Committee delivered its report with a Draft Convention on the Recognition and Enforcement of Foreign Arbitral Awards on 28 March 1955 (the Report), U.N. Doc. E/2704 and Corr. 1."

72 Freyer/Gharavi (1998), op. cit., 103/104.

73 Van den Berg (2007), op. cit., 28; Freyer/Gharavi (1998), op. cit., 102; Schwab/Walter (2005), op. cit., Ch. 57 para. 19; Sampliner (1996), op. cit., 23; Freyer/Gharavi (1998), op. cit., 104: The "binding" award requirement of Article V(1)(e) of the New York Convention prevailed over other proposed alternatives as well. See generally van den Berg, (1981), op. cit., 334-37.

74 For further details on the determination of finality in terms of the Geneva Convention see Sampliner, Enforcement of Nullified Foreign Arbitral Awards – Chromalloy Revisited, 14 J Int'l Arb (1997), 146 with reference to 92 League of Nations Treaties Series 302, 305, Article I(d) (1929-30); Lew (2000), op. cit., 587.

The New York Convention, in contrast, gives no reference to identify awards as binding, though it requires its signatories to recognise awards as such.[75] Basically two controversial concepts may be distinguished in determining an award's binding nature.[76]

(i) The apparently prevailing approach is to rely on the applicable law of the chosen forum state in order to determine whether an award has become binding.[77] Accordingly the applicable law determines the award's binding effect, and thereby its capability of being enforced abroad. Since the New York Convention provides for immediate recognition of "binding" awards, the legal effect is consequently extended throughout the recognising state.

In order to comprehend the weight given to the forum state in determining the binding character of an arbitral award, it is essential to recall the basic notions of legal systems at the time when the New York Convention was drafted, i.e. when far more value was attached to the national laws of the forum state than today. In the light of this historical context, it can hardly be assumed that the drafters conceived the binding nature of a 'foreign' award to derive solely from the Convention, utterly detached from the acceptance by national law.[78]

The most restrictive among the national approaches considered 'binding' as a synonym for 'final', thus similarly intending and reiterating the double exequatur requirement of the Geneva Convention, albeit "in a more condensed and abstract form".[79] This interpretation, however, was soon rejected due to its incompatibility

75 See New York Convention, Article III. "Professor Pieter Sanders, a member of the Dutch delegation to the Conference, predicted at that time the possible negative consequences of such omission: From "final" in the Geneva Convention, reintroduced in the text of the 1955-Draft as "final and operative" we come to "binding" in the New York Convention. What does this word "binding" mean? The term is the result of a compromise and will, I fear, cause a diversity of interpretations in countries where enforcement is sought and the defendant tries to prevent execution in proving to the competent authority that 'the award has not yet become binding on the parties'", Freyer/Gharavi (1998), op. cit., 103 with reference to Sanders, New York Convention on the Recognition and Enforcement of Foreign Arbitral Awards, VI Netherlands Int'l L. Rev 43, 55 (1959).

76 Van den Berg, Explanatory Note on the Hypothetical Draft Convention on International Enforcement of Arbitration Agreements and Awards (2008) para. 87, available online on http://www.arbitration-icca.org/media/0/12133703697430/explanatory_note_ajb_rev06.pdf

77 Freyer/Gharavi (1998), op. cit., 105; Gaillard/Goldmann (eds.) (1999), op. cit., para. 1677 et seq.; Schwab/Walter (2005), op. cit., Ch. 57 para. 20.

78 Gaillard/Goldmann (eds.) (1999), op. cit., para. 1682 with reference to Paulsson, Arbitre et juge en Suède –Exposé général et réflexions sur la délocalisation des sentences arbitrales, Rev. Arb. (1980), 467-68.

79 Ibid., para. 1679 with reference to Goldmann, Arbitrage (droit international privé), in Encyclopédie Dalloz – Droit International (1968), 288.

with the New York Convention's admitted intention to amend the double exequatur requirement of the Geneva Convention.

Another suggestion was to view an award as 'binding' if it was "not open to an arbitral – as opposed to a judicial – appeal",[80] or even to no appeal at all. The award could only be deemed as 'binding' if it were no longer subject to legal remedies, neither arbitral nor national.[81] Similarly it was proposed to consider an award as binding, provided it had not yet been set aside or suspended, which is the approach approved by English courts.[82] However, it might be assumed this approach would not entirely comply with Article V(1)(e) enumerating non-binding nature and setting aside or suspension as alternatives rather than in correlation.[83] But on the contrary, Article V(1)(e) contrasts the "not yet binding nature" of the award to its setting aside or suspension, which, in fact, implies that an award that has not yet become binding is as less binding as an award which has been set aside or suspended. As Article V(1)(e) expressly refers to the "competent authority" of the applicable law for deciding on a setting aside or suspension of the award, it appears "paradoxical" if the conception should not hold true to determine whether the award "has (not) yet become binding on the parties". Besides, in the context of Article V(1)(e) and Article VI, which provides for adjournment of the enforcement procedure while an annulment action is pending, it becomes apparent that a mere claim for annulment does not suffice to remove the award's binding nature.[84]

It is adduced that an award's binding nature cannot "exist in isolation", but must be recognised by a legal system. Even though it may be countered that the New York Convention's immanent legal order may substantiate the award's binding character, it is unlikely that the Convention in fact "intended to go that far" being clearly dedicated to "foreign" (as opposed to international or autonomous) awards.[85]

80 Ibid., para. 1679; Freyer/Gharavi (1998), op. cit., 106 at fn. 28.

81 Schwab/Walter (2005), op. cit., Ch. 57 para. 20.

82 Freyer/Gharavi (1998), op. cit., 106: "On at least two occasions, English courts have proceeded from the assumption that an arbitration award becomes "binding" immediately upon publication to the parties and continues to bind the parties unless it is set aside or suspended by a competent authority" see Rosseel NV v. Oriental Commercial & Shipping Co (UK) Ltd [1991] 2 Lloyds Rep. 625; Hiscox v Outhwaite [1991] 3 All E.R. 124 (Court of Appeal); aff'd on differènt grounds by the House of Lords [1991] 3 AII E.R. 641.

83 New York Convention, Article V(1)(e): The award has not yet become binding on the parties, or has been set aside or suspended by a competent authority of the country in which, or under the law of which, that award was made.

84 Freyer/Gharavi (1998), op. cit., 104/105; See also the District Court of Amsterdam's decision of 12 July 1984 in Southern Pacific Properties Ltd. v. The Arabic Republic of Egypt, X Y. B. Com. Arb. (1985), 487, 489.

85 Gaillard/Goldmann (eds.) (1999), op. cit., para. 1682.

Some reject the non-autonomous recourse to national laws as a quasi renewal of the "onerous double exequatur".[86] However, the mere determination of the award's binding nature in accordance with the applicable law of the forum state does not presuppose an official act in terms of a leave for enforcement (as required by the double exequatur).[87] Further, it is objected that the reference to particular national laws threatens a uniform enforcement practice under the New York Convention, since the preconditions for a binding award set out by distinct laws may vary.[88] But this objection does not take into account that the New York Convention's overarching aim is to facilitate enforcement, and not to harmonise it. A non-autonomous approach based on national laws is therefore well in accordance with the concept of the New York Convention.

(ii) The second approach taken to determine the binding nature of an arbitral award does not rely on national laws, but rather merely on the New York Convention itself, and is therefore an autonomous approach, which may be subclassified in variations.[89]

One sub-approach attempts to identify the award's binding character rather in a reverse way, focusing on the emergence of non-binding nature, and has *inter alia* been taken by a U.S. court.[90] It is held that the award's binding nature could not be disproved due to legal positions in the forum state, but only if defects of the arbitral procedure or the award itself capable of appeal to a second arbitration panel indicate the award's non-binding nature.[91]

The most popular notion of the binding nature among the autonomous approaches basically distinguishes between "ordinary and extraordinary recourse" and was even suggested for adoption into the New York Convention.[92] According

86 Schwab/Walter (2005), op. cit., Ch. 57 para. 20.

87 See Gaillard/Goldmann (eds.) (1999), op. cit., para. 1680.

88 Freyer/Gharavi (1998), op. cit., 105 with reference to the quote of van den Berg, The New York Convention of 1958: Towards a Uniform Judicial Interpretation (1981), 341.

89 Schwab/Walter (2005), op. cit., Ch. 57 para. 20.

90 Freyer/Gharavi (1998), op. cit., 106: Fertilizer Corp. v. IDI Mgmt., Inc. (517 F Supp. 948, 957-58 (S.D. Ohio 1981)), "where the court held that a pending court appeal in India, the place of arbitration, did not alter the "binding" effect of the award."

91 Gaillard/Goldmann (eds.) (1999), op. cit., para. 1679 with reference to David, Arbitration in International Trade, (1985), 441: „Compare with Henri Motulsky who defines „binding" as meaning „having an authority comparable to that of res judicata" (Ecrits – Vol. 2 – Etudes et notes sur l'Arbitrage 396 (1974) (L'exécution des sentences arbitrales étrangères")).

92 Freyer/Gharavi (1998), op. cit., 106; See also van den Berg's Hypothetical Draft Convention: "The Draft Convention retains the prevailing interpretation that the word "binding" means that an award is not binding if it is still open to appeal on the merits before an appeal arbitral tribunal or a court in the country of origin. Appeal arbitra-

to this approach an award that is still capable of *ordinary* recourse on its merits, be it to a national court or a second-tier arbitration, may not be considered as binding. An award still subject to *extraordinary* recourse like actions for annulment "on non-merits grounds" in contrast may be deemed as binding.[93] This approach also relies on notions of national law and therefore may equally produce inconsistent findings, as national laws may have distinct regimes and understanding of ordinary and extraordinary recourse, or even do not distinguish at all.[94] Therefore, it has been held that at least the "essence" of such distinction should be retained,[95] but was, however, not adopted by the authors of the New York Convention.

(iii) National courts generally agree that it is not necessary to submit a leave for enforcement of the forum state in order to recognise an award as "binding", which is in accordance with the New York Convention's intention of abolishing the double exequatur.[96] In contrast, national courts do not likewise agree when it comes to determining an award's binding nature.[97] While Italian, Swedish, Dutch and Belgian courts are deemed to favour an autonomous approach, French courts and the Swiss Federal Tribunal assess the binding nature of an award by reference to the law of the country of origin.[98] In 2002, a German court was asked to determine the binding nature of an arbitral award, when there were still second-tier' confirmation proceedings' pending in the forum state.[99] Notwithstanding the pending confirmation proceedings, the court assumed the award's binding nature

tion is allowed in a number of countries and specifically agreed to, in particular, in commodity arbitration. An appeal on the merits before a court is rare nowadays. The possibility of a setting aside or annulment of an arbitral award in the country of origin is not equivalent to an appeal on the merits. Consequently, in most cases an arbitral award can be enforced under the Draft Convention as soon as it is rendered.", van den Berg (2008), op. cit., para. 87, available online at *http://www.arbitration-icca.org/media/0/12133703697430/explanatory_note_ajb_rev06.pdf*

93 Gaillard/Goldmann (eds.) (1999), op. cit., para. 1679; Freyer/Gharavi (1998), op. cit., 105.

94 Ibid., 106 at fn. 27.

95 Ibid., 106 at fn. 26 with reference to van den Berg (1981), op. cit..

96 Freyer/Gharavi (1998), op. cit., 104 with reference to van den Berg (1981), op. cit., 337; Decision of the Court of First Instance of Strasbourg of October 9, 1970, Rev. Arb. (1970), 166, 169; Sanders, A Twenty Years' Review of the Convention on the Recognition and Enforcement of Foreign Arbitral Awards, 13 Int'l Law (1979), 275-76.

97 Van den Berg (2007), op. cit., 28 et seq.

98 S.E.E.E. v. Yugoslavia, Court of Appeal of Rouen decision of 13 November 1984, Rev. Arb. (1985), 115, 127; Swiss Federal Court in the matter of Joseph Muller A.G. v. Sigval Bergesen, on 26 February 1982, excerpt in IX Y. B. Com. Arb. (1984), 437, 438.

99 Plaßmeier, Vollstreckung nicht "endgültiger" Schiedssprüche – Zugleich eine Anmerkung zum Beschluss des BayOBLG vom 22. November 2002 (SchiedsVZ 2003, 142), SchiedsVZ 2004, 234.

and permitted for enforcement. This decision was criticised in Germany, as German procedural law[100] requires foreign court decisions to be final in order to be recognised if they are beyond the scope of the Brussels I Regulation.[101] As to arbitral awards, however, it is widely accepted in Germany that "binding nature" implies a lower standard than "finality". The German Code of Civil Procedure, for example, allows for the withdrawal of a leave for enforcement, if the award was set aside in its forum state.[102] Such provision would be dispensable, if arbitral awards were solely enforceable when they are already final.

(iv) In the light of the wording of the New York Convention, Articles III, V(1)(e) and VI, as well as in consideration of the Convention's subordinate purpose of harmonisation, it is more reasonable to determine an award's binding nature pursuant to the national law of its forum state. However, parties may achieve predictability by stipulating that their resulting award shall be "binding and enforceable" with issuance, or by choosing a corresponding set of arbitration rules.[103]

In practice, an absence of the binding nature has seldom caused a refusal of enforcement and the inconsistent approaches have not been of significant impact. However, the lack of clarity involved expensive litigation on identifying the substance of an award's binding character as well as redundantly protracted delays in the actual enforcement procedure.[104]

c) Preclusion of révision au fond

In order to ensure that arbitral awards are not reduced to mere "lower instance" of ordinary courts and to ensure finality of arbitral awards, it is essential to limit the possibility of review. The most significant restriction is that national courts may not set aside an award merely because they find that the arbitrators unduly interpreted the contract or the applicable law. The preclusion of any re-examination on

100 German Code of Civil Procedure, Section 723(2)(1).

101 Council Regulation (EC) No. 44/2001 of 22 December 2000 on Jurisdiction and the Recognition and Enforcement of judgements in Civil and Commercial Matters; see in greater detail below.

102 German Code of Civil Procedure, Section 1061(3): If the award is set aside abroad after having been declared enforceable, application for setting aside the declaration of enforceability may be made.

103 Most institutional arbitration rules govern that the award shall be (final and) binding on the parties: the International Arbitration Rules of the American Arbitration Association, Art. 27(1); the Rules of Arbitration of the International Chamber of Commerce, Art. 28(6); the London Court of International Arbitration Rules, Art. 26(8); and the Arbitration Rules of the United Nations Commission on International Trade Law (UNCITRAL Rules), Art. 32(2).

104 Freyer/Gharavi (1998), *op. cit.*, 102/103.

the merits of the award, a so-called révision au fond, is widely acknowledged and ruled by several national arbitration laws and courts,[105] and is also manifested in the New York Convention, as a review on the merits does not constitute a reason for refusal or adjournment.[106] Such preclusion is based on the conception that the admittance of arbitration by national legal orders implies a duty to occasionally tolerate undue awards, even if the award may infringe cogent law.[107]

d) Ordre Public Exception

With arbitral tribunals adjudicating instead of the national courts the call for state control arises, since each legal order and society have a fair interest in ensuring the observance of basic concepts of legal justice. Thus, there is one fundamental exception to the interdiction of re-examination of an arbitral award – once called the "emergency brake of preventing shocking outcomes":[108] A state's *ordre public*.

(i) In order to warrant their compliance with the local public policy, arbitral awards have to pass through national procedures, which are aimed at detecting any potential misuse of the far-reaching jurisdiction of the arbitrators.

As no state can be obliged to give effect to an award which is in breach of its fundamental legal concepts, the ordre public control may either be part of a judicial review conducted by a court of the state in which or pursuant to the law of which the arbitration took place, but may also take place in the context of the recognition and enforcement procedure of the state where a party seeks to rely on the award.

In the light of such potential impact of public policy on the effectiveness of the arbitral award, each arbitrator should carefully take into consideration the relevant ordre public at least of the state of the arbitration; (the state of enforcement is not

---

105 Representatively for many see Gaillard/Goldmann (eds.) (1999), *op. cit.*, para. 1693; van den Berg (2007), *op. cit.*, 16; Redfern/Hunter (2004), *op. cit.*, paras. 10-33; Reiner, *Zur Vollstreckung eines Schiedsspruchs nach dem Europäischen Übereinkommen von 1961 trotz Aufhebung im Ursprungsland und zum Umfang der ordre public-Kontrolle nach Artt. 81, 82 EGV*, IPRax 2000, 325 et seq. with reference to Austrian Supreme Court, decision of 23 February 1998 – 3 Ob 115/95; Mourre/di Brozolo (2006), *op. cit.*, 173; as will be seen in the U.S. judgement in the matter of Chromalloy.

106 *Ibid.*, 172.

107 Higher Regional Court of Thuringia, *Zum Umfang der Überprüfungskompetenz des Vollstreckungsgerichts nach erfolglosem Aufhebungsverfahren im Ursprungsstaat*, SchiedsVZ 2008, 45; Michaels, *Anerkennung internationaler Schiedssprüche und ordre public*, Anm. zu OGH 23.02.1998, 3 Ob 115/95 (OLG Wien 10.07.1995, 14 R 56/95; LG Wien 01.12.1994, 30 Nc 102/89), ZfRV 1999, 6.

108 This is not an official translation, but the personal translation of the authoress. Schwind, *Handbuch des österreichischen internationalen Privatrechts* (1975), 80.

necessarily known to the arbitrators). But for the sake of the finality of arbitral awards, national courts are required to resort to the public policy clause with caution.[109]

(ii) Although it is undisputed that public policy is to be respected in certain regards, the scope of its meaning is naturally rather vague.[110] While it is unanimously accepted that dispositive law is not part of ordre public, the ordre public relevance of substantive laws – provisions indispensible by party autonomy – is disputed. However, it is advisable not to consider each cogent provision as part of the ordre public, but rather laws properly deemed to provide appropriate guidance for the arbitration, such as basic rules and principles of law.[111] Therefore ordre public basically covers "all provisions of cogent law affecting the basis of public or economic life, as well as the fundamental conception of justice", constitutional rights such as personal liberty, equality and the prohibition of (any kind of) discrimination are of particular impact, as well as a minimum standard of procedural justice.[112] In this regard it is to be considered that the scope of the aforementioned fundamental concepts may not be confined and are subject to temporal changes, whereas the court in each case considers the ordre public that is relevant at the time of the decision on recognition and enforcement, not of the time when the award was rendered.[113]

Taking account of the exceptional character of the ordre public reservation not every discrepancy with national cogent law constitutes a breach of public policy.[114] A violation of public policy is only indicated, in the event the award's recognition is deemed to be "manifest incompatible" with the collective sense of justice.[115] These high requirements are necessary for maintaining the exceptional character of the remarkable ordre public reservation.

---

109 Reiner (2000), *op. cit.*, 325 et seq. with reference to Austrian Supreme Court, decision of 23 February 1998 – 3 Ob 115/95; Oberhammer, Gemeinschaftsrecht und schiedsrechtlicher ordre public, RdW 1999, 63/64.

110 *Ibid.*, 62.

111 *Ibid.*, 62, Higher Regional Court of Thuringia (2008), *op. cit.*, 45.

112 This is not an official translation but the personal translation of the authoress; Higher Regional Court of Thuringia (2008), *op. cit.*, 45; BGHZ 50, 370, 376; BGHZ 54, 140; BGH, NJW-RR 1991, 1213; Reiner (2000), *op. cit.*, 325 with reference to Austrian Supreme Court, decision of 23 February 1998 – 3 Ob 115/95; Oberhammer (1999), *op. cit.*, 62.

113 Reiner (2000), *op. cit.*, 326.

114 Different: Oberhammer (1999), *op. cit.*, 63.

115 Kropholler, Internationales Privatrecht (2006), 246 et seq.; Schütze/Tschernig/Wais, Handbuch des Schiedsverfahrensrechts (1985), para. 542; Siehr, Internationales Privatrecht (2001), 485; Brussels I Regulation, Article 34 No. 1; the German Code of Civil Procedure, Section 328(1)(4);

However, it is still disputed as to how far reaching the ordre public control in each case may be, if the judge is bound to the arbitrators' finding of the facts or whether the breach of the ordre public is to be apparent.[116] As an English court once outlined, the interplay of the acknowledged interdiction of révision au fond on the one hand, and the need for a review of serious defects on the other, before giving effect to an award is "the balancing exercise between the competing public policy considerations of finality and illegality".[117]

Since 2006 Austrian law has expressly provided for the setting aside of an arbitral award if it contradicts fundamental concepts of the Austrian legal order.[118] While such fundamental concepts derive from constitutional law, each constitutional right is not a part of the ordre public. Rather those provisions that manifest "indispensible fundamental concepts" constitute the ordre public.[119]

The Austrian Supreme Court manifested such limited scope of review holding that not every inconsistency with national law, nor even each violation of cogent provisions, may be interpreted as breaching Austrian ordre public. A considerable breach of public policy arises only if the finding of the award is "apparently incompatible with fundamental perceptions of the Austrian legal order".[120] Such an incompatibility is to be apparent, since a foreign arbitral award may by no means be comprehensively reviewed in respect of its factual or legal findings.[121]

In a more liberal manner, the German Federal Court of Justice, approved by German scholars, has repeatedly held that national courts may autonomously assess a violation of public policy, irrespectively of the finding of facts and legal perception of the arbitral tribunal in order to warrant legal justice, which would be vitiated if national courts were completely bound to the arbitrators' findings.[122] However, this approach is also criticised as expanding the ordre public control to a révision au fond, and infringing on the arbitrators' autonomous legal perception. Therefore, such expansion of court review is deemed to be a contravention of the purpose of international arbitration for providing an efficient and competent

116 Reiner (2000), *op. cit.*, 325.

117 Mourre/Radicati di Brozolo (2006), *op. cit.*, 174 with reference to Westacre Investments v. Jugoimport [1999] 3 All E.R. 864 (Q.B.); [1999] 3 W.L.R. 811 (C.A.).

118 Austrian Code of Civil Procedure, Article 611(2)(5): "An award shall be set aside if… the arbitral procedure was not carried out in accordance with the basic values of the Austrian legal system (ordre public)."

119 Oberhammer (1999), *op. cit.*, 62; Reiner (2000), *op. cit.*, 325 with reference to Austrian Supreme Court, decision of 23 February 1998 – 3 Ob 115/95.

120 *Ibid.*, 326 with reference to Austrian Supreme Court, decision of 23 February 1998 – 3 Ob 115/95.

121 *Ibid.*, 326 with reference to Austrian Supreme Court, decision of 23 February 1998 – 3 Ob 115/95.

122 Schwab/Walter (2005), *op. cit.*, Ch. 57 para. 23; Reiner (2000), *op. cit.*, 326.

mechanism for dispute resolution by rather subordinating arbitration to ordinary stages of appeal.[123]

Similarly, the Paris Court of Appeal restricted public policy controls over awards that were rendered in international arbitration in order to maintain the "final character" of the arbitrators' decision on the merits. For the sake of maintaining finality of arbitral awards, according to the Paris court, "a public policy argument can be accepted only when the enforcement of the award would violate in an unacceptable way our public policy, such violation having to affect in a manifest manner an essential rule of law or a principle of fundamental importance. (…) [A] violation of public policy must be 'flagrant, effective and concrete", which is unlikely if the violation could only be detected by an extended re-examination of the merits of the case.[124]

Courts in the United States also promote a narrow perception of public policy review of context of review of arbitral awards, since public policy is not intended "to protect parochial national interests (…) a circumscribed public policy doctrine was contemplated by the [New York Convention] framers and every indication is that the US, in acceding to the Convention, meant to circumscribe it to this supranational emphasis."[125]

An English court emphasised the counterpart of public policy considerations of illegality was the "great weight (…) attached to the public policy of sustaining the finality of international arbitration' and drew the 'conclusion that the public policy of upholding international awards on the facts' may overbalance" the public policy in discouraging international commercial corruption."[126]

Various court decisions and contributions of scholars and practitioners noted that the examination of an award's consistency with public policy "is a highly disciplined teleological exercise" and still not exhaustively confined and standardised.[127]

(iii) Further, it has yet to be clarified whether the judicial review involves the relevant domestic public policy, or should rather be guided by a higher level of public policy beyond the national legal order in terms of an international and transnational ordre public.[128]

---

123 *Ibid.*, 326 with further references.

124 Mourre/Radicati di Brozolo (2006), *op. cit.*, 177 with reference to André v. Tradigrain, Paris, 1e ch. C, 14 june 2001, Rev. Arb. (2001), 773.

125 *Ibid.*, 173.

126 *Ibid.*, 174 with reference to Westacre Investments v. Jugoimport, [1999] 3 All E.R. 864(Q.B.); [1999] 3 W.L.R. 811 (C.A.).

127 Reisman, ICCA Congress June 2006, ICCA Congress Series No. 18 (2007).

128 Schlosser, Das Recht der privaten internationalen Schiedsgerichtsbarkeit (1989), para. 868 et seq.

While national public policy is acknowledgedly maintained in national legislation, international public policy is deemed to be "much narrower",[129] therefore, not every issue that is subject to national public policy falls under international public policy.[130] International public policy is intended to refer to a particular part of public policy, which is either "common to many States" or covered by public international law and which, in case of violation, impedes giving effect to a foreign law, judgement, or award.[131]

Putting emphasis on the autonomy of international arbitration, the number of proponents interpreting international public policy "from a non-national, a-national or transnational standard" is growing, albeit without clear outlines.[132] Transnational public policy is, unlike its national or international counterparts, deemed to be independent of national laws, although it might involve "principles of public international law" while it additionally implies "public policy considerations that transcend state boundaries"[133] such as the maintenance of cultural goods, "labour standards, security matters and the right of indigenous peoples"

---

129 See also paragraph 11 of The International Law Association's Final Report on Public Policy as a Bar to Enforcement of International Arbitral Awards, New Dehli Conference (2002) cited by Pryles, *Reflections on Transnational Public Policy*, 24 J Int'l Arb (2007), 3.

130 Van den Berg (2007), *op. cit.*, 32.

131 Pryles (2007), *op. cit.*, 3 quoting paragraph 11 of The International Law Association's Final Report on Public Policy as a Bar to Enforcement of International Arbitral Awards, New Dehli Conference (2002).

132 Lew, *Achieving the Dream: Autonomous Arbitration*, 22 Arb Int'l (2006), 201.

133 Pryles (2007), *op. cit.*, 3 quoting The International Law Association's Interim Report on Public Policy as a Bar to Enforcement of International Arbitral Awards, London Conference (2000): *"The concept of 'transnational public policy' or 'truly international public policy' is of even more restrictive scope, but of universal application-comprising fundamental rules of natural law, principles of universal justice, jus cogens in public international law, and the general principles of morality accepted by what are referred to as 'civilised nations'. Whilst we know of no examples where a court has expressly applied 'transnational public policy', there are a few decisions which clearly make reference to the concepts as, for example, the Milan Court of Appeals decision ... Also the Swiss Federal Tribunal in W v. F (1994) was in favour of taking into account a 'universal conception of public policy, under which an award will be incompatible with public policy if it is contrary to the fundamental moral or legal principles recognised in all civilised countries.' And a number of cases have recognised certain activities, such as corruption, drug trafficking, smuggling and terrorism, to be illicit virtually the world over."* For further discussion on transnational public policy in international arbitration see Lalive, *Transnational (or Truly International) Public Policy and International Arbitration*, in *Comparative Arbitration Practice and Public Policy in Arbitration*, 3 ICCA Congress Series (1998).

and prevention of "sale and traffic of drugs, bribery and corruption, slavery and embargos of economic sanctions".[134]

A proponent of a transnational conception of public policy control is the Swiss Federal Tribunal, which clarified that a review of arbitral awards is to be "restricted to a limited number of transnational principles accepted not only by the forum, but by the international community at large."[135]

While proponents of transnational public policy emphasise that "we are living in a world of juridical pluralism" wherefore "transnational public policy is a must",[136] opponents assertively counter that the standard for the validity of an arbitral procedure "is the policy of the legal system which governs the dispute and not an artefact policy created by the arbitrators for that particular case."[137] Hence, the existence and necessity of transnational public policy is still intensely debated, as are its vague confines and application in international arbitration.[138] In other words, transnational public policy remains "a matter of some obscurity".[139]

(iv) In principle, the standard for violations of an international or even transnational ordre public is higher than in national terms. In this regard it appears questionable whether national courts of signatories to international conventions may at all merely rely on their domestic public policy in international issues or whether courts should rather be restrained in resorting to the public policy reservation. Restraint may be especially required, because in international regimes the reservation clause is appreciated as "international/transnational ordre public". Nevertheless, it is widely acknowledged that states may examine whether foreign judicial acts, which they intend to give effect to, comply with their national ordre public. But it remains undefined and controversial, to what extent such examination may be conducted or – differently put – how obvious potential violations have to occur in order to justify a judicial review.

A "minimalist trend" aims to restrict judicial controls of arbitral awards "to the most evident and manifest violations of principles and values of fundamental importance" without admitting a comprehensive re-examination of merits of the

---

134 Pryles (2007), *op. cit.*, 3 with reference to Lalive, Transnational (or Truly International) Public Policy and International Arbitration, in Comparative Arbitration Practice and Public Policy in Arbitration, 3 ICCA Congress Series (1998).

135 Mourre/di Brozolo (2006), *op. cit.*, 175 with reference to United Arab Emirates v. Westland Helicopters, Swiss Federal Tribunal, 19 April 1994. *"This solution applies only where the Swiss public policy is not at stake."*

136 Pryles (2007), *op. cit.*, 2 with reference to Catherine Kessedijan, ICCA Congress June 2006, ICCA Congress Series No. 18 (forthcoming 2007).

137 Reisman (2007), *op. cit.*

138 Pryles (2007), *op. cit.*, 6.

139 *Ibid.*, 1.

award, except under "exceptional circumstances".[140] However, in the light of the vague confines of this exception to the interdiction of a révision au fond, public policy might still be "a very dangerous instrument in the hands of a court seeking to review the merits of an award and to deprive it of effects."[141]

While the interplay of the interdiction of re-examination of the merits of the case and the maintenance of public policy is, in the first place, to be respected in the award's forum state, it is also to be considered within the recognition and enforcement procedure in another state, even though an English judge once held that "[public policy] is never argued at all but where other points fail."[142]

6. Application for Recognition and Enforcement

The core provisions on the recognition and enforcement procedure itself are contained in New York Convention, Articles IV, V and VI.

Article IV involves simplifications of the formal enforcement proceeding by providing merely for a minimum standard of documentation proof to be produced by the party applying for enforcement warranting authenticity and content of both the award and the underlying arbitration agreement.[143] As indicated above, a main achievement of the New York Convention in this context is redeploying the burden of proof from the pursuing party to the defending party.[144] The New York Convention obliges the enforcement seeking party to furnish the authenticated original or a duly certified copy of both the award and the arbitration agreement, if necessary supplemented with an official translation to the language of the enforcing state. As soon as these preconditions are supplied they constitute a *prima facie* evidence in favour of granting enforcement arbitral award.[145] The court may only reject

140 Mourre/di Brozolo (2006), *op. cit.*, 178.

141 *Ibid.*, 172.

142 Referred to by Redfern/Hunter (2004), *op. cit.*, para. 10-51.

143 Van den Berg (2007), *op. cit.*, 45; Gaillard/Goldmann (eds.) (1999), *op. cit.*, para. 1673.

144 In contrast to New York Convention, Article V(1), see Geneva Convention, Article 4(2) and (3): The party relying upon an award or claiming its enforcement must supply, in particular: (1) The original award or a copy thereof duly authenticated, according to the requirements of the law of the country in which it was made; (2) Documentary or other evidence to prove that the award has become final, in the sense defined in Article 1 (d), in the country in which it was made; (3) When necessary, documentary or other evidence to prove that the conditions laid down in Article 1, paragraph 1 and paragraph 2 (a) and (c), have been fulfilled.

145 Redfern/Hunter (2004), *op. cit.*, paras. 10-32.

enforcement on its own motion, if (at least) one of the reasons for refusal listed in Article V(2) that are to be examined *ex officio* is apparent.[146]

Unlike the former Geneva Treaties, the New York Convention thus does not burden the party applying for enforcement, but the respondent to prove relevant barriers in order to challenge the enforcement, which contributes to the major progress of the New York Convention and is even deemed to reflect "a radical change of attitude towards arbitral awards" recognising that "the award in itself constitutes a title capable of producing certain effects without the need for various extrinsic elements to be established".[147] Basically, the losing party can only defend enforcement if he proves the presence of at least one reason set out by Article V(1) lit. a-d.[148]

7. Reasons for Refusal of Enforcement

The restriction of such grounds for preventing enforcement is a further improvement in the efficiency of the recognition and enforcement regime of the New York Convention. Signatory states asked for enforcement of a New York Convention award may thus no longer rely on their domestic procedural law, involving potentially enforcement-adverse attitudes.[149]

The relevant provision in support of maintaining enforceability of foreign arbitral awards is Article V New York Convention:

> *"(1) Recognition and enforcement of the award may be refused, at the request of the party against whom it is invoked, only if that party furnishes to the competent authority where the recognition and enforcement is sought, proof that: (lit. a-e)"*

Article V intends to balance the two concurrent goals of finality of awards rendered in international arbitration against the warranty of fundamental principles of fairness and due process.[150] Therefore, it enumerates the only valid justifications to refuse recognition and enforcement of foreign arbitral awards, which likewise provide "a minimum standard" of procedural guarantees in respect of the parties, their arbitration agreement and the arbitral procedure.[151] Taking account of the

146 Van den Berg (2007), *op. cit.*, 45; Redfern/Hunter (2004), *op. cit.*, paras. 10-34.
147 Smit/Pechota (2005), *op. cit.*, 40; Gaillard/Goldmann (eds.) (1999), *op. cit.*, para. 1673.
148 Van den Berg (2007), *op. cit.*, 45; Redfern/Hunter (2004), *op. cit.*, paras. 10-34.
149 Smit/Pechota, (2005), *op. cit.*, 40; Gaillard/Goldmann (eds.) (1999), *op. cit.*, para. 1694 et seq.
150 Freyer (2008), *op. cit.*, 759.
151 *Ibid.*, 759.

New York Convention's "pro-enforcement bias" such reasons capable of impeding enforcement are to be interpreted in a narrower sense.[152]

The list of grounds contained in Article V is exhaustive,[153] and is divided into two subsections, and each subsection is divided into two categories. Article V(1) relates to defects of the arbitration procedure concerning the parties, and requires seeking to defeat enforcement to prove the defect.[154] The grounds contained in Article V(2) are relevant for the state giving effect to the arbitral award (like the arbitrability of the matter in dispute and the compliance with national public policy) and may therefore be asserted by the competent courts on their own motion.[155]

Incapacity of the Parties or Invalidity of the Arbitration Agreement[156]

The first reason justifying a refusal of enforcement relates to the Convention's requirement of a written arbitration agreement set out by Article II(2) and is apparent, if the party seeking to resist enforcement proves the invalidity of the arbitration agreement. The invalidity can be caused by the incapacity of a party, which means that a party is basically not capable of entering into legal transactions at his own instigation. In the terms of the New York Convention it is established that "incapacity" also covers a mere absence of the power to contract,[157] i.e. a party actually has the capacity to legal actions, but lacks authorisation to do so. The invalidity of the arbitration agreement can also derive from an inconsistency with the applicable law, which is the law of the agreement to arbitration or, alternatively, the law of the country where the arbitration took place.

While the Article V(1)(a) refers to the applicable arbitration law to determine the (in)capacity of the parties, no reference is made to identify the applicable choice of law rules. For the law governing the "substance of the arbitration agreement", the Convention, in contrast, provides for a choice of law rule. Thus, the applicable law is predominantly the one chosen by the parties, or alternatively, the law of the country where the award was made.[158]

---

152 Redfern/Hunter (2004), *op. cit.*, paras. 10-34.
153 *Ibid.*, paras. 10-33.
154 Gaillard/Goldmann (eds.) (1999), *op. cit.*, para. 1674.
155 *Ibid.*, para. 1674.
156 New York Convention, Article V(1)(a).
157 Gaillard/Goldmann (eds.) (1999), *op. cit.*, para. 1695.
158 Criticised by *ibid.*, para. 1695.

The losing party may also defend enforcement of an arbitral award, if he can prove that he "was not given proper notice of the appointment of the arbitrator or the arbitration proceedings, or was otherwise unable to present his case".[159] This Section provides a substantive rule that should be internationally warranted and whose violation is obviously deemed to be serious enough to constitute a reason to refuse enforcement.[160]

The Geneva Convention already established the fact that the failure to give a party proper notice of the appointment of the arbitrator and/or the arbitral procedure is sufficient to impede enforcement. It intends to put emphasis on the significance of these requirements for the parties.[161]

In order to assert any such violation of due process, the defending party needs merely to prove the actual violation, but is not required to substantiate a certain damage suffered in consequence. So this claim is often raised to resist enforcement in practice, but courts hesitate to admit its applicability.[162]

c) Non-Compliance with the terms of the Arbitration Agreement

According to Article V(1)(c) enforcement may be refused if the defending party asserts and proves that the arbitrators' decision went beyond the scope of the arbitration agreement by demonstrating that "[t]he award deals with a difference not contemplated by or not falling within the terms of the submission to arbitration; or it contains decisions on matters beyond the scope of the submission to arbitration".[163]

This justification relates to Article I(1)(a) concerning invalid arbitration agreements, as both provisions address decisions of an arbitrator who lacks authorisation, either because there was no valid arbitration agreement at all or the subject matter of the dispute was not covered by the existing agreement.[164] Modern arbitration laws therefore summarise both grounds by providing generally for a reason to refuse enforcement in case of an "absence of a valid arbitration agreement".[165] It may be pointed out that the Convention allows precluding recognition and

159 New York Convention, Article V(1)(b).
160 Gaillard/Goldmann (eds.) (1999), *op. cit.*, para. 1696.
161 *Ibid.*, para. 1696.
162 *Ibid.*, para. 1698 and 1699.
163 New York Convention, Article V(1)(c).
164 Gaillard/Goldmann (eds.) (1999), *op. cit.*, para. 1700.
165 *Ibid.*, para. 1700 with reference to Article 1502 of the French New Code of Civil Procedure and Article 1065 of the Netherlands Code of Civil Procedure.

enforcement for matters of an award not covered by the arbitration agreement, while matters effectively subjected to arbitration remain enforceable.[166] While justifications of Article V are generally to be construed narrowly and may not involve a comprehensive review of the merits these restrictions bear particular emphasis because even the verification of the arbitration's compliance with the underlying arbitration agreement is not intended to allow for a thorough factual and legal re-examination of the case.[167]

Irregularities in the Composition of the Arbitral Tribunal or in the Arbitral Proceeding

Enforcement may also be refused if the defending party asserts and proves that "[t]he composition of the arbitral authority or the arbitral procedure was not in accordance with the agreement of the parties or, failing such agreement, was not in accordance with the law of the country where the arbitration took place".[168]

While the Geneva Convention of 1927 required the constitution of the arbitral authority to comply with both the parties' arbitration agreement and the law of the forum state, the New York Convention predominantly refers to the parties' arbitration agreement and rather subsidiarily to the law of the country where the arbitration took place.[169] Modern arbitration laws may be even less restrictive, for example the French New Code of Civil Procedure ruling for the absence of a specified arbitral agreement between the parties that a mere irregularity under the governing law of the forum state is insufficient to refuse enforcement, and is rather only a deficient nomination of the arbitral authority.[170]

Non-Binding nature, Setting aside or Suspension of the Award

Among all reasons to deny enforcement under the New York Convention, interpretation and application of Article V(1)(e) was, from the outset, the most contended and debated by judges, arbitrators, and scholars.[171]

---

166 Van den Berg (2007), *op. cit.*, 24.

167 Mourre/di Brozolo (2006), *op. cit.*, 179 with reference to Pilliod v. Econosto, Paris, 30 June 2005, 2 Cahiers de l'arbitrage (2005), at para. 30.

168 New York Convention, Article V(1)(d).

169 Geneva Convention, Article I(2) lit. c.

170 French New Code of Civil Procedure, Article 1502 No. 2: "Appeal of a court decision granting recognition or enforcement is only available on the following grounds; – if the arbitral tribunal was irregularly constituted or the sole arbitrator irregularly appointed."

171 Freyer (2008), *op. cit.*, 759.

Article V(1)(e) essentially provides for a denial of enforcement if the defendant argues that "[t]he award has not yet become binding on the parties, or has been set aside or suspended by a competent authority of the country in which, or under the law of which, the award was made".[172] Accordingly, and as discussed before in the context of Article III, the New York Convention again requires the award to be 'binding' in order to obtain enforcement. The Geneva Convention, in contrast, required the award to be 'final', which was widely interpreted as a requirement for a leave of enforcement of the forum state and thus implying an exequatur in the state where the award was made,[173] – a formalistic obstacle that the drafters of the New York Convention aimed to remove.[174] Therefore the drafters of the New York Convention animatedly debated the wording of Article V(1)(e), primarily on the provision for a justification to refuse enforcement if the award had "not yet become binding on the parties". Therefore the wording approved after considerable debate is to be deemed to remedy this "key shortcoming" of the Geneva Convention.[175]

The defending party may avert enforcement by proving the setting aside of the award by a competent authority of either the state in which it was rendered, or of the state whose procedural law governed the arbitral procedure. By reference to a historical interpretation of this provision, it may be assumed that the basic intention is to give effect to the law of the state to which the parties agreled to submit their arbitration and the resulting award. Since the New York Convention itself does not provide for a list or any specification of valid grounds for setting aside or annulment decisions, such judgement is to be based on the applicable law of the forum state, and the relative grounds are of no significance to the (non) enforcement decision in the light of Article V(1)(e).[176]

Similarly, Article V(1)(e) allows for a refusal of enforcement if the award was suspended by a court of its forum state, but shows no regard for the fact that each Signatory to the New York Convention may have different requirements for the suspension of arbitral awards. Also, the Convention fails to confine the cases in which suspensions may be validly rendered. Presumably, Article V(1)(e) aims to cover merely those kinds of suspensions that were issued because the court of the forum state suspected a serious defect of the award and intended to stay the effectiveness until a judicial examination ascertained its (in)validity.[177]

---

172 New York Convention, Article V(1)(e).
173 See supra Ch. B II 2; van den Berg (2007), *op. cit.*, 28.
174 See supra Ch. B II 2; Haas (2002), *op. cit.*, para. 60; van den Berg (2007), *op. cit.*, 28.
175 Sampliner (1996), *op. cit.*, 23.
176 Schwab/Walter (2005), *op. cit.*, Ch. 57 para. 23; Abascal (2008), *op. cit.*, 168.
177 Gaillard/Goldmann (eds.) (1999), *op. cit.*, para. 1690; van den Berg (2007), *op. cit.*, 31.

In addition to setting asides, annulments, and suspensions in the forum state constituting valid reasons to refuse enforcement abroad, the enforcing state may also adjourn enforcement proceeding if an action for annulment is pending in the forum state in accordance with New York Convention, Article VI.[178] In this specification two diametrically opposed, though equally reasonable considerations are balanced: While in the light of the Convention's pro-enforcement bias it should not suffice for the losing party seeking to impede enforcement of the relevant award to trigger a challenge of the award before a court of the forum state, the drafters of the New York Convention likewise intended to maintain the principle of *ex nihilo nil fit*, i.e. an ineffective award should no longer benefit from the Convention, by precluding hasty enforcements abroad in the course of the legal challenge in the forum state.[179]

As to the complex regulation in particular of Article V(1)(e) it has been said "[t]he New York Convention breathes hot and cold; the double exequatur of the Geneva Convention is no longer required, but annulment in the country of origin may nevertheless be given effect."[180]

f) Lack of Arbitrability

As mentioned above, the second Section of provisions providing for a refusal of enforcement may be examined by the court concerned with such enforcement on its own motion, but may also be asserted by the party aiming to defend enforcement.[181]

The court may refuse enforcement if "the subject matter of the difference is not capable of settlement by arbitration under the law of that country". Accordingly a lack of arbitrability pursuant to national laws of the enforcing state constitutes a valid reason to deny enforcement.[182]

178 New York Convention, Article VI: "If an application for the setting aside or suspension of the award has been made to a competent authority referred to in article V(1)(e), the authority before which the award is sought to be relied upon may, if it considers it proper, adjourn the decision on the enforcement of the award and may also, on the application of the party claiming enforcement of the award, order the other party to give suitable security."

179 Gaillard/Goldmann (eds.) (1999), *op. cit.*, para. 1691; Whether the New York Convention in fact intends to maintain such rule and whether the provisions of the Articles V and VI are truly mandatory, will be discussed below.

180 Paulsson, Enforcing Arbitral Awards Notwithstanding a Local Standard Annulment (LSA), 9 ICC Bull (1998), 14; Paulsson (1996), *op. cit.*, 106.

181 Freyer (2008), *op. cit.*, 761.

182 New York Convention, Article V(2)(a); Redfern/Hunter (2004), *op. cit.*, paras. 10-50.

g) Breach of the National Ordre Public

A request for enforcement may also be rejected if enforcement of the award "would be contrary to the public policy of that country", in which enforcement is sought.[183] However, this reference to public policy is not intended to give consideration to principles of law in general – as previously permitted by the Geneva Convention – but rather involves fundamental concepts of justice.[184] Taking account of the Convention's pro-enforcement bias, the confines of ordre public need to be construed narrowly, thereby revealing the difficulties of defining its matter. Courts traditionally interpret the enforcement defences of the New York Convention restrictively and assume a breach of ordre public merely in case of "violations of the 'most basic notions of morality and justice'".[185]

h) General Remarks on the Enforcement Defences of Article V

In order to prevent enforcement of an award under Article V(1), the defending party must furnish proof of the fulfilment of the preconditions to the relevant court.

In view of the few enforcement conditions and the limited reasons for a refusal, it is basically easier to obtain recognition and enforcement of awards rendered in international arbitration proceedings than of judgements issued by foreign national courts. Further, arbitral awards are principally also less vulnerable than court decisions, since the reasons for nullification are very limited and a review of the substance of the award is interdicted, whereas court decisions may be subject to an exhaustive review by the court of higher instance.[186]

8. Effects on National Law

In addition to public policy considerations, the New York Convention gives further reflections on national law providing "[t]he provisions of the present convention shall not (…) deprive any interested party of any right he may have to avail himself of an arbitral award in the manner and to the extent allowed by the law (…) of

183 New York Convention, Article V(2)(b); Redfern/Hunter (2004), *op. cit.*, paras. 10-52.

184 Smit/Pechota (2005), *op. cit.*, 41.

185 See supra Ch. B II 5 d; Freyer (2008), *op. cit.*, 761, fn. 18, 19 with further references, and Redfern/Hunter (2004), *op. cit.*, para. 10-51 et seq.

186 Plaßmeier (2004), *op. cit.*, 237; Higher Regional Court of Thuringia (2008), *op. cit.*, 45.

the country where such award is sought to be relied upon."[187] Accordingly, the pursuing party does not necessarily need to seek for enforcement of a New York Convention award under the Convention's regime, but may also rely on adequate national or international legislations.

Even if the so-called "more favourable right" clause seems to contravene the Convention's purpose of harmonisation, it is well in accordance with its pro-enforcement bias, since it promotes the application of the most arbitration-friendly law, may it be international or domestic, as long as it favours enforcement. Accordingly, in case of conflicting provisions on enforcement New York Convention, Article VII(1) allows for application of the provision best promoting enforcement of the award. Consequently, the New York Convention intends by no means to impede enforcement of an award, which would have been in accordance with the national laws or international treaties in effect in the state of enforcement.[188] In fact, the "more favourable law" clause of Article VII outright embodies the pro-enforcement bias of the New York Convention. Nevertheless, the 'more favourable law' clause may not be interpreted as a provision for 'cherry-picking' a single more favourable rule on a particular issue of the enforcement procedure, but rather promotes a comprehensive application of a more favourable set of provisions on the entire enforcement proceeding.[189]

While some subsequent – *leges posterior* – treaties, like the 1965 ICSID Convention on the Settlement of Investment Disputes between States and Nationals of Other States; the 1972 Moscow Convention on the Settlement by Arbitration of Civil Law Disputes Resulting from Economic, Scientific and Technical Cooperation; and the 1975 Inter-American Convention on International Commercial Arbitration, rank as *leges speciales* to the New York Convention, the 1961 European Convention on International Commercial Arbitration is deemed merely to supply the New York Convention on its Article V(1)(e) – as will be discussed below. For the Geneva Treaties, the 'more favourable law' clause does not apply, since they are in no respect more favourable, and besides, the New York Convention sets out their ineffectiveness in relation to New York Convention signatories.[190]

As will be discussed in detail below, the interplay of the Article V(1)(e) and Article VII(1) causes remarkable intricacies in view of enforcement of nullified awards and the issue of applicable laws. Repeatedly an "apparent tension" was detected in the relation of the permissive language of Article V(1)(e) to the "more

187 New York Convention, Article VII.

188 Sampliner (1996), *op. cit.*, 24, for further detailes on the 'most favourable law' clause see Schwab/Walter (2005), *op. cit.*, Ch. 42 para. 24.

189 Schwab/Walter (2005), *op. cit.*, Ch. 42 para. 25.

190 New York Convention, Article VII(2).

favourable right" clause contained in Article VII,[191] and there is still no unanimity on whether the character of both provisions is permissive or mandatory.[192]

9. Intertemporality of the New York Convention

Finally, it is questionable whether the New York Convention enjoys retroactive applicability, as the text of the Convention is silent on this matter.[193] The diplomatic conference, when concerned with a final endorsement of the Convention, did not incorporate a proposed provision for an exclusive applicability merely to future awards, although it was previously overwhelmingly accepted. This was partly noticed with surprise and partly interpreted in favour of a retroactive applicability.[194] Since the 1970s there has been a common trend to apply the New York Convention to all arbitral procedures in a Signatory State from the date of its accession[195] – though some national acts implementing the New York Convention contain preclusions of retroactive applicability.[196] Also, on international law basis it must be emphasized that retroactive applicability basically requires explicit stipulation. International treaties principally only apply *ex nunc* (*see* Article 28 of the 1969 Vienna Convention on the Law of Treaties).[197] In summary, a retroactivity of the New York Convention is to be denied. Further difficulties may arise, if signatories fail to implement the Convention as a national legislative act as required by most countries in order to give effect to international treaties.[198]

10. Appreciation of the New York Convention

Despite the inconsistencies in interpretation and application, the New York Convention, is a great achievement and a true milestone for the establishment and effectiveness of international arbitration as a convenient and neutral dispute resolu-

191 Freyer, United States Recognition and Enforcement of Annulled Foreign Arbitral Awards – The Aftermaths of the Chromalloy Case, 17 J Int'l Arb (2000), 1 et seq; Freyer (2008), *op. cit.*, 758.
192 Freyer (2000), *op. cit.*, 5 with further reference.
193 Van den Berg (2007), *op. cit.*, 37.
194 Smit/Pechota (2005), *op. cit.*, 42; Schlosser, Das Recht der internationalen privaten Schiedsgerichtbarkeit (1989), 112.
195 Schlosser (1989), *op. cit.*, 112.
196 Smit/Pechota (2005), *op. cit.*, 42.
197 Völkerrechtsprechung: Ausgewählte Entscheidungen zum Völkerrecht in Retrospektive, Menzel/Pierlings/Hoffmann (eds) (2004), 85.
198 Van den Berg (2007), *op. cit.*, 38.

tion mechanism. Generally, the New York Convention relies on the arbitral award itself rather than on the arbitration procedure in the forum state and prevents undue interference of national courts.[199] The administrative minimum of Article IV of the New York Convention, requiring only submission of arbitration agreement and award, the fairly limited possibilities for foreign courts to deny enforcement and the shift of the burden of proof in view of Article V and additionally the option for reliance on even more favourable law permitted by Article VII contributed to the facilitation of recognition and enforcement of foreign arbitral awards. However, the uncertainties in the interpretation of the Convention have led to national court decisions, which hindered an efficient enforcement.[200] The interplay of Articles V and VII generally gave rise to inconsistent judgements on enforcement of awards, which were previously vacated in their forum state. Another shortcoming of the New York Convention is its less comprehensible renunciation of the Geneva Convention's double exequatur by replacing 'final' with 'binding', without any guidance on what constitutes a binding award.[201]

However, since its entry into force the New York Convention has significantly contributed to the effectiveness of awards rendered in international arbitration and has thus likewise contributed to the effectiveness of international arbitration in the past 50 years. It is certainly an important incentive for parties choosing arbitration as a means to resolve their disputes in cross-boarder business affairs.[202]

III. European Convention on Commercial Arbitration, (1961)

1. Historical Development

Similar to the New York Convention, the European Convention on International Commercial Arbitration has its origins in the difficulties arising from the economic environment after the Second World War, and actually "pre-dated" the United Nations' Conference in New York.[203] At that early stage of first commercial relations, when Eastern and Western states were becoming increasingly opposed to each other, arbitration was deemed to be the only acceptable mechanism for dispute resolution.[204] Though the parties more frequently and unanimously opted for neutral non-state dispute resolution in terms of international arbitration, grave

199 Gaillard (2007), *op. cit.*; Freyer/Gharavi (1998), *op. cit.*, 102.
200 Freyer/Gharavi (1998), *op. cit.*, 102.
201 *Ibid.*, 107.
202 Sampliner (1997), *op. cit.*, 150.
203 Gaillard/Goldmann (eds.) (1999), *op. cit.*, para. 274.
204 *Ibid.*, para. 284.

problems occurred in the context of the arbitration procedure itself, due to ineffective arbitration agreements. The United Nations established subdivisions in several parts of the world in order to promote international trade. In 1954 the division concerned with the region of Europe (the Economic Commission for Europe, seated in Geneva) assigned a board of experts to draft a multilateral treaty providing for international commercial arbitration between the Western European States and the Eastern States of the *Comecon* (Council for Mutual Economic Assistance). Aiming for independence from national legal systems, the drafted Convention was simplified, and to the greatest extent, detracted from national jurisdiction.[205] Its purpose was to cover all essential stages of the arbitral procedure from the conclusion of the arbitration clause to the enforcement of the arbitral award. After the New York Convention was signed in 1958, the expert board decided to concentrate its effort to draft an amendment to the New York Convention for European East-West trade relations, with particular focus on the arbitral process *per se*. Without intending to affect the New York Convention's effectiveness, the drafters of the European Convention considered it essential to surpass the effort made by the New York Convention.[206]

The *European Convention on Commercial Arbitration* was signed in Geneva on April 21, 1961 by 22 European countries, and has had a significant impact on the field of international arbitration, even as a mere regional treaty. Though it is worth noting the Council of Europe (today 47 member states) has meanwhile significantly grown, and so the geographical scope of application may outreach the territory of the European Union (today 27 member states). According to its preamble, the European Convention is "desirous of promoting the development of European trade by, as far as possible, removing certain difficulties that may impede the organisation and operation of international commercial arbitration in relations between physical or legal persons of different European countries".[207] By providing for specified rules of commercial arbitration and promoting an interpretation in the light of "international trade rather than national law",[208] the European Convention encouraged a progressive "emancipation" of international commercial arbitration from the prevalence of national jurisdictions.[209]

205 *Ibid.*, para. 284.
206 *Ibid.*, para 286.
207 European Convention, Preamble.
208 Smit/Pechota, *European Convention on International Commercial Arbitration*, in International Arbitration Treaties (2005), 102.
209 See Schwab/Walter (2005), *op. cit.*, Ch. 41 para. 4; Schütze/Tschernig/Wais (1985), *op. cit.*, para. 795; Smit/Pechota (2005), *op. cit.*, 101; Gaillard/Goldmann (eds.) (1999), *op. cit.*, para. 274 et seq., Redfern/Hunter,(2004), *op. cit.*, paras. 10-56.

The authors of the European Convention assumed that each of its prospective parties would also be affiliated to the New York Convention, an assumption which ultimately came to fruition.[210] According to the general applicability of the New York Convention, the European Convention does not predominantly focus on the recognition and enforcement of arbitral awards, but – for the first time – focuses on the organisation of commercial arbitration in its entirety, therefore establishing standardised rules for the particular phases of commercial arbitration.[211]

Strictly speaking, the European Convention applies to all arbitral agreements "concluded for the purpose of settling disputes arising from international trade between physical or legal persons having, when concluding the agreement, their habitual places of residence or their seats in different Contracting States".[212] Despite being related to "commercial matters", the Convention is silent as to the scope of this term, and is thus to be interpreted in accordance with national law.[213]

While the applicability of the New York Convention is dependent only on the diversity of the enforcing state and the seat of the arbitration, unless reservations were made, the European Convention refers to the habitual residence of the parties and does not require the arbitration to be held in another contracting state.[214] This modern approach is deemed to reflect a liberalised perception of international arbitration, "no longer confined to – and in fact largely ignoring – the enforcement of an award in a country other than that where it was made."[215]

However, it is worth noting that the European Convention requires both parties to be subject to the jurisdiction of different signatory states when concluding their arbitration agreement. This is contrary to the New York Convention and analogous to the Geneva Treaties. A later relocation of a party would not affect the Convention's applicability.[216] The revival of the "nationality" requirement and the consequent limitation of the Convention's range are to be considered in the context of the European Convention's concept of promoting East-West trade,

---

210 Gaillard/Goldmann (eds.) (1999), *op. cit.*, para. 286.

211 *Ibid.,* para. 277 et seq.

212 European Convention, Art. I(1)(a).

213 Neuteufel, Das Europäische Übereinkommen über die internationale Handelsschiedsgerichtsbarkeit, Anwaltsblatt 2004, 547 with reference to Art. I(3) New York Convention.

214 Gaillard/Goldmann (eds.) (1999), *op. cit.*, para. 280.

215 *Ibid.,* para. 280.

216 Smit/Pechota (2005), *op. cit.*, 102; Neuteufel (2004), *op. cit.*, 547; Gaillard/Goldmann (eds.) (1999), *op. cit.*, para. 279.

and providing concessions to the Soviet regime, which solely recognised disputes evolved between parties of different nationalities.[217]

3. Scope of Provisions

Aiming to govern the organisation of the arbitral procedure, the provisions of the European Convention cover issues of arbitrability, validity of the arbitration agreement, appointment of the arbitrator(s), competence of both the arbitral tribunal and the national courts, and the course of the arbitral proceeding itself. Hence, the issue of recognition and enforcement of foreign awards by national courts is covered in a rather confined manner as the drafters were well aware of the profound impact of the New York Convention.[218] Article IX of the European Convention is the only provision related to the recognition and enforcement of arbitral awards, or, more precisely, producing valid reasons to refuse recognition and enforcement.[219]

As previously mentioned, the European Convention applies exclusively to arbitral matters related to "international trade" – however, the term is conceived to be used in a wider sense.[220] According to the authors, 'international trade' embraces "any operations characterised by the movement of goods, services, or currencies across national boundaries"; and was later identified as also involving "the transfer of technology and joint ventures between enterprises of different countries".[221]

Like the New York Convention, the European Convention encompasses arbitral agreements and awards submitted to or rendered by *ad hoc* arbitration, and permanent arbitration institutions.[222]

4. Reasons to Refuse Recognition and Enforcement

As indicated, the European Convention principally leaves it to other treaties to govern the course of recognition and enforcement of foreign arbitral awards, pri-

217 Smit/Pechota (2005), *op. cit.*, 102; Gaillard/Goldmann (eds.) (1999), *op. cit.*, para. 279.
218 Gaillard/Goldmann (eds.) (1999), *op. cit.*, para. 281.
219 Redfern/Hunter (2004), *op. cit.*, paras. 10-56.
220 European Convention, Article I as to the Scope of the Convention; Smit/Pechota (2005), *op. cit.*, 102.
221 *Ibid.*, 102.
222 European Convention, Article I(2)(b).

marily the New York Convention. There is only one exception and this concerns the issue of recognition and enforcement of vacated awards.[223]

While Article V of the New York Convention provides an exhaustive list of reasons to deny recognition and enforcement of a foreign arbitral award, Article IX of the European Convention supplements the New York Convention's list and enumerates grounds for annulment of awards, which it considers being serious enough for causing a refusal of enforcement.[224] Strictly speaking, the European Convention allows contracting states to refuse recognition and enforcement of a vacated foreign arbitral award, if the vacating decision was based on one of the grounds set out by the Convention, and which, in turn, correspond closely to the first four reasons for refusal listed in New York Convention, Article V(1) lit. a-d. Accordingly, the European Convention provides that an award may not be denied enforcement if previously vacated in its forum state based on a valid ground (in that state), but not listed in Article IX lit. a-d. Therefore, it may be said that the European Convention goes beyond the New York Convention in respect to the enforcement of vacated awards. It is worth noting that the award which is supposed to be enforced, must have been rendered and annulled in another signatory state in order to fall under the scope of European Convention, Article IX(1) lit. a-d.

In concreto, Art. IX(1) lit. a-d allows for a refusal of enforcement if the decision to vacate the award was based on one of the subsequent grounds, which are, as indicated above, similar to those of Article V(1) lit. a-d of the New York Convention:

"(1) The setting aside in a Contracting State of an arbitral award covered by this Convention shall only constitute a ground for the refusal of recognition or enforcement in another Contracting State where such setting aside took place in a State in which, or under the law of which, the award has been made and for one of the following reasons: (lit. a-d)"

a) Incapacity of the Parties or Invalidity of the Arbitration Agreement

In the light of the European Convention the court asked for enforcement of a nullified award may deny it, if the nullification was founded on the fact that the parties were under some incapacity according to their applicable law, or their agreement is not valid either due to the law chosen by the parties or, alternatively, due to the law of the country of the seat of the arbitration.

223 Redfern/Hunter (2004), *op. cit.*, paras. 10-56.
224 Smit/Pechota (2005), *op. cit.*, 104.

b) Violation of Due Process

If an award was vacated because the party was not given proper notice of the appointment of the arbitrator or the arbitral procedure, or was otherwise incapable to present his case, courts in a European Convention state may refuse to enforce such an award.

c) Non-Compliance with the terms of the Arbitration Agreement

An application for enforcement may further be rejected if an award is related to a dispute, or contains a decision beyond the scope of the arbitration agreement, and was therefore annulled. Assuming the award to be divisible, the valid portion is not to be set aside, and may still be enforced.

d) Irregularities in the Composition of the Arbitral Tribunal or the Arbitral Proceeding

Finally, the court of the addressee state may refuse enforcement of a vacated award if it was vacated due to a defect in either the composition of the arbitral authority, or the course of the arbitral proceeding due to the agreement of the parties or, alternatively, due to Art. IV of the European Convention.

The European Convention's approach of limiting the effect of a national annulment decision and minimising its impact on recognition and enforcement in another signatory state is widely appreciated. Proponents point out that arbitration is not integrated as a lower "court" into the forum state's judicial system. Accordingly, arbitral awards are suitable for autonomous assessment by the courts of the state where enforcement is sought without respect to the findings of the courts in the first jurisdiction.[225]

In contrast, critics argue that violations of national public policy might never be considered under Article IX of the European Convention, particularly if the agreed procedure prohibits the tribunal from applying the substantive law of the forum.[226] However, the primary concern is the arbitral award's compliance with the public policy of the state in which it is to be given effect, i.e. in which it is to be enforced. In the event that the arbitral award will only be enforced abroad, violation of the local public policy at the forum state is not of notable consequence. If enforcement is also sought within the forum state, the state is naturally free to deny such requests in the light of the award's incompatibility with the prevalent fundamental concepts

225 See in detail below; Michaels (1999), *op. cit.*, 6.
226 *Ibid.*, 6.

of the domestic law. Similarly, the enforcing state is free to refuse enforcement of an award that violates the national public policy. Article IX(1) does not justify a denial of enforcement in the enforcing state, only because the award was set aside for public policy reasons at the forum state.

Nevertheless, opponents argue that the public policy of the enforcing state could, in turn, be violated if cogent principles of a foreign legal system were infringed. The public policy of the enforcing state concerning the legal recognition would not only require observance of the national public policy, but also of general principles of international trade. Thus it is deemed to reflect a rather international concept of public policy.[227] This approach should be rejected, as it aims to bypass Article IX(1) of the European Convention, which specifically prohibits a public policy violation within the forum state from justifying a refusal of enforcement.

e) 'Priority Clause'

Since the drafters of the European Convention presumed contracting states would also be signatories to the New York Convention, they sought to maintain the Article IX(1) lit. a-d justifications for a refusal of enforcement. Accordingly, Article IX(2) of the European Convention governs that its restrictive provisions of Subsection (1) lit. a-d are given precedence over the reasons for refusal enumerated in Article V(1) lit. a-d of the New York Convention.

5. Final Clauses

The European Convention's 'priority clause' reflects the drafters' careful considerations of the assumed double-membership of its perspective signatories, and it impacts the interplay with the New York Convention.[228]

While the drafters placed emphasis on the European Convention's precedence over the New York Convention's justifications for a refusal of enforcement, the European Convention yields precedence on other issues to the New York Convention by providing that it would not "affect the validity of existing or future multilateral or bilateral agreements concerning arbitration entered into by Contracting States".[229]

---

227 *Ibid.*, 8.
228 Gaillard/Goldmann (eds.) (1999), *op. cit.*, para. 286 with reference to CA Rouen, Nov. 13, 1984, S.E.E.E..
229 European Convention, Article X(7).

IV. Relation Between New York Convention and European Convention

After this introduction to the two major Conventions within Europe governing the effectiveness of awards rendered in international commercial arbitration, it is essential to examine their interaction and their particular decisiveness. Ratified by more than 148 nations, the New York Convention has by far the widest range and is principally the starting point when it comes to the recognition and enforcement of foreign arbitral awards.[230] All members of the European Union are signators of the New York Convention, even though some of these states have yet to adopt the European Convention.

1. Distinct Ambitions of both Conventions

While the New York Convention outlines a specific regime for the recognition and enforcement of foreign awards beyond their forum state, the European Convention focuses on regulating the procedure of international commercial arbitration in general. However, there is one substantive point of intersection: the justifications for refusals of enforcement of arbitral awards, or, strictly speaking, the justifications for refusals of enforcement of annulled awards. Accordingly, the recognition and enforcement of an annulled award in a country, which is party to both the New York Convention and the European Convention is to be considered within the constraints imposed upon the enforcing state by the interplay of these two conventions.

As mentioned above the drafters of the European Convention set out from the assumption that each of their prospective signatories is also affiliated with the New York Convention, thus necessitating, in its final clause, Article X(7) which provides that the European Convention will not affect the validity and effect of the New York Convention.

2. Coinciding Issue

The European Convention deals with two issues of international arbitration, which are not covered by the New York Convention. One such issue is Article VIII's obligation to provide a justified award "unless [the parties] expressly declared that reasons shall not be given or (...) assented to an arbitral procedure under which it is not customary to give reasons for awards". The second issue not addressed

230 Webster (2006), *op. cit.*, 203.

in the New York Convention is the limitation of grounds on which an annulment decision is based, and, accordingly, may justify a refusal of enforcement.[231]

As indicated above, the present treaties focus on the examination of the latter, as to which the provisions of the European Convention are in conflict with corresponding provisions of the New York Convention.

On the one hand, the New York Convention, Article V(1) lit. a-e sets out an exhaustive list of justifications for the refusals of recognition and enforcement of arbitral awards in a country other than the country of origin. Therein, Subsection (e) qualifies a setting aside, or suspension of an award by a competent authority of the forum state as a reason for refusal.

On the other hand European Convention, Art. IX(1) lit. a-d intends to follow up on the second alternative of this provision by stipulating restrictively that a foreign court decision annulling the award may only justify a refusal of enforcement, if the decision was based on one of the grounds listed in Article IX(1) lit. a-d of the European Convention.[232]

3. Controversial Outcomes

A controversial outcome may occur if a pursuing party seeks enforcement of its award in a country that is signatory to both Conventions and if a competent authority in the forum state has previously set aside the award for public policy reasons.

According to the New York Convention, the court concerned with the request for enforcement may only consider that the award has been set aside, without particular respect to the grounds of such annulment decision. The enforcement of such an award may thus be refused in accordance with New York Convention, Article V(1)(e).

In contrast, the European Convention requires the court concerned with the request for enforcement to take into account the grounds on which the award has been set aside. If such grounds are enumerated in Article IX(1) lit. a-d, enforcement may be refused. With regard to the case in hand, it must be emphasized that an annulment for public policy reasons is not listed in Article IX(1) lit. a-d, and thus may not be given consideration during the determination of enforcement. Therefore, under Article IX(1) lit. a-d enforcement of an award that was

231 *See* European Covention, Article IX(1) lit. a-d.

232 Smit/Pechota (2005), *op. cit.*, 104, Gaillard/Goldmann (eds.) (1999), *op. cit.*, para. 274.

previously set aside on public policy grounds may not be denied enforcement in a European Convention state.

As the application of both the New York and the European Conventions results in controversial findings on identical request for enforcement, it is questionable which of the two international treaties deserves priority.

4. Question of Priority

Generally speaking, the New York Convention applies even to the enforcement of arbitral awards rendered by tribunals principally falling under the Geneva Convention.[233] However, there is a significant exception:

a) Appreciation of the European Convention

Since the drafters of the European Convention set out the assumption of their parties' affiliation with the New York Convention, they took account thereof in the conception of the European Convention. In particular they did not only warrant that the applicability of other bi- or multilateral treaties like the New York Convention, would not be affected by the provisions of the European Convention,[234] but also established a priority of the European Convention's justifications for a refusal of enforcement over those listed in the New York Convention.[235]

Consequently, Article IX(1) lit. a-d of the European Convention takes precedence in the field of enforcement applications for an award that has been annulled in its forum state.

b) Appreciation of the New York Convention

The authors of the prior New York Convention also intended to give consideration to subsequent bi- and multilateral treaties and thus precautionarily involved the 'more favourable law' clause.[236] Accordingly, the New York Convention admits a flexible adjustment of distinct regimes on recognition and enforcement in order to promote a maximal effectiveness of arbitral awards.[237]

In the context of conflicting international conventions (on private law) it is noteworthy that "more favourable law" clauses do not refer to a generally more

233 Neuteufel (2004), *op. cit.*, 548.
234 European Convention, Article X(7).
235 European Convention, Article IX(2):
236 New York Convention, Article VII.
237 Schwab/Walter, (2005), *op. cit.*, Ch. 42 para. 24.

favourable law, but to the law that is more favourable in the end, and thus requires a case-by-case approach. Guidance for such a case-by-case approach is provided by three conflict rules set out by Ferenc Majoros.[238]

(i) The first indication for "more favourable law" is the "maximum efficacy". If there is a subject covered by more than one international convention and all conventions are obviously aiming for the same goal, the most effective convention is the one that is to be applied. Indeed, the New York and the European Convention do not actually "have clearly recognizable uniform goals":[239] while the New York Convention aims to facilitate recognition and enforcement, the European Convention provides a general regime for international commercial arbitration. Nevertheless, Article V(1)(e) of the New York Convention, principally permits the refusal of enforcement of a vacated award, while Article IX(1) lit. a-d of the European Convention limits such a refusal to four justified grounds. To pick up the previous example: The award set aside for public policy reasons must be granted enforcement under the European Convention, but not necessarily under the New York Convention, since Article V(1) gives the enforcing court great discretionary powers. Consequently, the European Convention is rather more efficient for enforcement of annulled arbitral awards.

(ii) The conflict between the New York and the European Convention may also be resolved due to Majoros' second rule. According to this rule, the convention providing for a "specific rule on the subject matter in conflict" deserves preference over the more general convention. Since Article V(1) of the New York Convention i. a. generally allows for a refusal of enforcement of arbitral awards in case of annulment, Article IX(1) of the European Convention goes further by defining only four grounds for annulment that are capable of justifying a refusal of enforcement. In this regard, Article IX(1) of the European Convention is more specific than Article V(1) of the New York Convention and thus deserves preference, according to Majoros.

(iii) Additionally, also Majoros' third rule supports a preference of the 1961 European Convention over the 1958 New York Convention: the traditional international law rule *"lex posterior derogat priori"*.

Consequently, European Convention Article IX(1) lit. a-d is to be considered as more favourable than New York Convention Article V(1)(e). Hence, in countries affiliated to both the New York Convention and the European Convention, the latter is given priority due to the 'more favourable law' provision of New York Convention, Article VII.

---

238 Majoros, Konflikte zwischen Staatsverträgen auf dem Gebiete des Privatrechts, RabelsZ 1982, 84 et seq.

239 Majoros (1982), *op. cit.*, 116.

c) Basic Principles of Law

Besides the provisions in favour of a priority of the European Convention involved in the international treaties themselves, the priority of the 1961 European Convention over the 1958 New York Convention as to coinciding matters may i. a. also be reasoned by the basic principle of *lex posterior derogat lex priori*, though it depends on each Signatory's individual date of accession.[240] By all means, the European Convention provisions on recognition and enforcement of nullified awards enjoys priority over New York Conventions Article V(1)(e).

5. Dogmatic Evaluation

Strictly speaking and taking the language of both the New York Convention Article V(1)(e) in connection with Article VII(1), and the European Convention, Article IX Subsection (1) lit. a-d in connection with Subsection (2) into proper consideration, the sole due and valid conclusion to be drawn is that the European Convention's justifications to refuse enforcement of set aside awards take precedence.

In practice, the issue of precedence mainly arises with requests for enforcement despite a public policy annulment. The European Convention takes into consideration that the award in fact neither infringes the domestic public policy, nor even mandatory law in the enforcing state.[241] In addition to this consideration there is also a resonating political aspect, which is widely appreciated. Given that an annulment has no effect at all in any European Convention state, it impedes the fundamental concept that decisions of foreign jurisdictions may extend to other legal orders.[242]

However, it must be emphasized that Article IX of the European Convention only limits the justifications for refusal set out under Article V(1)(e) of the New York Convention. Enforcing states may still avail themselves of the justifications provided by Article V(2), which provides for a refusal of enforcement if the award violates national public policy.

240 Gottwald/MüKo, *ZPO* (2008), UNÜ Art. VII, para. 8; van den Berg (2007), *op. cit.*; Schwab/Walter (2005), *op. cit.*, Ch. 42 para. 27.

241 Schwab/Walter (2005), *op. cit.*, Ch. 57 para. 26.

242 Braumüller, Das Schicksal im ehemaligen Jugoslawien ergangener „internationaler“ Schiedssprüche nach dessen Zerfall an einem Beispiel – Staatsverträge im Widerspruch, WBl 1996, 99 et seq; Austrian Supreme Court 3Ob221/04b; Neuteufel (2004), op. cit., 548.

Generally speaking, the European Convention's restriction on refusing enforcement constitutes "a significant contribution to the development of international commercial arbitration."[243]

V. More Favourable National Arbitration Laws

Beside the scope of both the New York and the European Convention there are national regimes governing the recognition and enforcement of foreign arbitral awards. A state, indeed signatory to both Conventions, may attempt to facilitate enforcement even more by adopting a national arbitration law providing for less reasons to refuse enforcement – for example, when enforcement of a set aside/annulled/suspended award – as set out in Article V of the New York Convention – may nevertheless only be refused, if the award is in "manifest incompatibility"[244] with the state's national public policy.

Such a restriction of reasons for refusal of enforcement not only makes enforcement more *efficient*, but also provides a more *specific* regime than Article V(1) of the New York Convention in terms of Majoros' rules.[245] In consequence, this kind of national arbitration law may warrant a more favourable treatment than the New York Convention. In this context, Article VII of the New York Convention enables the enacting state to disregard the regime set out by Article V(1) lit. a-d by instead relying on the more favourable national law.

Arbitration laws adopting such progressive enforcement preference may be found in various states, including France, Belgium, Netherlands and Luxembourg. They involve favourable autonomous provisions on recognition and enforcement of international arbitral awards. The French regulation is even more progressive than Article IX(1) lit. a-d of the European Convention and provides that annulments of arbitral awards in their forum state do not constitute a valid reason to refuse enforcement. Accordingly, an arbitral award that has previously been set aside in its forum state (Sweden, Germany, Austria, Spain or Italy for example) can easily be recognised and enforced in France.[246]

In addition to Article VII of the New York Convention, Article III provides also for application of national laws requiring the state where enforcement is sought to "recognize arbitral awards as binding and enforce them", while admitting to do so "in accordance with the rules of procedure of the territory where the award is

243 Smit/Pechota (2005), *op. cit.*, 105.
244 See Chapter II.5.d.
245 See supra 61 et seq.
246 Koch, The Enforcement of Awards Annulled in their Place of Origin: The French and U.S. Experience, 26 J Int'l Arb (2009), 291.

relied upon", i.e. its national law. Therefore the actual enforcement depends to a large extent on national arbitration laws in enforcing states.[247]

1. Belgian and Swiss Arbitration Law

Since 1999 the Swiss Private International Law Act has been setting out progressive, arbitration-friendly substantive rules[248] which permit arbitrators to govern the arbitration proceeding at their own discretion; unless the parties have made distinct agreements,[249] the interference of Swiss courts is limited to 'judicial assistance' for the appointment or challenging of the arbitral authority,[250] the taking of evidence, and injunctions.[251]

Both Swiss and Belgian law permits preclusion of annulment actions for arbitral awards in their respective courts, if neither the parties nor their dispute is particularly connected to the forum state.[252] Even if parties do not waive their right for annulment, awards rendered in Switzerland may only be annulled in case of defective constitution of the arbitral authority, a lack of jurisdiction of the arbitral tribunal, ultra or infra petitia, a lack of due process of law or a breach of the Swiss ordre public, according to Article 190 of the Swiss Private International Law Act.

The Belgian Judicial Code was amended in 1998. Article 1717(4) now permits parties to international arbitration to exclude "any application for the setting aside of an arbitral award" when neither party is connected to Belgium by means of nationality or residence.[253] Already in 1985 the Belgian Judicial Code was amended by Article 1717(4) which then generally precluded annulment proceedings in Bel-

---

247 Freyer (2008), *op. cit.*, 757.

248 Article 178 (as to arbitration agreement).

249 Articles 183, 184, 187 (as to taking of evidence, interim relief, applicable law).

250 Articles 179, 180.

251 Articles 183, 184, 185.; see also Lew (2006), *op. cit.*, 192.

252 Swiss Federal Statute of Private International Law (*Swiss Private International Law Act*).

253 Belgian Judicial Code, Article 1717 (adopted 4 July 1972, amended 27 March 1985 and 19 May 1998):

(1) Except for the provisions of paragraph 2 of Article 1719, the court that has jurisdiction to apply part VI of this Code is the court designated in the arbitration agreement or in a later agreement, concluded before the place of arbitration is determined.

(2) If the parties have reached no agreement, the court of the place of arbitration has jurisdiction. If such place of arbitration has not yet been determined, the court has jurisdiction in whose district the court is situated that would have had jurisdiction if the dispute had not been submitted to arbitration.

(3) (deleted)

gian courts, if neither party of the arbitration had the nationality of, or its habitual residence or seat within Belgium. The main purpose of the Belgian amendment was to prevent procrastinations in the courts of the arbitration preceding, but also during the enforcement procedure.[254] However, after the 1985 amendment Belgium was not a popular or frequently chosen venue for international arbitration proceedings.[255] Therefore the Belgian legislator enacted the 1998 amendment, which now permits even foreign parties to initiate an annulment proceeding in Belgian courts, even though they still have the option to exclude such recourse.

2. French Arbitration Law

When it comes to recognition and enforcement of foreign arbitral awards, French courts do not consider the New York Convention, Article V(1) lit. a-e. French courts rather apply their national arbitration law, which is based on the New York Convention's 'more favourable law' clause.

In 1981 France adopted the new Decree on International Arbitration, a progressive arbitration law, providing for the parties extensive rights to autonomously govern their arbitration procedure independent of national procedural law either by their arbitration agreement or by reference to a "resolution by arbitration".[256] In the absence of such a choice of law by the parties, the arbitral panel is authorised to determine the proceedings. A particular amendment of the Decree is Article 1502, which provides that awards rendered in international arbitration may be set aside in France on only five grounds – including the absence or invalidity of the arbitration agreement, a deficient composition of the arbitral tribunal, an exceeding by the arbitrator(s) of the mandate to arbitrate or a violation of due process or public policy.[257] This exhaustive list is also called on for enforcement

(4) The parties may, by an explicit declaration in the arbitration agreement or by a later agreement, exclude any application for the setting aside of an arbitral award, in case none of them is a physical person of Belgian nationality or a physical person having his normal residence in Belgium or a legal person having its main seat or a branch office in Belgium.

254 Statistical data provided by the International Arbitration Court of the ICC referred to by Verbist, Reform des belgischen Rechts der Schiedsgerichtsbarkeit, BB 1998 Suppl., 5.

255 *Ibid.*

256 French New Code of Civil Procedure, Article 1494.

257 French New Code of Civil Procedure, Articles 1502 (inserted by Decree No.81-500 of 12 May 1981, sec.5 and 52, Official Journal of 14 May 1981, amendment JORF of 21 May 1981): An appeal against the decision which shall confer recognition or enforcement shall be open only in the following cases: 1° where the arbitrator has

decisions and is perceived as confining the only valid justifications for rejections of enforcement. Accordingly, a nullification of an award in its forum state does not constitute a valid reason to refuse enforcement in France,[258] nor does the New Code of Civil Procedure allow for court appeals in international arbitration.[259] Relying on Article VII of the New York Convention, French courts, when faced with a request for enforcement, scrutinise whether the arbitral award may be given effect in accordance with the applicable French law, particularly Article 1502 of the New Code of Civil Procedure French – irrespective of previous foreign court's decisions.[260] Hence French courts have decided at least five times to enforce an arbitral award notwithstanding its nullification in the respective forum state,[261] reflecting France's basic attempt of granting finality of international awards to the greatest possible extent and to subject them only to limited review by the courts considering the *"integrity of the arbitral process"*.[262]

---

ruled upon the matter without an arbitration agreement or where this agreement is null or has lapsed; 2° where the arbitration tribunal has been unlawfully constituted or a sole arbitrator unlawfully appointed; 3° where the arbitrator has ruled upon the matter contrary to the assignment given to him; 4° where the adversarial principle has not been respected; 5° where the recognition or enforcement shall be contrary to public international order. See also Lew (2006), *op. cit.*, 192; Abascal (2008), *op. cit.*, 170 with reference to Gaillard/Goldmann (eds.) (1999), *op. cit.*, para. 1603.

258 Sampliner (1996), *op. cit.*, 24 with reference to Société Pabalk Ticaret Sirketi v. Société Anonyme Norsolor, 95 Dalloz Sirey 101 (Cour de Cassation, 1984), English excerpt in XI Y. B. Com. Arb. (1986), 484; Polish Ocean Lines v. S.A. Jolasry, 120 J. D. I. (Clunet) 360, Rev. Arb. 1993, 258 (Cour de Cassation 1993), English excerpt in XIX Y. B. Com. Arb. (1994), 662; Société Hilmarton v. Société OTV, Rev. Arb. 1994, 327 (Cour de Cassation 1994).

259 French New Code of Civil Procedure, Article 1507; Abascal (2008), *op. cit.*, 170 with reference to Derains/Goodman-Everard, France, Annex I-II, in International Handbook on Commercial Arbitration, Paulsson (ed), Suppl 26 (February 1998).

260 Gaillard, L'exécution des sentences annulées dans leur pays d'origine, 3 J.D.I. (1998).

261 See in detail below; Sampliner (1996), *op. cit.*, 24 with reference to Société Pabalk Ticaret Sirketi v. Société Anonyme Norsolor, 95 Dalloz Sirey 101 (Cour de Cassation, 1984), English excerpt in XI Y. B. Com. Arb. (1986), 484; Polish Ocean Lines v. S.A. Jolasry, 120 J.D.I. (1993), 360, Rev. Arb. (1993), 258 (Cour de Cassation 1993), English excerpt in XIX Y. B.. Com. Arb. (1994), 662; Société Hilmarton v. Société OTV, Rev. Arb. (1994), 327 (Cour de Cassation 1994).

262 Delaume, Reflections on the Effectiveness of International Arbitral Awards, 12 J Int'l Arb (1995), 5-20.

3. Swedish Arbitration Law

While Sweden has long since been an approved venue for international arbitration, and has always displayed an arbitration-friendly attitude,[263] in 1999 Sweden adopted a new Arbitration Act, which permits the arbitration panel to govern the arbitral procedure,[264] while court interference is restricted to the providence of judicial assistance.[265] Arbitral awards may only be appealed under restricted circumstances such as exceeding the arbitration agreement or a deficient arbitration proceeding.[266]

4. Comment

The validity and preference of such more favourable national laws as Article V of the New York Convention is without controversy due to the "more favourable law" clause provided by Article VII of the New York Convention. But since the European Convention does not provide for a comparable clause, it is questionable what effect these more favourable national laws have on Article IX(1) of the European Convention.

Undoubtedly, Article IX(1) of the European Convention takes precedence over Article V(1) of the New York Convention in the field of enforcement of nullified awards (due to Subsection 2 of Article IX of the European Convention).[267]

Likewise, more favourable national laws take precedence over Article V(1) of the New York Convention for general enforcement of arbitral awards, whether nullified or not (due to Article VII of the New York Convention).

In consequence, it may occur that the New York Convention in fact provides for application of a (national) law which particularly facilitates enforcement of nullified awards – even more than Article IX(1) of the European Convention. Many signatory states with such modern arbitration laws rely merely on their (more favourable) national law, as permitted by Article VII of the New York Conven-

---

263 Lew (2006), *op. cit.*, 192 with reference to Gaillard/Goldmann (eds.) (1999), *op. cit.*, para. 164, citing Paulsson, Arbitrage international et voies de recours: La Cour supreme du Suede dans le sillage des solutions belge er helvetique, 117 J.D.I. (1990), 589.

264 See Swedish Arbitration Act of 1999, Sections 21-25.

265 Swedish Arbitration Act of 1999, see for example Sec. 4, 14-17 and 20 as to the constitution of the arbitral tribunal.

266 Lew (2006), *op. cit.*, 192.

267 See Chapter IV.

tion – or are they necessarily bound by Article IX(1) of the European Convention when it comes to enforcement of nullified awards?

Basically, these states are equal signatories to both the New York and the European Conventions. Hence, this is again an issue of conflicting international conventions and may thus be resolved in accordance with the three conflict rules set out by Ferenc Majoros.

a) The rule of "maximum efficacy"

Though neither Convention principally pursues a uniform goal,[268] it may be said that parts of the European Convention, Article IX in particular, and the New York Convention in general, are both directed at facilitating recognition and enforcement of an arbitral awards. In this context, the more favourable national arbitration laws promoted by Article VII of the New York Convention may be, in particular cases, more effective for enforcement of nullified awards than Article IX of the European Convention.

For example, when a state basically assesses the enforceability of even annulled awards only due to their compatibility with public policy, with no regard to the particular reasons for the foreign annulment decision, this approach facilitates enforcement even more than Article IX(1) of the European Convention does, which explicitly allows refusing enforcement of nullified awards in four distinct cases.

In the light of such enforcement-friendly national laws, Article VII of the New York Convention is more efficient as to enforcement of nullified awards than Article IX of the European Convention.

b) The rule of "specificity"

While the New York Convention expressly allows for application of these favourable enforcement laws, the European Convention is silent on the matter. So when it comes to giving effect to the most efficient provisions in order to facilitate enforcement of nullified awards, the New York Convention Article VII provides a specific rule. The European Convention, in contrast, merely promotes its own regime as manifested in Article IX, with no expressed option for further facilitation of enforcement. In this regard, the specific rule in terms of the "more favourable law" clause contained in Article VII of the New York Convention, is to be given preference over the more general regime of the European Convention.

268 See Chapter III 2.

c) *The rule of "lex posterior derogat legi priori"*

According to the international basic principle of "lex posterior derogat legi priori" the 1961 European Convention basically may have priority over the 1958 New York Convention, though it depends on the particular date of accession.[269] Besides, the enforcement-friendly national laws in question may be more recent, which may in particular cases lead to a precedence of these national laws over Article IX(1) of the European Convention.

d) *General Considerations*

The purpose of the European Convention is not to provide for an exhaustive regime on international commercial arbitration, but to clarify some core issues its drafters considered to be relevant for international trade. This intention determines the relation between the European Convention and the national laws of its signatories.[270] The provisions of the European Convention are supposed to amend the national regulations, but take preference as far as they are more specific.

By adopting Article IX, the European Convention derogated the principle of dependency of the recognition and enforcement of an arbitral award by its continued existence in its country of origin.[271] According to the wording of Article IX(1) of the European Convention, the nullification of an arbitral award "...shall only constitute a ground for the refusal of recognition or enforcement..." in certain enumerated cases. Thus, recognition and enforcement of nullified awards may not be refused for other reasons than those listed in Article IX(1). It does not mean recognition and enforcement must be refused in any such case, but a further restriction of the listed reasons for refusal on national law basis is consistent with the spirit of the Convention. In summary, more favourable national laws on refusals of enforcement also take preference over Article IX(1) of the European Convention.

269 Adolphsen/MüKo, *ZPO* (2008), Art. VII UNÜ, para. 6 et seq.
270 Mezger (1965), *op. cit.*, 290.
271 Mezger (1965), *op. cit.*, 290.

C. Recognition and Enforcement of Nullified Awards

In the light of international comity, national courts generally favour recognition of decisions rendered by competent authorities of other sovereign states.[272] A foreign court decision annulling an arbitral award would thus generally be recognised, whereupon the principle of 'ex nihilo nil fit' would hinder enforcement of the award.[273] However, despite the multitude – or maybe due to the multitude – of national and international legislation on enforcement of foreign awards, inconsistent approaches to enforcement of vacated awards are to be recorded.

I. Local Standard Annulment

Such awards, annulled by a competent authority in their forum state or in accordance with the stipulated applicable law, and therefore on the basis of "local particularities" have been identified as "Local Standard Annulments".[274] In order to maintain arbitration as an internationally approved and feasible mechanism of alternative dispute resolution, the upholding of an utterly "Local Standard Annulment" should be avoided, to the greatest possible extent, since "[t]he choice of a particular place of arbitration should not facilitate such subterfuge by dint of an unusual or internationally unusual local rule".[275] While opponents object that "ignorance" of such annulments "is no excuse", the author of the "Local Standard Annulment" conception counter "it would be unfortunate and unnecessary to allow the system of international arbitration to be a minefield for the unwary."[276]

To date, a number of national courts, including those in the United States, France, Belgium, Austria and Germany, have favoured enforcement of an award that had previously been set aside. In contrast, several state courts have refused to enforce vacated awards. These states include (again) Germany and the United States.

272 Horvath (2009), *op. cit.*, 250; Abascal (2008), *op. cit.*, 173;
273 Van den Berg, Enforcement of annulled awards, 9 ICC Bull. (1998), 15, 16.
274 Paulsson (1998), *op. cit.*, 14.
275 Paulsson (1996), *op. cit.*, 99.
276 Ibid,, 99.

The issue of whether an award which was previously set aside in its forum state, or in accordance with its applicable law, may be or should (not) be enforced is still controversially discussed in the light of the distinct and apparently inconsistent court decisions, which emerged due to confusion as to the multitude and diversity of possibly applicable national and international regimes on the matter of recognition and enforcement of foreign arbitral awards and uncertainties in their interpretation.

II. The Quality of Guidance Provided by the New York Convention

As indicated above, the New York Convention has the widest range and effect on the recognition and enforcement of foreign awards, and applies to the majority of awards, which are to be enforced abroad. With respect to the enforcement of annulled awards Article V(1)(e) of the New York Convention provides a justification for refusal. Strictly speaking, it provides that "[r]ecognition and enforcement of the award *may* be refused,… if [t]he award… has been set aside… by a competent authority of the country in which, or under the law of which, that award was made".

1. Lack of Clarity

It may be said that the ambiguous Article V(1)(e) of the New York Convention provides the main source of uncertainty, and opinions particularly differ on "[t]he conditional 'may'" of which it has actually been said that it "leaps out at any lawyer. Since 'may' necessarily contemplates 'may not'",[277] but nevertheless is frequently deemed to mandatorily postulate the refusal of enforcement in the listed cases.[278] However, uncertainties arise not only on whether 'may refuse' indicates a latitude of judgement, but there is also a significant discrepancy in the official versions of the New York Convention on Recognition and Enforcement of Foreign Arbitral Awards, issued in 1958 by the United Nations.

In order to approach a consistent perception of the interplay of the regimes governing the recognition and enforcement of awards, it is essential to determine whether the New York Convention allows for discretion of the enforcing court or

277 Paulsson (1996), *op. cit.*, 102; Freyer (2008), *op. cit.*, 757 with reference to Paulsson (1998), *op. cit.*.

278 So even deemed by the Explanatory Note to the UNCITRAL Model Law, para. 7 (b).

precisely indicates a certain outcome – strictly speaking, whether Article V of the New York Convention is permissive or mandatory.

2. Comparative Analysis of the Authentic Convention Texts

The New York Convention was – as displayed above – adopted under the auspices of the United Nations. The United Nations acknowledges six official languages, namely Arabic, Chinese, English, French, Russian and Spanish. While the latter five were already chosen when the United Nations was founded, Arabic was added in 1979. The text of the 1958 New York Convention was therefore primarily issued in five versions, including English, French, Chinese, Spanish and Russian. According to Article XVI these versions are equally authentic, though they are partially distinct in their tenor of Article V(1).[279]

As illustrated above, Article V(1) of the English text using the expression 'may' suggests permission, but no obligation to deny a request for enforcement of an arbitral award, if one of the reasons listed in the subsequent subparagraphs has been asserted and proved by the defending party or on the court's own motion..

The relevant portion of the French Article V(1), on the contrary, reads as follows: "La reconnaissance et l'exécution de la sentence *ne seront refusées*, sur requête de la partie contre laquelle elle est invoquée, *que si* cette partie fournit à l'autorité compétente du pays où la reconnaissance et l'exécution sont demandées la preuve: Que....". The phrase "...ne seront refusées que..." does not perfectly match with the formulation "...may be refused if..." used in the English text, but rather states "shall not be refused, unless...".[280] Accordingly, a French court faced with an application for enforcement of an award which contains a procedural default as enumerated in subparagraphs (a)-(e), would, unlike its English equivalent, feel obliged to reject the application.[281] As to the question of whether the

279 New York Convention, Article XVI: 1. This Convention, of which the Chinese, English, French, Russian and Spanish texts shall be equally authentic, shall be deposited in the archives of the United Nations.

280 Paulsson, May or Must Under the New York Convention: An Exercise in Syntax and Linguistics, Arb Int (1998), 227; see also Redfern/Hunter (2004), *op. cit.*, paras. 10-34.

281 Gaillard (1998), *op. cit.*, 661: *"Aux yeux d'un lecteur francais, il n'est pas impossible de lire l'article VI comme n'exprimant qu'une faculté, traduite par le 'ne-que' don't l'objet est de souligner le caractère limitatif des causes possibles de refus de reconnaissance. L'article VII confirme aussitôt cette lecture et ne laisse subsister aucun doute sur le fait que les auteurs de la Convention n'ont voulu fixer que les hypothèses minimales de reconnaissance des sentences, laissant à chaque Etat le soin d'apprécier s'il y a lieu d'être plus libéral."*

notion of Article V(1) is to be interpreted as permissive or mandatory, comparing the authentic English version with the equally authentic French version, in fact, rather complicates a conclusive perception. Just as Jan Paulsson amplified, "[t]he problem is not the negative formulation in French... Rather it is the use of the future indicative *ne seront...que si* (*shall* not...unless) instead of the conditional *ne pourront etre refusées...que si* (*may* not be...unless). The latter wording would have had precisely the same meaning as the English and would leave no doubt as to the element of discretion".[282]

While the official English and French versions remain in conflict, the other authentic versions of the New York Convention might be of assistance in identifying a common meaning.

The Spanish Section of Article V(1) provides: "*Sólo se podrá denegar* el reconocimiento y la ejecución de la sentencia,...*si* esta parte prueba ante la autoridad competente del país en que se pide el reconocimiento y la ejecución: Que..." (Emphasis added). Although, like the French text, using the future tense corresponding to "it will only be possible to be denied if...", the Spanish version also manifests a permissive nature, which is of superior relevance due to the "linguistic proximity" of the Romance languages Spanish and French.

Since the authoress is not well grounded in either Chinese or Russian, she relies on the findings of the esteemed Jan Paulsson, who came to the conclusion that both the Chinese and the Russian versions "correspond fully" with the permissive language used in the English text.[283]

In the Chinese text of the New York Convention Article V(1) reads as follows:[284]

第五條

一．裁決唯有於受裁決援用之一造向聲請承認及執行地之主管機關提具證據證明有下列情形之一時，始得依該造之請求，拒予承認及執行：

282 Paulsson (1998), *op. cit.*, 227

283 *Ibid.*, 227; Accordingly the Mandarin expression '*ke yi*' means – dependent on the context – either '*can*' or '*may*', while the Russian phrase '*mozhet byt*' equates to '*may be*' or '*can be*'.

284 The full Chinese text is available on: *http://www.uncitral.org/uncitral/zh/uncitral_texts/arbitration/NYConvention.html*

And the relevant Section of the Russian version of the New York Convention is:[285]

> 1. В признании и приведении в исполнение арбитражного решения может быть отказано по просьбе той стороны, против которой оно направлено, только если эта сторона представит компетентной власти по месту, где испрашивается признание и приведение в исполнение доказательства того, что

The Arabic version of the New York Convention has not been examined by Paulsson, but may be deemed to be of particular significance, as it is the most recent official translation by the United Nations. Its wording is as follows:[286]

> ١- لا يجوز رفض الاعتراف بالقرار وتنفيذه ، بناء على طلب الطرف المحتج ضده بهذا القرار ، الا اذا قدم ذلك الطرف الى السلطة المختصة التي يطلب اليها الاعتراف والتنفيذ ما يثبت :

In the light of the preceding discussions on the permissive or mandatory nature of Article V(1), the UN has thus had the chance to clarify its genuine intention by keeping the Arabic version in a clear use of language. It may be said that the Arabic text, similar to the four other versions, expresses a permissive interpretation of Article V(1)(e).

As five of the six official languages of the United Nations drafted Article V(1) of the New York Convention in a permissive manner, it may be assumed that the wording is in fact intended to give discretion to the enforcing courts. The distinct French reading of the Convention's Article V(1) does not suffice to rebut such an assumption, according to the International Law Commission's "presumption that the terms [of plurilingual treaties] are intended to have the same meaning in each text", it rather swims against the tide.

285 The full Russian text is available on: *http://www.uncitral.org/uncitral/ru/uncitral_texts/arbitration/NYConvention.html*

286 The full Arabic text is available on: *http://www.uncitral.org/uncitral/ar/uncitral_texts/arbitration/NYConvention.html*

Admittedly, the New York Convention's use of the term 'may' is in contrast to the language provided by the Geneva Convention, which provided that enforcement "shall be refused" for vacated arbitral awards. On the other hand, the language of the European Convention Article IX is equally permissive, and since its drafters deliberately linked their ideas to the New York Convention Article V(1), it may be assumed that they realised and approved such discretion given to the enforcing courts – otherwise, they would have had the opportunity to renounce the permissive wording.[287]

However, it is held that tension is apparent between Article V's 'may' and the language of the New York Convention Articles III and VII. Article III states that each signatory "*shall* recognize" and enforce arbitral awards, provided the preconditions set out by the New York Convention and the applicable procedural law are met. Article VII similarly provides the Convention "*shall* not" deprive a pursuing party of any rights to enforce his award to the extent permitted by the applicable national law or adopted international treaties. When assessing the quality of 'guidance' provided by Article V of the New York Convention, it is also clear that the authors admittedly intended to facilitate enforcement, and accordingly, carefully considered the language used to manifest such intention. While it is reported that the drafters had considerable discussions on the adoption of the term 'binding' instead of 'final', it might be assumed that they also deliberately inserted the mandatory expression 'shall not' in Articles III and VII, as they provide obligations in favour of recognition and enforcement. Article V, in contrast, constitutes the single significant (but appropriate) exception from the Convention's 'pro-enforcement bias', which should not, however, culminate in a denial of enforcement. The language of Article V therefore provides that contracting states 'may' instead of 'shall' refuse enforcement of awards in the presence of a listed justification.[288]

It is argued that according to the Preparatory Works of the New York Convention it appears that the drafters had "remarkably little discussion of the portion" of Article V(1) permitting courts to deny enforcement of vacated awards, while they extensively debated the change of terminology from 'final' to 'binding'. They did not give an explanation "why the final language of Article V(1)" sets out that enforcement of arbitral awards 'may be refused' under certain circumstances, as

287 Gaillard (1998), *op. cit.*, 665: *"La Convention de Genève ne laisse subsister aucune ambiguïté, ... les Etats n'ont nullement l'obligation de refuser de reconnaître les sentences ainsi annulées. ... Certains pourront en effet y voir une clarification de son [la Convention de New York] caractère facultatif."*

288 Sampliner (1996), *op. cit.*, 23.

it "strongly suggests, ... that it is up to the discretion of the enforcing courts" to frankly decide on an application for enforcement as to which the defending party asserted and proved an justification for rejection. Even if there were no extensive debates or specific explanatory notes, it may be assumed that the drafters knew what they intended when they adopted the permissive "may" in the language of Article V(1). Maybe there was no such reference or merely little discussion, due to the very fact that 'may' "leaps out at any lawyer" as non-mandatory.[289] Drawing a comparison to the considerable discussion held on the "binding"-requirement in order to expose the deficient "minus" of discussion on the 'may' language is misleading. The adoption of the term "binding" was intended to replace 'final', the former language used by the Geneva Convention. Such a displacement requires *a priori,* a solid rationale, which in turn requires preparatory discussions. Since both terms are rather complex, their actual meanings do not "leap out" at first glance. In fact it is the intricate distinctness between the terms "final" and "binding" that calls for a step-by-step approach, as generally performed by the authors of the Convention. The language of Article (V)(1), in contrast, manifests a novel perception of international arbitration as a fairly autonomous mechanism, and thus reflects the pro-enforcement bias from the outset, though not by using juridical terminology, but rather a language familiar to any perceptive reader – which might alienate jurisprudents.

With such indications arguing in favour of unambiguous wording, the discussion presumably did not flare up *ab initio* due to the 'woolly' language of Article V(1). The permissive character was rather discussed because its proper application promoted undesired results, namely when the concerned court realises it 'may', but in fact does not wish to refuse enforcement. Therefore, it may be deemed, that in particular the language of Article V(1)(e) was, due to its definitive nature, beyond dispute until the first remarkable, so much the more controversial decision originated therefrom: the almost revolutionary decision to give full effect to an award which was actually deemed to be extinct due to a valid annulment through a respectable competent foreign court.

For the grounds discussed above it may be concluded that Article V(1) leaves it to the courts faced with an application of enforcement against which the defending

289 As to the discussions held at the New York Conference: *"During the preparation of the Conventions, a draft providing that enforcement "shall be refused" when an award had been annulled in its country of origin was not adopted"*, Paulsson (1996), *op. cit.,* 107 at fn. 13; *"It would seem neither fair nor appropriately respectful of the distinguished drafters of the Convention... to attribute this ultimate change to oversight, and to read in a mandatory proscription against enforcing nullified awards when none exists in the final language."*, Sampliner (1997), *op. cit.*, 149; Freyer/Gharavi (1998), *op. cit.*, 104.

party asserts and proves a reason for refusal, to decide on such an application at its own discretion. Courts in contracting states did not merely realise, but increasingly availed themselves of the provided option to either refuse, or provide for enforcement under certain circumstances. Actually, the regime of Article V(1)(e) of the New York Convention permits disregard for the common principle of 'ex nihilo nil fit'. But it was – and still is – held that the authors of the New York Convention may impossibly have intended such permission – even though the language in fact seemed to be permissive. Consequently, the language was deemed to be a lapse.

However, the language of Article V(1) is as little a lapse or in need of correction as the outcome is. Facts should not be confused with preferences, nor should legal exegesis be subordinated to international comity. For all these reasons, and despite the fact that such a perception is still opposed by some authors,[290] Article V(1) is clearly permissive and allows for discretion of the enforcing courts within signatory states.[291]

Because Article V is supplemented with the 'more favourable law' clause of Article VII, parties to the New York Convention can either strictly provide for enforcement of annulled awards or leave it to their courts' discretion for the in-

---

290 In support of a mandatory interpretation of Article V(1): Schwab/Walter (2005), *op. cit.*, Ch. 57, para. 21 ("*sind zu versagen*"); Gaillard/Goldmann (eds.) (1999), *op. cit.*, para. 1687 (*"If an award is set aside in its country of origin it loses the benefit of the New York Convention. ...According to the Convention all other jurisdictions must refuse to acknowledge the effects of a decision to set aside made elsewhere, and such a decision will have no effect on the Convention's operation."*)

291 *"[T]he convention does not as suggested by a prominent commentator impose an obligation to refuse enforcement, on the contrary it leaves it to the court in the second state free to grant recognition"*, Smit, The Internationalization of Law and Legal Practice: A-National Arbitration, 63 Tul. L. Rev. (1989), 641 with reference to van den Berg, The New York Convention of 1958 (1981), 349-351; Further in support of a permissive perception of Article V(1): Schwab/Walter (2005), *op. cit.*, 22; Freyer (2008), *op. cit.*, 758; Gaillard (2007), *op. cit.*; Delaume, Enforcement Against a Foreign State of an Arbitral Award Annulled in the Foreign State, RDAI (1997), 254; Alvarez, The Enforcement of Arbitral Awards, Comm. Arb. (Continuing Legal Education, June 1996) at 1.1.19; Schwartz, A Comment on Chromalloy: Hilmarton à l'américaine, 14 J Int'l Arb (1997), 133; Park, Arbitration of International Business Disputes: Studies in Law and Practice (2006), 185; Webster (2006), *op. cit.*, 223; Mallmann, Die Bedeutung der Schiedsvereinbarung im Verfahren zur Anerkennung und Vollstreckbarerklärung ausländischer Schiedssprüche, SchiedsVZ (2004), 157; similarly Section 207 of the United States Federal Arbitration Act provides that U.S. courts *"shall confirm the [foreign] award unless it finds one of the grounds for refusal or deferral of recognition or enforcement of the award specified in the... Convention."*

dividual case. By all means, signatories cannot compel their courts to necessarily refuse enforcement of awards under the New York Convention.[292]

It is somewhat contradictory that countries which are parties to both the New York and the European Conventions should not respect a foreign annulment decision based on public policy reasons due to Article XI, if the award was rendered in another European Convention state while recognising such an award in accordance with Article V, if it was rendered in a non-European Convention state.[293] For example, if enforcement of an award issued and annulled on public policy basis in Germany is sought in Austria, the Austrian court would have, in the light of Article IX, no other choice than to grant enforcement. However, if such an award were rendered and annulled on public policy basis in England, which is not a party to the European Convention, the Austrian court would have discretion and may decide to refuse enforcement in accordance with Article V. Even though such outcomes seem contradictory, they are well in accordance with current international legislation.

III. The Quality of Guidance Provided by the European Convention

Only Article IX(1) lit. a-d of the European Convention sets out rules for the recognition and enforcement of foreign arbitral awards – strictly speaking, for refusal of recognition and enforcement of arbitral awards that were previously set aside in their country of origin.

In this context it is to be examined whether the guidance provided by Article IX is permissive or mandatory. It is clear that enforcement of an annulled award may not be refused if the annulment was based on grounds not listed in Article IX(1) lit. a-d. But it may be questioned whether given a ground listed in Article IX(1) lit. a-d the refusal of enforcement is permissive or mandatory. In other words, if Article IX(1) lit. a-d requires courts to refuse enforcement of an award that was set aside based on a listed ground, or whether the enforcing court retains discretion to grant enforcement notwithstanding the valid annulment. In favour of a mandatory nature is the European Convention's intention of maintaining a minimum standard of internationally recognised annulment reasons. Therefore, Article IX(1) lit. a-d allows for a denial of enforcement in limited cases. For a permissive interpretation of Article IX(1) lit.a-d, on the contrary, it is important to consider that the European Convention's major purpose is to promote the

292 Paulsson (1996), *op. cit.*, 107, however with remark that *"a country bound by the Convention may require its judges to refuse enforcement under the circumstances defined in Article V"*.

293 Gaillard (1998), *op. cit.*, 666.

effectiveness of international arbitration, including enforcement of arbitral awards to the greatest possible extent. Therefore it even confined the limited reasons for refusal of enforcement under the New York Convention, which demonstrates the European Convention's arbitration-friendly attitude. Article IX(1) rules that "[t]he setting aside... of an arbitral award... *shall only* constitute a *ground* for the refusal of... enforcement" (emphasis added) if based on one of the listed reasons. Unlike the mandatory language in the French text of Article V(1)(e) of the New York Convention, Article IX(1) of the European Convention does not rule that enforcement itself "*shall* be refused", but merely that a ground allowing for refusal *shall* only be constituted in certain cases. Accordingly the European Convention does not generally preclude enforcement of set aside awards. But it merely intends to leave it to the discretion of the enforcing courts to grant enforcement even though the award has been set aside on a ground listed in Article IX(1) lit. a-d. The European Convention's justifications for a refusal of enforcement are therefore of a permissive nature.

IV. Distinct National Case Law and Approaches

When a national court is asked to grant enforcement of an award that was handed down by an international arbitration, but has meanwhile been nullified by a competent authority in the forum state, it has to determine which regime is to be applied and whether such a regime provides permissive or mandatory guidance. As for European courts, the interplay of the two principal Conventions in the field of recognition and enforcement, the New York Convention, and the European Convention has been displayed with the result that the European Convention – for different reasons – takes precedence over the earlier New York Convention, while the character of Article V(1) New York Convention has finally been identified as permissive.

Today, few courts have been faced with requests for enforcement of a previously nullified award. As will be shown, some countries clearly rely on their domestic arbitration law in accordance with Article VII of the New York Convention. Others properly obey the elaborated international regime, whilst yet others are seemingly inconsistent in their approaches; whereas such 'inconsistency' may as well be caused by alternative memberships of the respective forum states.

Although the relevance of such decisions in numbers is rather negligible,[294] its relevance as to their indicative effect is significant. Assuming that in the economic, or at least the international arbitration world the belief prevails that once a party

294 Sampliner (1996), *op. cit.*, 24.

succeeds in obtaining recovery in arbitration, even though such recovery may be withdrawn, the succeeding party could still carry out the award, and enforce assets of the defeated debtor – at least in one of several contemplable countries.

It is also said that such a course of action entails some principally undesirable 'forum shopping' features.[295] However, "forum shopping" rather refers to an active endeavour of a party to benefit from the most favourable regime out of different competent jurisdictions involving a tactical distribution of assets.[296] But a party seeking for enforcement of a nullified award, in contrast, merely aims to benefit from the different approaches thereto taken by the countries where the counterpart has located his assets. These tactical considerations when seeking for enforcement of an annulled award are rather reminiscent of a "chase for enforcement" than of "forum shopping".

Basically, it is not objectionable to seek for enforcement where it is likely to be the easiest and most efficient – as long as there is a valid arbitral award. But as soon as the rendered award is challenged or has already been set aside, such ambition may add up to a misuse of rights. Parties have consistently entered into arbitration in order to obtain a fair and just settlement of the disputed issue and generally aim to continue their existing business relations. None of the parties (re)considers the location of his assets before entering into arbitration. Usually, the assets are where the parties need them or hope for economic benefits, but not where they are safe from enforcement of nullified awards. Parties do not anticipate that they might be involved in an international arbitration where the rendered award might be vacated by a national court in the forum state, but nevertheless be granted enforcement by a national court in this or that state.

However, even the pursuing party still encounters obstacles when seeking enforcement.

1. French Case Law

Following a comment of the U.S. Second Circuit in *Baker Marine* (*see below*) it may be said that French courts have shown a rather "mechanical application of domestic arbitral law" in several judgements of both lower and higher instances.

---

295 Gharavi, The International Effectiveness of the Annulment of an Arbitral Award (2002), 125; Gharavi, Chromalloy: Another View, 12 Mealey's Int Arb Rep (1997), 22; see also Kreindler, Arbitral Forum Shopping, in Parallel State and Arbitral Procedures in International Arbitration – Dossiers of the ICC Institute of World Business Law, Cremades/Lew (eds.) 153 et seq.

296 Siehr (2001), *op. cit.*, 479.

a) Société Berardi v. Société Clair (1980)[297]

The first (unpublished) case in which a French court was asked to enforce a nullified award was Berardi v. Clair in 1980 – before the adoption of the New Code of Civil Procedure.

Subject of the arbitration was the value of shares in the Gabonese S. A. "Routière", which was – according to the Parties' agreement – to be determined on the basis of the balance sheet of December 31 1972. Although Berardi had guaranteed "the correctness and sincerity" of the relevant balance sheet, the arbitral tribunal considered this guarantee as pointless. In the opinion of the arbitrators, it was crucial that Clair had participated at a general meeting of shareholders where the balance sheet had been approved, "without making any objections". In consequence, they dismissed Clair's claim.

At Berardi's request, the Paris Court of First Instance granted enforcement of the award, though meanwhile a Swiss Court found the award "arbitrary", because the arbitral tribunal failed to assess the correctness and sincerity of the balance sheets autonomously despite their obligation to do so under the terms of reference. The award was, hence, set aside in accordance with national laws (*in concreto* Art. 36(f) of the Swiss Concordat on Arbitration).[298]

Subsequently, the Paris Cour d'Appel revoked its prior recognition of the nullified award, because it considered Article V(1)(e) New York Convention – in the light of the French authentic version – to be of mandatory character and thus providing that the enforcing court *must* refuse enforcement in case of an annulment of the award.

b) Société Pabalk Trcaret v. Société Norsolor (1984)[299]

The first time a state court decided to deflect from the New York Convention provisions for (non)enforcement of nullified awards by relying on domestic arbitration law, was the 1984 French Supreme Court decision known as *Norsolor*.

---

297 Unpublished Case No. 11542; Translated excerpt in XII Y. B. Com. Arb. (1982), 319 referred to by Sampliner (1996), *op. cit.*, 24.

298 The decision is not published.

299 Award of 26 October 1984 in ICC Case No. 3131, IX Y. B. Com. Arb. (1984), 109-110; Reference by Gharavi (2002), *op. cit.*; French Supreme Court, decision of 09 September 1984, Rev. Arb. 1985, 341, commentary of Goldmann, J.D.I. (1985), 679, note Khan, Rev. Crit. D.I.P. (1985), 551, commentary of Dutoit, Dalloz (1985), 101, commentary of Robert, Retour sur l'arret Pabalk Norsolor, Dalloz (1985), Chronique 83, 2 J Int'l Arb. (1985), 67.

The original dispute submitted to international arbitration arose out of an agency agreement concluded between the French company, Norsolor, and a Turkish company, Pabalk Trcaret. Rather based on *lex mercatoria* than domestic law of either party, the arbitral tribunal, seated in Vienna, found Norsolor breached its obligation of good faith and awarded Pabalk Trcaret damages amounting to 800,000 French Francs. On appeal the Vienna Court of Appeal partially set aside the award holding inter alia, that the tribunal's application of *lex mercatoria* rather than the applicable national law exceeded its competency. Nevertheless, Pabalk Ticaret sought enforcement against Norsolor, in France. While the lower French court granted enforcement, Norsolor, subsequent to the annulment decision of the Austrian court, appealed against such enforcement, whereupon the Paris Court of Appeal overruled the earlier leave for enforcement relying on New York Convention, Article V(1)(e).

Finally, at the request of Pabalk Ticaret the French Supreme Court revived the leave for enforcement holding that the Paris Court of Appeal had violated Article VII of the New York Convention by simply refusing enforcement on basis of Article V(1)(e) without particular scrutiny as to whether Pabalk Ticaret was deprived of more favourable French law. Strictly speaking, the French Supreme Court emphasised with respect to the 'more favourable law' clause, Article VII, that enforcement of a nullified award may not be refused merely on the basis of Article V(1)(e), but rather if even French law provides a justification for a refusal. The 'more favourable law' clause was accordingly perceived not as a privilege of the parties, but rather as an obligation for the courts to examine and apply *ex officio* their domestic law if more enforcement-friendly.[300]

c) Société Polish Ocean Line v. Société Jolasry (1993)

It was only after nearly a decade had passed that a U.S. court confirmed the *Norsolor* case with the *Polish Ocean Line* v. *Jolasry* decision. After arbitration between Polish Ocean Line and the French company Jolasry was held in Poland and resulted in an award for Jolasry, Polish Ocean Line appealed to a Polish court, and also obtained a stay of enforcement pending the relevant outcome. Nonetheless, Jolasry applied for enforcement of the award in France. In the end, the *Cour de Cassation* upheld the decision of the Court of Appeal, which in turn had confirmed the leave for enforcement of the ultimately vacated award. Again, France's highest court provided guidance in favour of disrespect of local standard annulments and held that:

300 See also Freyer/Gharavi (1998), *op. cit.*, 108.

"[A] French court may not deny an application for leave to enforce an arbitral award which was set aside or suspended by a competent authority in the country in which the award was rendered, if the grounds for opposing enforcement, although mentioned in Art. V(1)(e) of the 1958 New York Convention, are not among the grounds specified in Art. 1502 of the New Code of Civil Procedure."[301]

Hence, the French Supreme Court turned away from its less restrictive notion in *Palbalk v. Norsolor* that Article V(1) lit. a-e reasons would simply not suffice for justifying a denial of enforcement, but only if even French law provides for refusal. Now the court rather held that French courts may not at all rely on Article V(1) to refuse enforcement, since Article VII of the New York Convention would clearly give precedence to French arbitration law, in particular Article 1502 of the New Code of Civil Procedure, over Article V(1) lit. a-d.[302] Local standard annulments are not enumerated among the justification for refusal of enforcement of Article 1502 New Code of Civil Procedure; accordingly the French leave for enforcement was consistent.[303]

d) Société Hilmarton Ltd. v. Société OTV (1994)[304]

Finally in 1994, the French Supreme Court manifested such an approach in its most noted decision on this issue, *Hilmarton v. OTV*.[305] In the first instance, Hilmarton, an English company initiated an arbitration proceeding, governed by Swiss law and seated in Geneva, against a French company, Omnium de Traitement et de Valorisation (OTV), claiming allegedly due payments for performed work. As the sole arbitrator considered the contract to be governed by Algerian law and again in violation of its mandatory principles, he denied Hilmarton's claim.[306] However, the Geneva Court granted Hilmarton's appeal,[307] and found the arbitral award 'arbitrary' and thus capable of nullification pursuant to Article 36(f) of

301 Cour de Cassation, 10 March 1993 in XIX Y. B. Com. Arb. (1994), 662-663.

302 For Article 1502 see fn. 285.

303 Generally see Gharavi (2002), *op. cit.*

304 Soc. Hilmarton Ltd. v. Soc. OTV, French Supreme Court, decision of 23 March 1994, XIX Y. B. Com. Arb. (1994), 665; Rev. Arb. (1994), 329, commentary of Jarosson, J.D.I (1994), 701, note Gaillard, Rev. Crit. DIP (1995), 359, commentary of Oppetit.; RTD Com. 1994, 702 commentary of Dubarry et Loquin; 5 Mealey's Int Arb Rep (1994), 6.

305 See i. a. Webster (2006), op. cit., 212.

306 ICC Case No. 5622, XIX Y. B. Com. Arb. (1994), 105 et seq.

307 Cour de Justice du canton de Genève, 17 November 1989, in 2 Rev. Arb. (1993), 327.

the Swiss Intercantonal Concordat on Arbitration.[308] The Swiss Federal Tribunal subsequently confirmed the decision.[309] While Hilmarton initiated new arbitration proceedings in Switzerland, OTV sought for recognition and enforcement of the original award in France, which was granted by the Court of First Instance in Paris and later confirmed by the Paris Court of Appeal. The Court again identified Article V(1)(e) as rather mandatory by stating:

"The provision of Art. V(1)(e) of the Convention – according to which exequatur must be denied to an award which has been set aside in the country in which it was made – does not apply when the law of the country where enforcement is sought permits enforcement of such an award."[310]

Hence, a French court once more manifested the exclusive relevance of Article 1502 New Code of Civil Procedure in contrast to Article V(1)lit. a-d New York Convention. In 1994, the French *Cour de Cassation* ultimately supported the decision, holding that *"the award rendered in Switzerland is an international award which is not integrated in the legal system of that State, so that it remains in existence even if set aside and its recognition in France is not contrary to international public policy."*[311] In addition to the afore-noted argumentation of French arbitration law, particularly Article 1502 New Code of Civil Procedure being more favourable, and thus taking precedence over Article V(1)(e) of the New York Convention the *Cour de Cassation* this time established its fundamental perception of international arbitration entailing truly international awards.

Meanwhile the pending arbitration proceeding in Switzerland resulted in a new award, this time in favour of Hilmarton. As Hilmarton's subsequent application for enforcement at the Nanterre Court of First Instance was granted,[312] OTV promptly appealed against the leave, arguing that the first Paris judgement on the

308 Swiss Concordat on (in effect from 1969 to 1984), Article 36(f): An action for annulment of the arbitral award may be brought before the judicial authority provided for in Article 3, where it is alleged: (f) that the award is arbitrary in that it was based on findings which were manifestly contrary to the facts appearing on the file, or that it constitutes a clear violation of law or equity.

309 Tribunal Fédéral, 17 April 1990 in 2 Rev Arb (1993), 322.

310 Cour d'Appel, Paris, decision of 19 December 1991 90–16778 in XIX Y. B. Com. Arb. (1994), 655 – 657.

311 Webster (2006), *op. cit.*, 201-226, 213 with reference to Hilmarton, XX Y. B. Com. Arb. (1995), 663-65.

312 *"Après...coexistaient donc dans l'ordre juridique français,...une sentence stuant dans un sens donné, une sentence postérieure statuant, sur le même litige entre les mêmes parties, en sens contraire et un jugement annulant la première sentence. Il va sans dire que la situation ne pouvait demeurer en l'état."* Gaillard (1998), *op. cit.*, 652 et seq.

enforceability of the original award had become *res judicata*, and that enforcing a contradictory award on the same issue between the same parties would infringe French *ordre public*. Nevertheless, the Versailles Court of Appeal confirmed the leave to enforce the second award, although it acknowledged the lately developed approach of enforcing nullified awards pursuant to Article 1502 of the New Code of Civil Procedure, but denied that French *ordre public* opposes *"the recognition of a foreign arbitral award rendered after a previous award, which has been declared enforceable in France, has been set aside in the country of rendition"*. Additionally the court emphasised:

"To reach a different conclusion would mean to allow the systematical prevalence of the award which has been first recognized or enforced in France, whatever its value in the foreign legal system. It would also mean to accord to enforcement an effect which by far exceeds its object: it is certainly not the purpose of the enforcement to maintain awards in France which have been set aside in the State of rendition."[313]

On appeal the French Supreme Court clarified that *"the existence of a final French decision bearing on the same subject between the same parties creates an obstacle to any recognition in France of court decisions or arbitral awards rendered abroad which are incompatible with it..."*.[314] The French Supreme Court therefore succinctly reversed the Versailles decision due to its disregard of Article 1351 of the French Civil Code, which governs the *res judicata* effect.[315]

It should be noted that the second award, rendered in Hilmarton's favour, was ultimately granted enforcement in England, since the English court found the second award to be in accordance with the national public policy of the country of the proper law (Switzerland), the crucial law (Swiss law) and English public policy.[316]

e) S.A. Lesbats et Fils v. Esterer WD GmbH (Dr. Volker Grub) (2007)

The French company S.A. Lesbats et Fils holding a saw mill, and the German company Esterer WD GmbH entered into a contract including an agreement on

---

313 Versailles Cour d'appel, XXI Y. B. Com. Arb. (1996), 524 – 531.

314 Gaillard (1998), *op. cit.*, 653: *"Cette décision de la Cour de cassation a ainsi pleinement restauré la cohérence, qui avait paru un instant incertaine, de la jurisprudence française relative à la reconnaissance des sentences annulées dans le pays d'origine."*

315 Article 1351: "The force of res judicata takes place only with respect to what was the subject matter of a judgment."

316 *See* High Court of Justice, Queen's Bench Division (Commercial Court), 24 May 1999, excerpts published in XXIVa Y. B. Com. Arb. (1999), 777 – 785.

ICC arbitration for arising disputes. In fact later on, a dispute arose and was settled in Belgium by an ICC award of a sole arbitrator in favour of Esterer, which its court-appointed judicial administrator subsequently successfully sought to enforce in France. While Lesbats appealed against the leave of the Paris Court of First Instance, the Brussels Court of First Instance set aside the arbitral award due to an invalidity of the arbitration agreement. Nevertheless the French Court of Appeal confirmed the enforcement decision again based on French procedural law, which applied by virtue of the New York Convention, Article VII and does not provide for refusal of enforcement only due to an annulment at the court of the forum state. The Court precisely held:

"As Dr. Grub correctly stresses, Art. VII(1) of the 1958 New York Convention encourages, for efficacy's sake, the application of a national law which is more favourable to the enforcement of awards that the Convention's own provisions. This is precisely the case of French law, whose Art. 1502 [New Code of Civil Procedure] does not list annulment of the award in the country of the place of arbitration as a ground for refusing enforcement. In fact, it is a fundamental principle of French law in respect of the denial of enforcement of awards rendered abroad that annulment by a court of the seat does not affect the existence of the awards, hindering its recognition and enforcement in other legal systems, because the arbitrator is not an integral part of the juridical system of the country of the seat – in the present case, Belgium."[317]

This decision of the Paris Court of Appeal is another consequent confirmation of the established approach to enforcement of set aside foreign awards. However, the French court did not expressly consider the European Convention, Article IX(1) although the arbitral award rendered between a German and a French company is actually also a European Convention award. Since the annulment of the arbitral award was based on the invalidity of the parties' arbitration agreement, the French court might have refused enforcement in accordance with Article IX(1)(a) of the European Convention.

Société PT Putrabali Adyamulia v. Société Rena Holding (2007)[318]

The most recent French case in favour of enforcement of a (partially) vacated award is fairly similar to the Hilmarton case: Putrabali, an Indonesian company, initiated an arbitration proceeding against (later named) Rena Holding, a French company, due to a dispute arising out of a sales contract on spices, which were lost during a shipwreck. The arbitral tribunal, seated in London, held Rena Holding

317 Paris Court of Appeal, 18 January 2007, No. 05/10887, in XXXII Y. B. Com. Arb. (2007), 297.

318 PT Putrabali Adyamulia v. Rena Holding, in XXXII Y. B. Com. Arb. (2007), 299.

capable of defending payment of the lost cargo. On Putrabali's appeal, an English judge found Rena's failed payment in breach of contract, and accordingly partially nullified the award, remanding it to the arbitral tribunal.[319]

However, Rena successfully applied for recognition and enforcement of the original award at the Paris Court of First Instance,[320] while the tribunal in a second arbitration awarded Putrabali payment of €163,086.04.[321] While Putrabali's appeal against the enforcement decision in favour of the first award failed at the Paris Court,[322] it nevertheless obtained likewise enforcement of its second award from the Paris *Tribunal de Grande Instance*.[323] Though upon Rena's appeal, the Paris Court of Appeal overruled the recognition of the second award due to the *res judicata* effect of the former recognition of the original award.[324] Putrabali in turn appealed against both decisions of the Paris Court of Appeal, albeit the French Supreme Court rejected the appeal and first confirmed enforcement of the premier award, manifesting that an arbitral award, *"which is not linked to the legal order of a particular country, is a ruling of international justice, the validity of which is examined in the light of the rules of the country in which its recognition and enforcement is sought"*.[325] Therefore, Rena Holding could by virtue of Article VII of the New York Convention rely on the award issued in London revoking *"the rules of French law pertaining to international arbitration, which do not provide for the setting aside of an award in its country of origin as a ground to refuse to recognize and enforce the award handed down abroad."*[326]

In its second finding, the Supreme Court confirmed the previous Paris Court of Appeal decision holding that *"res judicata attached to the ruling... – which confirmed and enforced the... award at the request of Rena Holding"*,[327] rendering it impossible to recognise and enforce the later award in favour of Putrabali due

319 His Honour Judge Havelock-Allan, Q.C. in PT Putrabali Adyamulia v. Société est Espice (2003) 2 Lloyd's Rep. 700.
320 By order of 30 September 2003.
321 Havaron, Enforcement of Annulled Foreign Arbitral Awards: The French Supreme Court Confirms The Hilmarton Trend, 22 Mealey's Int Arb Rep (2007), 2.
322 Paris Court of Appeal, 3 March 2005, Société Putrabali Adyamulia v. S.A. Rena Holding et alt., note by Gaillard, 3 Rev. Arb. (2006), 665.
323 By order of 10 February 2004.
324 Cour de Cassation, 1st Civil Chamber, 29 June 2007, Société Putrabali Adyamulia v. S.A. Rena Holding et alt., n° 05- 8.053.
325 Cour de Cassation, 1st Civil Chamber, 29 June 2007, Société Putrabali Adyamulia v. S.A. Rena Holding et alt., n° 05- 8.053; Translation from Haravon (2007), *op. cit.*, 33.
326 Translation from *ibid.*, 33.
327 Cour de Cassation, 1st Civil Chamber, 29 June 2007, Société Putrabali Adyamulia v. S.A. Rena Holding et alt., n° 06-3.293; Translation from Haravon (2007), *op. cit.*, 33.

to its inconsistency with the *res judicata* award. Hence, French courts once more consequently demonstrated a strict application of their domestic laws, allowing for the enforcement of a set aside award, and furthermore conceding *res judicata* effect to such enforcement.

However, the reasoning of the Supreme Court has been disputed within the international arbitration world.[328] Some authors have criticised that the legal effect of arbitral awards would thus rather depend on the assessment of the courts at the enforcement state, than of the courts at the forum state.[329] This was, on the contrary, objected by reference that precluding the enforcement state from an autonomous assessment would contravene the New York Convention, Article V(1) and besides would impede the enforcing state's legitimate interest of controlling the assets within its territory.[330] Besides, some commentators are concerned that the French approach would encourage seeking for judicial enforcement as soon as they suspect the underlying party of seeking to set aside the award, which would contribute to a "chase for exequatur".[331]

g) Conclusions on the French Approach

From the first encounter with a request for enforcement of a nullified award, French case law has systematically observed the interaction of national and international legislation. Thus, pursuant to the new Decree on International Arbitration – which did not yet apply in Berardi v. Clair – and admitted by Article VII of the New York Convention, French courts are willing to enforce arbitral awards notwithstanding a former nullification in the forum state, as demonstrated in six cases.[332] A core pro-

328 Note by Gaillard, 3 Rev. Arb. (2006), 665.

329 *For example* Bollée, Les methodes du droit international privé à l'épreuve des sentences arbitrales N° 8, Economica (2004), para. 369; Paris Court of Appeals, International Bechtel Company Limited v. Department of Civil Aviation of the Government of Dubai, September 29, 2005 with commentary by Muir-Watt, Rev. Arb. (2006), 695.

330 See Gaillard's note, 3 Rev. Arb. (2006), 665, and in L'execution des sentences annulées dans leur pays d'origine, 3 J.D.I. (1998); Fouchard, La portée internationale de l'annulation de la sentence arbitrale dans son pays d'origine, Rev. Arb. 1997, 329; Paulsson, L'éxecution des sentences arbitrales en dépit d'une annulation en fonction d'un critère local (ACL), 1 ICC. Bull. (1998), 14.

331 Loquin, Commentary on Chromalloy, RTD Com. (1994), 702.

332 Sampliner (1996), *op. cit.*, 24 with reference to Société Pabalk Ticaret Sirketi v. Société Anonyme Norsolor, 95 Dalloz Sirey 101 (Cour de Cassation, 1984), English excerpt in XXI Y. B. Com. Arb. (1986), 484; Polish Ocean Lines v. S.A. Jolasry, 120 J.D.I. (1993), 360, Cour de Cassation 1993, Rev. Arb., 258, English excerpt in XIX Y. B. Com. Arb. (1994), 662; Société Hilmarton v. Société OTV, Cour de Cassation 1994, Rev. Arb. (1994), 327.

vision enabling such outcomes is primarily the New York Convention, Article VII allowing France – which is in fact bound by the New York Convention to provide recognition and enforcement due to the particular regime governed therein – to apply its own, more favourable arbitration law, namely Article 1502 of the New Code of Civil Procedure commanding – *e contrario* – enforcement of nullified awards, which in turn finally became *res judicata* pursuant to Article 1351 French Civil Code.[333]

French courts did not have considerations for international comity towards foreign annulment decisions, but rather strictly applied their national law as permitted by the New York Convention. Out of six requests for enforcement of set aside awards, French courts decided four times in favour of their own nationals and twice in favour of the foreign party. None of the courts ever examined or even considered the applicability of Article IX of the European Convention. In the matter of Palbak v. Norsolor, a Turkish and a French company, the European Convention would today apply; however, at the time of the enforcement decision, Turkey was not yet a party to the European Convention. Otherwise enforcement might have been denied pursuant to Article IX(1)(c) of the European Convention, since the tribunal had exceeded its competence.[334] At least in the enforcement decision on the award between the French company Lesbats et Fils and the German company Esterer WD, the European Convention actually should have been taken into consideration. As the award was even set aside, due to the invalidity of the arbitration agreement, the French would have been justified if they had denied enforcement pursuant to Article IX(1)(a) of the European Convention, and actually even required to do so. Likewise Article IX of the European Convention could have been applied in Polish Ocean Line v. the French company Jolasry. However, the enforcement was granted while the annulment proceeding was still pending, and the European Convention applies merely to enforcement requests of already set aside awards. Polish Ocean Line could only rely on the European Convention to challenge the enforcement decision, if the annulment was already issued and based on a reason listed in Article IX(1) lit. a-d.

---

333 Gaillard (1998), *op. cit.*, 655: *"L'annulation d'une sentence dans un pays dans lequel elle a été rendue ne constitue pas, en elle-même, une cause de refus d'exequatur de cette sentence en France. Le contrôle de la sentence s'effectue au regard des seuls critères du droit français qui sons identiques que les juridictions françaises soient par la voie d'une demande en annulation de la sentence, recevable si elle a été rendue en France, ou par la voie d'une damande d'exequatur, si la sentence a été rendue à l'étranger."*

334 Turkey ratified the European Convention on International Commercial Arbitration on 24 January 1992.

Apparently, French arbitration law is quite arbitration-, or rather enforcement-friendly, reflecting the country's effort of promoting France as a progressive partner in international arbitration. There is also a principle perception of international arbitration as a procedure rendering delocalised awards, without any dependence on a particular national legal system. French courts do not consider an arbitral award as integrated into or emerging from a particular jurisdiction, not even the legal system of the country where the arbitration took place[335], or rather not until the award is sought to be enforced in a particular jurisdiction, as merely recognition and enforcement of an award affiliates it to the relevant legal system, whereupon it is deemed *res judicata*. Accordingly, pursuant to the French perception of international arbitration, awards are not connected to a national legal system, thus capable of 'co-existence' until one of them is sought to be enforced in France, thus "leaving the scene of international justice to crystallize in the French legal order", and with becoming *res judicata* at the time of enforcement leave, it precludes enforcement of the second award on the same issue between the same parties, at least within France.[336]

2. U.S. Case Law

Similar to France, U.S. courts have examined the option of recognition and enforcement of annulled awards and evidenced their discretionary power.

a) Chromalloy Aeroservices Inc. v. Arab Republic of Egypt (1996)[337]

The first time a U.S. court was faced with a request for enforcement of an award which had been set aside by a competent authority in its country of origin, was in 1996 in the matter of the arbitration between *Chromalloy Aero Services v. The Arab Republic of Egypt*.[338] Initially Chromalloy obtained an award in its favour, obliging Egypt on the basis of Egyptian private law to pay more then US$ 18 million. Subsequently Chromalloy sought enforcement in the United States, while the Egyptian Ministry of Defence challenged the award at the Court of Appeal

---

335 Gaillard (1998), *op. cit.*, 654.

336 Haravon (2007), *op. cit.*, 34; See infra 144 et seq.

337 Chromalloy Aeroservices v. The Arab Republic of Egypt, 939 F. Supp. 907 (D.D.C. 1996).

338 See Sampliner (1996), *op. cit.*, 22 et seq. with reference to Civ. No. 94-2339 in Mealey's Int Arb Rep (1996), C-54; Freyer (2000), *op. cit.*, 2 et seq; Paulsson (1996), *op. cit.*, 100 et seq; Gharavi (1997), *op. cit.*, 21 – 27, and The Legal Inconsistencies of Chromalloy, 12 Int. Arb. Report (1997).

of Cairo. The Cairo Court of Appeal considered the parties' underlying contract as an 'administrative contract' subject to Egyptian administrative law, rather than private law. While the Egyptian court decided to set the award aside as "manifestly null",[339] the U.S. District Court of Columbia noted that *"Article V provides a discretionary standard"*, but Article VII of the New York Convention would require application of more favourable national laws.

"In other words, under the Convention, Chromalloy maintains all rights to the enforcement of this arbitral award that it would have in the absence of the Convention. Accordingly, the Court finds that, if the Convention did not exist, the Federal Arbitration Act would provide Chromalloy with a legitimate claim to enforcement of this arbitral award."[340]

Therefore, the American Court did not rely on Article V(1) New York Convention, but on Article VII in order to 'not deprive' Chromalloy of its right ascertained by national U.S. law. Unlike the 'more favourable law' revoked by French judges, the Federal Arbitration Act the District Court referred to does not exactly provide a limited list of valid justifications for a denial of enforcement, but rather lists some valid grounds for nullification if the award is deficient of "fraud, corruption, bias, procedural misconduct, or exceeding the arbitrators' powers in any way, including 'manifest disregard' of the law".[341] However, the Court considered that Federal Arbitration Act, Section 10,[342] also implies the only valid justification for a denial of enforcement if one such listed ground is apparent. Assuming that the

339 Sampliner (1996), *op. cit.*, 25.

340 District Court of Columbia, 13 July 1996, 939 F. Supp. 907, in XXII Y. B. Com. Arb. (1997), 1001–1012.

341 Sampliner (1996), *op. cit.*, 26.

342 U.S. Federal Arbitration Act, Section 10:

(a) In any of the following cases the United States court in and for the district wherein the award was made may make an order vacating the award upon the application of any party to the arbitration

1. Where the award was procured by corruption, fraud, or undue means.
2. Where there was evident partiality or corruption in the arbitrators, or either of them.
3. Where the arbitrators were guilty of misconduct in refusing to postpone the hearing, upon sufficient cause shown, or in refusing to hear evidence pertinent and material to the controversy; or of any other misbehaviour by which the rights of any party have been prejudiced.
4. Where the arbitrators exceeded their powers, or so imperfectly executed them that a mutual, final, and definite award upon the subject matter submitted was not made.
5. Where an award is vacated and the time within which the agreement required the award to be made has not expired the court may, in its discretion, direct a rehearing by the arbitrators.

application of Egyptian private law instead of administrative law constitutes rather a mistake of law than a 'manifest disregard', the Court adjudged that *"as a matter of U.S. law, the award is proper"*.[343] Afterwards, in determining whether to give effect to the Egyptian judgement, the District Court relied on previously established guidelines on enforcement of foreign state court decisions, postulating that the court proceeding had been properly conducted, and the original claim would not be in breach of U.S. public policy. Considering that *"[t]he U.S. public policy in favour of final and binding arbitration of commercial disputes is unmistakable, and supported by treaty, by statute, and by case law"*, the Court deemed the judgement invalid for recognition in the United States, as it presumed jurisdiction in disregard of the parties' agreement which stipulated that the finding of the arbitral tribunal *"shall be final and binding and cannot be made subject to any appeal or other recourse"*.

While the District Court took into consideration that principles of international comity constitute an acknowledged exception to public policy, which could require recognition of the Cairo judgement,[344] it concluded:

> *"[n]o nation is under an unremitting obligation to enforce foreign interests which are fundamentally prejudicial to those of the domestic forum. [C]omity never obligates a national forum to ignore 'the rights of its own citizens or of other persons who are under the protection of its laws.'"*[345]

After all, the District Court found the Egyptian judgement, which disregarded the parties' waiver of recourse, in breach of U.S. 'public policy in favour of final and binding arbitration', precluded an obligation for enforcement in light of international comity and granted recognition and enforcement of the award notwithstanding its former annulment, since non-application of the more favourable Federal Arbitration Act would contravene Article VII New York Convention. Section 10 of the Federal Arbitration Act was perceived as providing the only relevant rule for determining the award's validity, whereas the law of the country of origin would not matter at all, while the Court also deemed the 'international policy in favour of arbitration' to be strong enough to rescind international comity principles.

(b) The United States district court for the district wherein an award was made that was issued pursuant to Section 590 of title 5 may make an order vacating the award upon the application of a person, other than a party to the arbitration, who is adversely affected or aggrieved by the award, if the use of arbitration or the award is clearly inconsistent with the factors set forth in Section 582 of title 5.

343 Abascal (2008), *op. cit.*, 173.

344 Sampliner (1996), *op. cit.*, 26.

345 See also supra, Freyer (2000), *op. cit.*, 4.

b) Yusuf Ahmed Alghanim & Sons v. Toys "R" Us and TRU (HK) Ltd. (1997)

The second time a vacated award should be enforced in the U.S. the concerned court took advantage of the opportunity to specify the interplay between the New York Convention and the Federal Arbitration Act. Alghanim, an Iraqi company, initiated and prevailed in an arbitration proceeding pursuant to the rules of the American Arbitration Association, situated in New York, against Toys "R" Us (U.S.) and TRU (Hongkong), alleging a breach of the concluded license agreement.[346] While Alghanim applied for enforcement of the promotive award under the New York Convention, Toys "R" Us challenged the award by relying on the Federal Arbitration Act, Section 10. Both requests were likewise admissible, as the District Court held that – given an award rendered in the U.S. is nonetheless considered as non-domestic – there may emerge an "overlapping coverage" of regimes set out by the New York Convention and the Federal Arbitration Act – providing for enforcement on the one hand, and nullification on the other hand. Basically confirming this finding, the Court of Appeal clarified whether the Federal Arbitration Act, Section 10 implicit grounds for refusal of enforcement may be asserted in enforcement proceedings under the New York Convention. The Court denied raising the vacatur grounds of Section 10 Federal Arbitration Act while enforcement under New York Convention:

"There is now considerable case law holding that, in an action to confirm an award rendered in, or under the law of, a foreign jurisdiction, the grounds for relief enumerated in Art. V of the Convention are the only grounds available for setting aside an arbitral award.[347] ... This conclusion is consistent with the Convention's pro-enforcement bias... We join these courts in deciding to read into the Convention the FAA's implied defenses to confirmation of an arbitral award."[348]

Another issue to clarify for the Court of Appeal was the nullification of a non-domestic award. As the New York Convention regards the authority of the country where the award was made as competent to make decisions on the continued existence of the award, it seems questionable if this remains true, even though the award is considered as non-domestic in such a country. However, the Second

346 *Yusuf Ahmed Alghanim & Sons v. Toys "R" Us*, Inc., 126 F.3d 15, 19 (2nd Cir. 1997), (13) cert. denied, 522 U.S. 1111, 118 S.Ct. 1042, 140 L.Ed.2d 107 (1998), in XXXIII Y. B. Com. Arb. (1998), 1058 et seq.

347 The Court referred to "M&C, 87 F.3d at 851 (concluding that the Convention's exclusive grounds for relief 'do not include miscalculations of fact or mainfest disregard of the law')."

348 United States Court of Appeals, Second Circuit, 10 September 1997, No. 1757, Docket 96-9692, in XXXIII Y. B. Com. Arb. (1998), 1058 et seq.

Circuit Court of Appeal clarified for all awards rendered in arbitrations that were seated in the U.S. regardless of their categorisation, the Federal Arbitration Act is the relevant *lex arbitri*, and thus may be applied in order to determine the award's validity:

"In sum, we conclude that the Convention mandates very different regimes for the review of arbitral awards (1) in the state in which, or under the law of which, the award was made, and (2) in other states where recognition and enforcement are sought. The Convention specifically contemplates that the state in which or under the law of which, the award was made, will be free to set aside or modify an award in accordance with its domestic arbitral law and its full panoply of express and implied grounds for relief. See Convention Article V(1)(e). However, the Convention is equally clear that when an action for enforcement is brought in a foreign state, the state may refuse to enforce the award only on the grounds explicitly set forth in Article V of the Convention."[349]

Accordingly, the U.S. Court acknowledged the jurisdiction of the state where the arbitration was held to review and control the arbitral award by means of a setting aside based on national law. Likewise, the Court admitted that a sort of review is also triggered by the courts of the state where enforcement is sought, though enforcement may only be denied under the constraints of Article V(1) of the New York Convention.

c) Baker Marine (Nig.) Ltd. v. Chevron (Nig.) Ltd., 191 F.3d 194 (1999)

Another case, similar in fact, but different in outcome, was Baker Marine.[350] Baker Marine, a Nigerian company had initiated arbitration proceedings in Nigeria against its contractual partners the Nigerian companies Danos and Curole Marine Contractors, Inc. and the companies Chevron Ltd. and Chevron Corp., Inc., which had agreed on transportation services for the oil exploration business in Nigeria. The tribunal awarded Baker Marine US$ 2.23 million to be paid by Danos and another US$ 750.000 from Chevron. Baker Marine subsequently sought for enforcement in Nigeria, while the losing parties successfully challenged the award. The Nigerian courts found that there was not sufficient evidence for the tribunal's conclusions as to Danos' case, and in Chevron's case it found that the arbitral tribunal had exceeded its mandate for arbitration, inappropriately adjudicated punitive damages and improperly took parole evidence. Baker Marine, nonetheless, applied for recognition and enforcement of its original award in the U.S. under the auspices of the New York Convention, which was denied by the District Court of

349 XXIII Y. B. Com. Arb. (1998), 1066.

350 United States Court of Appeals, Second Circuit, 12 August 1999, Nos. 97-9615, 97-9617, in XXIVa Y. B. Com. Arb. (1999), 909 et seq.

the Northern District of New York, holding it inappropriate under the New York Convention and in light of international comity to enforce an award issued and annulled in Nigeria. Baker Marine appealed the judgement, arguing that the District Court deficiently neglected the provision of New York Convention, Article VII, which would allow for Baker Marine to obtain enforcement of the award under the more favourable regime of the Federal Arbitration Act. As its Section 10 in turn does not allow for vacatur of the award for such grounds determined by the Nigerian courts, both awards would be capable of enforcement in accordance with the Federal Arbitration Act. However, Baker Marine's assertion apparently did not convince the Court of Appeal:

"Nothing suggests that the parties intended United States domestic arbitral law to govern their disputes. The primary purpose of the FAA is ensuring that private agreements to arbitrate are enforced according to their terms. Furthermore Baker Marine has made no contention that the Nigerian courts acted contrary to Nigerian law."[351]

In addition, the Court clarified the interaction of the New York Convention and national arbitration law, in concreto the American Federal Arbitration Act:

"Furthermore, as a practical matter mechanical application of domestic arbitral law to foreign awards under the Convention would seriously undermine finality and regularly produce conflicting judgements. If a party whose arbitration award has been vacated at the site of the award can automatically obtain enforcement of the awards under the domestic laws of other nations, a losing party will have every reason to pursue its adversary 'with enforcement actions from country to country until a court is found, if any, which grants enforcement.'"[352]

This is a clear renunciation by the second Circuit of the position taken in Chromalloy, although the Court distinguished both cases.[353] With the parties' agreement on arbitration in Nigeria, they did not stipulate American law; accordingly there is no pointer to subject the award to the Federal Arbitration Act. Whereas in Chromalloy the foreign nullification proceeding entirely disregarded the parties' express waiver of any recourse, and thus violated U.S. public policy. The Court of Appeal differentiated as follows:

"Unlike the petitioner in Chromalloy, Baker Marine is not a United States citizen, and it did not initially seek confirmation of the award in the United States. Furthermore, Chevron and Danos did not violate any promise in appealing the arbitration award within Nigeria.

351 XXIVa Y. B. Com. Arb. (1999), 912.
352 XXIVa Y. B. Com. Arb. (1999), 914 at fn. 3; the Court further cites van den Berg (1981), *op. cit.*, 355.
353 Haravon (2007), *op. cit.*, 34.

Recognition of the Nigerian judgement in this case does not conflict with United States public policy."[354]

However, even if the Court distinguished the Baker Marine case from the circumstances given in Chromalloy, the judgement reflects a novel shade in the U.S. perception as to the interplay of regimes governing international arbitration, which was even manifested after only two months.

d) Martin Spier v. Calzaturificio Technica, S.p.A. (1999)

Martin Spier sought enforcement of an award fourteen years after it was rendered, and subsequently vacated by an Italian court. Originally Spier initiated arbitration proceedings against Calzaturificio, an Italian ski boot manufacturer, due to a dispute arising out of a consulting contract for the production of plastic footwear and ski boots. The tribunal awarded Mr. Spier an entitlement amounting to US$ 672,000. The enforcement proceeding Spier subsequently triggered, was recessed by the U.S. District Court for the Southern District of New York, while a nullification procedure initiated by Cazaturificio was pending in Italy. After the Italian courts ultimately set the award aside, Spier revived his application for enforcement. The District Court pursued the trend set in *Alghanim v. Toys "R" Us and TRU* and *Baker Marine v. Chevron*, rather then the principles established in *Chromalloy v. Egypt*. Nevertheless, the Court pointed out that the award issued in Italy is a truly foreign and not just a 'non-domestic' award by emphasising that *"where (as in the case at bar) an arbitral award is made in one State adhering to the Convention and sought to be enforced in another adhering State, the grounds for resisting the award are limited to those found in Article V of the Convention."*[355] In qualifying Spier's reference to Chromalloy, the judge clarified:

"In some respects Chromalloy bears a superficial resemblance to the case at bar, since Spier is a United States citizen and seeks confirmation of the award in the United States. But I read this footnote in Baker Marine to identify as the decisive circumstance Egypt's repudiation of its contractual promise not to appeal an arbitral award. Only that circumstance is singled out as violating American public policy articulated in the Federal Arbitration Act, thereby justifying the district court's enforcement of the Egyptian award."[356]

In the light of such finding, U.S. jurisdictions (at least in the second circuit) have progressively shifted away from the initial Chromalloy approach.

354 XXIVa Y. B. Com. Arb. (1999), 911, fn. 5.
355 XXV Y. B. Com. Arb. (2000), 1048.
356 *Ibid.*,1048.

e) Pertambangan Minyak Dan Gas Bumi Negara (Petramina) v. Karaha Bodas Company, L.L.C. (KBC) (2004)

Nevertheless, the occurrence of 'Petramina' shows that there was still no uniform approach of U.S. courts to the issue of (non)enforcement to offshore-vacated awards.

Petramina, an Indonesian state oil company, and KBC concluded a contract on the development of KBC's geothermal project in West Java, Indonesia. The contract was governed by Indonesian law, and provided that disputes should be submitted to arbitration under the UNCITRAL rules, with the seat of the arbitration in Geneva, Switzerland. When the Indonesian government decided to discontinue the project, KBC duly initiated an arbitration proceeding, and obtained a final award in its favour, Petramina was ordered to make payments amounting US$ 261 million compensation. The Swiss Federal Tribunal dismissed Petraminas' subsequent appeal.

Petramina thereupon not only sought nullification of the award in Indonesia, but also requested the Central Jakarta District Court to issue an enjoinder impeding enforcement of the award anywhere in the world. When KBC gained knowledge of such request, it in turn successfully demanded from the U.S. District Court for the Southern District of Texas an anti-suit injunction obligating Petramina to recall its injunctive relief pending in Jakarta. However, Petramina consequently challenged the anti-suit injunction obtained by KBC, whereupon the U.S. Court of Appeal for the Fifth Circuit had to determine the Texan District Court's injunctive power in the light of an award subjected to the New York Convention (Petramina I).[357] The Court of Appeals' considerations on potential justifications as anti-suit injunctions involved national judicial concerns, strictly speaking the necessity to prevent *"vexatious or oppressive litigation"*, and principles of international comity. The Court conceived such "vexatious and oppressive litigation" to be present in case the foreign lawsuit inflicts (i) *"inequitable hardship"* for one party, (ii) an obstacle to *"speedy and efficient determination of the cause"*, and (iii) a protracting doubling of litigation, however the Court found none of the justifications to be apparent in the present Indonesian injunctive relief.[358] In fact, the Court of Appeal pointed out:

"[u]nder the Convention, a court maintains the discretion to enforce an arbitral award even when nullification proceedings are occurring in the country where the award was rendered.

357 United States Court of Appeals, Fifth Circuit, 18 June 2003, No. 02-20550 in XXVIII Y. B. Com. Arb. (2003), 908 et seq.

358 *Ibid.*, 953 et seq.

Furthermore, an American court and courts of other countries have enforced awards, or permitted their enforcement, despite prior annulment in courts of primary jurisdiction."

In addition, the Court clarified that *"[b]y allowing concurrent enforcement and annulment actions, as well as simultaneous enforcement actions in third countries, the Convention necessarily envisions multiple proceedings that address the same substantive challenges to an arbitral award."*[359] While this judgement was deemed to reflect an endorsement of the trend set by *Hilmarton* and *Chromalloy*, it must be emphasised that *Petramina I* was not concerned with the issue of enforcement of a vacated award, but rather with potential justifications for anti-suit injunctions. Therefore, it illustratively listed the various types of proceedings under the New York Convention that may be simultaneously held in different jurisdictions relating to the very same award, but never intended to support any of these proceedings, nor in particular concurrent enforcement and annulment proceedings. The last KBC's request for anti-suit injunction was not justified, as the Indonesian injunctive relief proceeding was not considered as overly burdensome.

In a second decision, this time on enforcement, the Court of Appeal had to determine whether the Indonesian court's annulment of the award issued in Geneva precluded enforcement in the U.S. in the light of the New York Convention (Petramina II).[360] Petramina opposed enforcement arguing Indonesia had primary jurisdiction to review of the award, as the parties had agreed to subject their contract to Indonesian law, they also intended Indonesian procedural law to govern the arbitration notwithstanding that the (mere) seat of the arbitration was Geneva. In accordance with the "under the law of which" phrase of New York Convention, Article V(1)(e) the Indonesian nullification of the award hinders its enforcement in the U.S. Again, the U.S. Court of Appeal for the Fifth Circuit was in fact not asked to determine whether enforcement of a vacated award is possible, but rather which jurisdiction pursuant to the New York Convention is given the competence to vacate an award. In this context the Court of Appeal remarked

"[t]he New York Convention provides a carefully structured framework for the review and enforcement of international arbitral awards. Only a court in a country with primary jurisdiction over an arbitral award may annul that award. Courts in other countries have secondary jurisdiction; a court in a country with secondary jurisdiction is limited to deciding whether the award may be enforced in that country. The Convention 'mandates very different regimes for the review of arbitral awards (1) in the [countries] in which, or under the law of which, the award was made, and (2) in other [countries] where recognition and enforcement are sought.' Under the Convention 'the country in which, or under the [arbitration] law of which [an] award was made' is said to have primary jurisdiction over

359 *Ibid.*, 908 et seq.
360 United States Court of Appeals for the Fifth Circuit, 364 F.3d 274.

the arbitration award. All other signatory states are secondary jurisdictions, in which parties can only contest whether that state should enforce the arbitral award. It is clear that the district court had secondary jurisdiction and considered only whether to enforce the Award in the United States."[361]

While Petramina I appeared as a confirmation of the Chromalloy trend giving considerable discretion and weight to the enforcing court's assessment of the awards' legal effect even when it was previously set aside, Petramina II however more restrictively attributed the "primary" jurisdiction of the forum state the exclusive competence to assess the award's effectiveness.

f) TermoRio & LeasCo GroupS.A. E.S.P. v. Electranta S.P., et. al. (2007)

The latest American judgment on the enforcement of a previously vacated award was in *TermoRio v. Electrana.*

TermoRio, a wholly owned subsidiary of the U.S. American LeaseCo Group, initiated arbitration proceedings in Colombia against the Colombian state-owned electrical utility, Electranta, whereby all participants were formally to be considered as Colombian. TermoRio obtained an award obligating Electranta to payments amounting to US$ 60.3 million. However, Electrana successfully sought annulment, because the ICC arbitration clause was in breach of Colombian law at the time of conclusion. TermoRio subsequently applied for enforcement in the United States, but both the District Court for the District of Columbia[362] as well as the Court of Appeal for the District of Columbia Circuit, rejected such a request on the following rationale:

"The Convention does not endorse a regime in which secondary States (in determining whether to enforce an award) routinely second-guess the judgement of a court in a primary State, when the court in the primary State has lawfully acted pursuant to 'competent authority' to 'set aside' an arbitration award made in its country. Appellants go much too far

361 364 F.3d 274 at para. 26; Prof. Michael Reisman initially distinguished between "primary" and "secondary" jurisdiction in: Systems of Control in International Adjudication and Arbitration, Duke University Press (1992), which was criticised by Paulsson (1998), *op. cit.*, 14-31, as: *"...pure products of his own reflection... The Convention itself does not define the categories "primary" and "secondary", as conceived by Mr. Reismann, and I find them unwarranted. If anything, the primary jurisdiction should be the one where the economic or other consequences of an award are sought."*

362 TermoRio S.A. E.S.P. and LeaseCo GROUP, LLC v. ELECTRANTA S.P., et al., 487 F.3d 928 (D.C. Cir. 2007) United States District Court, District of Columbia, 17 March 2006; *http://www.altlaw.org/v1/cases/1143876*; XXXI Y. B. Com. Arb. (2006), 1457 et seq.

in suggesting that a court in a secondary State is free as it sees fit to ignore the judgment of a court of competent authority in a primary State vacating an arbitration award. It takes much more than a mere assertion that the judgement of the primary State 'offends the public policy' of the secondary State to overcome a defence raised under Article V(1)(e)."[363]

In the light of the "strong public policy in favour of final and binding arbitration" attested in Chromalloy, the Court of Appeal adds that *"[t]he test of public policy cannot be simply whether the courts of a secondary State would set aside an arbitration award if the award had been made and enforcement had been sought within [their] jurisdiction."*[364] Accordingly, a U.S. court may only disregard a foreign vacatur against the principles of international comity, if the party applying for enforcement asserts and proves that the vacatur is in breach of U.S. ordre public. Which is solely the case if the foreign court decision violates fundamental notions of justice, or if the vacatur contravenes the public interest and the public confidence in the legal system.[365]

Although the Court of Appeal for the District of Columbia Circuit modified the Chromalloy approach as to strong 'public policy in favour of final and binding arbitration', with the single admitted exception of the principles of international comity, it did not undertake to overrule the basic notion of Chromalloy.[366] However, the Senior Circuit Judge noted *"[a]n arbitration award does not exist to be enforced in other Contracting States if it has been lawfully 'set aside' by a competent authority in the State in which the award was made."*[367]

While deciding the request for enforcement the U.S. Court considered that the annulment decision was 'the judgement of a court of competent authority', which U.S. courts may not 'second-guess', rather than examining the actual enforceability of the award in light of the Federal Arbitration Act.[368] The TermoRio decision is contradictory to the permissive language and the enforcement-friendly purpose of the New York Convention, while it was also deemed to encourage the defending

363 Termorio S.a. E.s.p. and Leaseco Group, Llc, Appellants v. Electranta S.p., et al., No. 03cv02587, United States Court of Appeals for the District of Columbia Circuit, decided 25 May 2007, U.S. App. LEXIS 12201 (2007 WL 1515069).

364 *Ibid.*

365 See supra „ordre public exception", 31 et seq, with reference to corresponding U.S. case law.

366 In this regard the Court of Appeals stated: *"We need not decide whether the holding in Chromalloy is correct, because, as appellees point out, 'the present case is plainly distinguishable from Chromalloy where an express contract provision was violated by pursuing an appeal to vacate the award."*

367 Haravon (2007), *op. cit.*, 35.

368 Gaillard (2007), *op. cit.*

party to commence redundant proceedings at courts in the forum state, even if no enforcement actions were initiated or envisaged.[369]

g) Conclusions on the U.S Approach

To summarise the various remarks on the U.S. judicature, it may be said that the courts do not manifest "bright-lined rules" as to the applicability of local law on the recognition and enforcement of New York Convention awards. However, the Petramina decision was criticised for its general considerations on the effect of foreign annulment decisions, instead of proper examination of the particular case.[370] Basically, the most distinguished essence is, enforcement of an award, which was nullified in its forum state will not be "readily" approved within the United States.[371] In fact, only in *Chromalloy* were U.S. courts willing to grant enforcement by virtue of the Federal Arbitration Act and the New York Convention's 'more favourable law' clause and merely due to the 'solemn promise' set out in the arbitration agreement to preclude any form of appeal against the award. Likewise the judge of the District Court concerned with *Spier* case admitted the 'decisive circumstance' for the leave for enforcement in *Chromalloy* was the explicit 'no recourse language' stipulated by the parties.[372] The judgments in *Spier* itself and *Baker Marine* reflect rather a reluctance of U.S. courts to grant enforcement to awards, which have been validly annulled by competent authorities of the "primary jurisdiction", i.e. in their forum states, unless the parties selected U.S. Federal Arbitration Act to govern their arbitration.[373] However, unlike French courts, the U.S. courts have never been faced with the intricacy of two contradictory arbitral awards.

3. Austrian Case Law

While a vacated award is usually said to be a legal *nullum* inapplicable for recognition and enforcement,[374] the European Convention – as displayed before – provides in the majority of the cases, for recognition and enforcement

369 *Ibid.*
370 Gaillard, Anti-suit injunctions et reconnaissance des sentences annulées au siège: une evolution remarquable de la jurisprudence américaine, J.D.I. (2003), 1112.
371 Freyer (2000), *op. cit.*, 1-9.
372 See supra 92; *Ibid.*, 8.
373 *Ibid.*, 8.
374 Horvath (2009), *op. cit.*, 249 et seq..

even for such vacated awards, therefore making this original approach no longer sustainable.[375]

Compared to France and the U.S, the issue of whether to allow for enforcement of a previously vacated award rarely occurred in Austria.

a) Do Zdravilisce Radenska v. Kajo-Erzeugnisse Essenzen GmbH (1993)[376]

Radenska, a Slovenian company and Kajo, an Austrian company, entered into a contract for the production and distribution of low-calorie soft drinks within the territory of the Federal Republic of Yugoslavia. The contract further included an arbitration clause, whereby all claims asserted by the Yugoslavian party were to be submitted to the competent arbitration board of the Austrian Chamber of Industry and Commerce, or rather, all claims of the Austrian party were to be submitted to the competent arbitration board of the Yugoslavian Economic Chamber. Each arbitral board should apply its own national law.

Kajo duly initiated an arbitration proceeding before the competent arbitration board of the Yugoslavian Economic Chamber in Belgrade, and obtained an arbitral award in its favour, subsequently Radenska sought an annulment at a Yugoslavian Court of First Instance (now lying in Slovenia), but the court rejected the request, confirmed by the Court of Appeal. Kajo meanwhile applied for and was granted enforcement by the Austrian County Court of Bad Radkersburg. Thereafter, the Supreme Court of Slovenia (former Yugoslavia) assumed that the rights granted by the original contract amounted at least to a particularly privileged situation, if not even a monopoly, for Kajo, which was in breach of the relevant ordre public. Thus, the Vienna Supreme Court finally set aside the award and encouraged Radenska to appeal against the Austrian leave for enforcement, arguing that in the light of the vacation the award was neither recognisable nor enforceable. Moreover, Radenska raised objections to alleged violations of the Austrian ordre public and European Community competition law, and requested to stay the execution. The Bad Radkersburg County Court rejected the request for suspension of the exequatur, thus admitting enforcement, on the ground that even though Austria had recognised Slovenia as an independent state in 1992, the legal ramifications were not yet perfectly clear, therefore the Slovenian Supreme Court's annulment had no legal effect in Austria.[377] The Court of Appeal in Graz, in contrast, assumed the effectiveness of the Slovenian judgement as it was issued after Austria's recognition of Slovenia as a sovereign

375 Schwab/Walter (2005), *op. cit.*, Ch. 57 para. 24.

376 Do Zdravilisce Radenska v. Kajo-Erzeugnisse Essenzen GmbH, decision of 23 February 1998, in XXIVa Y.B. Com. Arb (1999), 925; Rev. Arb. (1999), 385.

377 County Court Bad Radkersburg E 237/89.

state. The Court further approved the applicability of the Bilateral Treaty between Austria and the Federal Republic of Yugoslavia on the Mutual Recognition and Enforcement of Arbitral Awards in Commercial Matters, and deduced its priority as *lex specialis* as to the European Convention on International Commercial Arbitration. According to the Treaty, the law of the enforcing state (Austria) governs the enforcement procedure. In the light of Austrian procedural law, the nullification of the award causes a lapse of title for the exequatur. Therefore, the Graz Court of Appeal overruled the leave for enforcement of the lower court of Bad Radkersburg.[378]

On Kajo's subsequent appeal the Austrian Supreme Court revived the initial decision of the County Court allowing for enforcement. This decision, based on a review of two potentially applicable treaties, namely the European Convention and the Bilateral Treaty between Austria and the Federal Republic of Yugoslavia on the Mutual Recognition and Enforcement of Arbitral Awards in Commercial Matters, which was considered effective as to Slovenia on the one hand pursuant to a "pragmatic" application,[379] on the other hand based on an exchange of notes between Austria and Slovenia as to the continued application of particular Austrian-Yugoslavian treaties. However, while such an approach is unsuitable in matters of multilateral treaties, the Austrian Supreme Court discovered that Slovenia had avowed itself to be also continually bound by the European Convention.[380]

With the bilateral treaty providing for non-derogation of other international treaties on recognition and enforcement of arbitral awards, the Austrian Supreme Court assumed a parallel applicability of both treaties, which was in accordance with Section 614 of the Austrian Code of Civil Procedure, approving the applicability of such international treaties in Austria. Subsequently, the Austrian Supreme Court concluded enforcement might only be refused if it is justified pursuant to each of the two treaties. (As mentioned before, Austria is also a contracting party to the New York Convention; however, due to the preferential applicability of European Convention, Article IX between the Austrian and Slovenian party, New York Convention, Article V(1) lit. a-e justifications were

378 Higher Regional Court of Graz 4 R 746/92.

379 Austrian Supreme Court, decision of 20 October 1993, 3Ob117/93.

380 While no declaration of Slovenia's continuation into Yugoslavia's participation had been announced in the Austrian Federal Law Gazette (Bundesgesetzblatt), the Supreme Court obtained information from the Federal Ministry of Justice (in analogy to Section 4(1) of the Austrian Act on Private International Law) that Slovenia already escrowed a 'declaration of continuance' by the General Secretary of the United Nations on 6 July 1992 with effect frome 25 June 1991, which had not yet been proclaimed, but is to be announced in the Austrian Federal Law Gazette.

subsidiary.) With European Convention, Article IX(1) lit. a-d not listing a violation of foreign public policy among the grounds justifying a rejection of enforcement, the annulment of the award on a Yugoslavian public policy basis did not cause a valid reason to deny enforcement under the European Convention. In the light of the Court's initial finding, it precluded a further review, as a justification merely granted by the bilateral treaty would, in fact, not suffice for a due refusal of enforcement. The Supreme Court emphasised the interdiction of *révision au fond*, by the court of enforcement. Finally, the Austrian Supreme Court granted Kajo enforcement of the vacated Slovenian award against Radenska.

In 1998, the Austrian Supreme Court had used the opportunity to confirm its position in a further decision on the very case.[381]

b) The Austrian Supreme Court (2005)

In another decision in 2005 Austrian courts (names undisclosed) were asked to enforce an arbitral award rendered by the Foreign Trade Arbitration at the Chamber of Commerce and Industry of Serbia in Belgrad between an Austrian buyer and a seller from Serbia and Montenegro. The defending party objected that the award would violate public policy due to a false testimony and an invalid arbitration agreement. The pursuing party, in contrast, found that these objections should have been better raised in an annulment proceeding in Serbia, than during the enforcement proceeding in Austria. The District Court of Feldkirchen partially granted enforcement, whereas the Klagenfurt Court of Appeal in turn overruled the leave for enforcement. The Austrian Supreme Court finally clarified that the pursuing partie's reference to annulment proceedings in the forum state were not substantiated:

"Pursuant to Art. IX(1) European Convention, even the annulment of the award for violation of the public policy of the country of origin – which is not argued here – is not one of the grounds for refusal exhaustively listed in the European Convention, and is therefore not a ground for refusing enforcement in the enforcement state.[382] *[Hence], even if the buyer obtained the annulment of the arbitral award in the state of the seat because the award was allegedly based on a false witness statement, this would not be a ground for refusing*

381 Austrian Supreme Court, decision of 23 February 1998, 3Ob115/95; XXIVa Y. B. Com. Arb. (1999), 925; Rev. Arb (1999), 385.

382 The Court referred to 3 Ob 115/95 with commentary of Reiner (2000), *op. cit.*, 323 et seq.; Heller//Berger/Stix, Die Exekutionsordnung, Angst/Jakusch (eds.) (1988), 787 et seq.

recognition and enforcement in Austria pursuant to Art. IX European Convention together with Art. V(1)(e) New York Convention." [383]

Therefore, the Austrian Supreme Court did not consider it appropriate to refer the defending party to annulment proceedings due to a violation of public policy at the country of origin, "*and thus (...) proceedings that are irrelevant for enforcement and execution in Austria.*"[384]

c) Conclusions on the Austrian Approach

The Austrian Supreme Court quite clearly adhered to the specified interaction of the New York Convention and the European Convention, as well as to the parallelism of international treaties provided by the Austrian Code of Civil Procedure. In fact, no other European Convention state would have been justified to decide differently. The Austrian Supreme Court duly realised that the annulment of an award based on a violation of the ordre public in the forum state does not provide a valid ground to refuse enforcement by virtue of European Convention, Article IX(1) lit. a-d.[385]

4. German Case Law

In contrast to Austria, German courts have been faced with the question of granting enforcement to a nullified award more than once. Whilst the majority of requests for enforcement were rejected, only one court was willing to grant enforcement of such an annulled award.

a) Do Zdravilisce Radenska v. Kajo-Erzeugnisse Essenzen GmbH (1995)

The Higher Regional Court of Munich received the very same request as the Austrian Supreme Court.[386] After having obtained enforcement in Austria, Kajo

383 Austrian Supreme Court, decision of 26 January 2006, 3 Ob221/04b, translation from XXX Y. B. Com. Arb. (2005), 426.

384 Austrian Supreme Court, decision of 26 January 2006, 3Ob221/04b, translation from XXX Y. B. Com. Arb. (2005), 426.

385 To the Austrian case law see inter alia: SZ 66, 131; ZfRV 1999, 24; IPRax 2000, 314; Reiner (2000), *op. cit.*, 323; Oberhammer (1999), *op. cit.*, 62; Michaels (1999), *op. cit.*, 24; Braumüller (1996), *op. cit.*, 99.

386 *See* Higher Regional Court of Munich, decision of 13 February 1995, Vollstreckbarerklärung eines ausländischen (jugoslawischen) Schiedsspruchs, OLG Report München (1995), 57.

also applied for enforcement in Germany, which Radenska again attempted to defend. However, the Higher Regional Court, similar to the Austrian court, granted enforcement notwithstanding the former nullification of the award in Slovenia, in the light of European Convention, Article IX(1) lit. a-d. While Radenska relied on the defences set out in the New York Convention, the Court admitted that Article V(1)(e) indeed provides for justifications to deny enforcement irrespective of whether the award was nullified for ordre public reasons, but clarified that the New York Convention does not apply in the present case as the parties are also parties to the European Convention. In the light of the apparent vacation due to public policy violations, the European Convention, Article IX(1) lit. a-d supersedes the New York Convention, Article V(1) lit. a-d as more favourable, arbitration-friendly law providing more restrictive grounds allowing for rejection of enforcement, which does not include nullifications based on alleged violations of a domestic ordre public.

However, the Court questioned whether the Slovenian Supreme Court which had annulled the award, embodies a valid 'competent authority' in terms of Article V(1)(e) New York Convention, since the award was originally issued in the Former Federal Republic of Yugoslavia and Slovenia is not Yugoslavia's successor in terms of international law. The Court saw no need to determine the competency of the Slovenian Court, as the *"absolute effect of the annulment decision accordant to the New York Convention, Article V(1)(e) is confined to annulments based on the exhaustive reasons listed in Article IX(1) lit. a-d of the European Convention"* in the light of the more favourable law provision of New York Convention, Article VII and the priority mode set out in Article IX(2) European Convention.[387] The Higher Regional Court of Munich concluded that *"the legal consequence resulting from Article IX(2) European Convention – namely the recognition of a foreign arbitral award notwithstanding a former annulment in the state of origin for other reasons than those listed in Article IX(1) lit. a-d European Convention, like the ordre public of the state of origin – is generally acknowledged"*.[388]

b) Higher Regional Court of Rostock (1999)[389]

The parties (names undisclosed) A and B entered into a contract on reinstatement works on the motor vessel of A. B later initiated an arbitration proceeding at the Maritime Commission at the Chamber of Commerce and Industry of the Rus-

387 See *ibid.*, 59.

388 See *ibid.*, 59.

389 *See* Higher Regional Court of Rostock, 28 October 1999 – 1 Sch 3/1999; Add. 8 to BB 2000, 20; Kröll, Antragsvoraussetzungen und Präklusion im Verfahren zur Vollstreckbarerklärung ausländischer Schiedssprüche, IPRax 2002, 384 et seq.

sian Federation, Russia, claiming payments due by A for the partially performed reinstatement works. While A did not appear during the proceedings, the tribunal issued an award in favour of B allotting, approximately, Russian Rouble 1,17 million. A thereupon successfully appealed against the award at the Municipal Court of Moscow, as the Court approved that the arbitral tribunal lacked jurisdiction, as the parties' arbitration clause merely provided for submission to the "arbitration commission of Moscow", which does not automatically allow for arbitration under the auspices of the Maritime Commission at the Chamber of Commerce and Industry of the Russian Federation. Even though Article 34 Number 2 of the Russian International Commercial Arbitration Act allows for nullification if the defending party asserts and proves a violation of the confines of the arbitration agreement, the Municipal Court of Moscow vacated the award. The Court Council for Civil Matters of the Russian Supreme Court subsequently confirmed this finding, noting that Article 7 of the Russian International Commercial Arbitration Act requires arbitration agreements to be in writing, however, the contract between the parties did not provide for arbitration under the Maritime Commission at the Chamber of Commerce and Industry of the Russian Federation in Moscow.

Nevertheless, B sought to enforce the award in Germany and thus applied for recognition and enforcement at the Higher Regional Court of Rostock, additionally requesting a leave for compulsory execution, while the proceeding was pending. B contested no valid judgement had been rendered on the continued existence of the award. The Rostock Higher Regional Court assumed the validity of B's application in the light of Section 1061(1) of the German Code of Civil Procedure with the implied reference to the 1958 New York Convention, and granted preliminary enforcement and compulsory execution of the award in order to provide security for B's potentially existing rights under the award. However, the Court remarked that it was obliged to scrutinise *ex officio* the award's binding nature in the light of the applicable foreign (i.e. Russian) procedural law, while it may be assumed if the award is no longer subject to any legal remedies.[390] Besides, the award is no longer binding if a foreign competent authority has already issued an annulment or suspension as *"this decision must be recognised [in Germany] regardless whether it were a part from that recognisable according to the rules governing the recognition of foreign judgements."*[391] While the Court admitted that the New York Convention, Article V burdens the defending party to assert and prove the fulfilment of the preconditions, in the event that the pursuing party previously

390 Higher Regional Court of Rostock, 28 October 1999, 1 Sch 3/99 at No. 39 with reference to Federal Court of Justice in NJW 1984, 2763/2764.

391 This is no official translation, but the authoress' personal translation of Higher Regional Court of Rostock, decision of 28 October 1999, 1 Sch 3/99 at No. 39, with reference to Meier/MüKo, Sec. 1044 para. 7.

proved the fulfilment of the formal requirements as set out by Article IV, it assumes that the vacatur of the award is not in dispute, B rather asserted that the Russian judgements were not yet binding in the light of Russian procedural law. The Rostock Court, however, concluded that *"this is not essential pursuant to New York Convention, Article V(1)(e)(2nd Alternative)"* and therefore *"the recognition and enforcement of the award must be denied pursuant to Article V(1)(e) of the aforementioned New York Convention."*[392] The Higher Regional Court of Rostock did not examine the Russian *vacatur*, but rather assumed that the foreign vacating judgement had to be recognised, independent of further fulfilment of the requirements on the recognition of foreign judgements set out by the German Code of Civil Procedure, Section 328.

On remonstration of the representative chairman of the Russian Supreme Court against the previously issued judgement confirming the annulment of the award, that judgement as well as the prior annulment by the Municipal Court of Moscow was vacated. Thus, when the German Federal Court of Justice had to deal with a further appeal from the pursuing party, the original award was already revived.[393] The Court therefore acknowledged that as the justification for refusal of enforcement pursuant to Article V(1)(e) New York Convention was no longer given, the rebinding award was to grant recognition and enforcement in Germany, in accordance with Section 1061(1)(1) with reference to the New York Convention. Besides, the Federal Court of Justice clarified enforcement proceedings in Germany are in case of dispute dependent on the outcome on the award's binding nature or setting aside in the country of its origin: *"If the award has not yet become binding or has been vacated in the state where it was made, recognition must be refused in the state of enforcement (Article V(1)(e) New York Convention); if a petition for annulment of the award has been filed in the state where it was rendered, the enforcement proceeding may be adjourned (Article VI New York Convention)."*[394] Apparently, the German court assumed the New York Convention, Article V(1) to be mandatory in terms of requiring a refusal of enforcement in case of set aside awards. Within the scope of the European Convention, Article IX(1) such a refusal might have been invalid, however the court did not consider the applicability of the European Convention, and such an approach could not be questioned as the habitual seat of the parties had not been disclosed.

---

392 This is no official translation, but the authoress' personal translation of Higher Regional Court of Rostock, decision of 28 October 1999, 1 Sch 3/99 at No. 38 and 40.

393 Federal Court of Justice, 22 February 2001, III ZB 71/99.

394 This is no official translation, but the authoress' personal translation of Federal Court of Justice, 22 February 2001, III ZB 71/99, 8 no. 4.

c) *Higher Regional Court of Berlin (2006)*[395]

The Higher Regional Court of Berlin was asked to grant enforcement to an arbitral award notwithstanding its previous annulment in China.

Initially, the parties X and Y (names undisclosed) had entered into a contract for the construction of a plant in Wuxi, China, involving an arbitration clause stating that for any arising dispute "Arbitration 15.3 ICC Rules, Shanghai shall apply". Arbitration 15.3 ICC Rules is a model arbitration clause of the General Conditions (FIDIC Green Book), which provides for final and binding dispute resolution by a sole arbitrator, who is to be appointed by the authority specified in the annex, unless differently agreed by the parties, whereby the arbitration's seat is in Shanghai, while proceedings are to be conducted in English. After X had duly commenced an arbitration procedure, the sole arbitrator issued a final award on behalf of the International Court of Arbitration of the International Chamber of Commerce in Shanghai, obligating Y to pay the sums of RMB 4,578,597 and US$ 55,000. Thereupon, Y successfully appealed against the award at the People's Court in Wuxi, which found the arbitration clause to be invalid according to Chinese law, which requires the nomination of the particular arbitral authority in the arbitration clause. The award was thus found to be in breach of Chinese public policy.

While the X, notwithstanding the Chinese nullification, applied for enforcement in Germany, Y attempted to defend such enforcement by relying on the Chinese judgement. The Higher Regional Court of Berlin stated:

"[I]t is due to the valid judgement of the People's Court of Wuxi... bindingly ascertained, that the agreed arbitration clause was invalid. This judgement must be recognised pursuant to Section 328 of the Code of Civil Procedure. The grounds for refusal of recognition are not manifest, and thus do not require a detailed review."[396]

While Section 328 Code of Civil Procedure[397] *inter alia* requires reciprocal recognition of foreign court decisions pursuant to either international treaties, or a trend of mutual enforcement, the Berlin Court assumed mutual recognition of judgements in absence of obverse indication, although there was in fact no such international treaty between Germany and China. Indeed, the Court considered

395 Higher Regional Court of Berlin, decision of 18 May 2006, SchiedsVZ 2007, 100 et seq.

396 This is no official translation, but the authoress' personal translation of the Higher Regional Court of Berlin, decision of 18 May 2006, Anerkennung einer ausländischen Gerichtsentscheidung zur Wirksamkeit einer Schiedsvereinbarung, SchiedsVZ 2007, 101.

397 German Code of Civil Procedure, Section 328.

that the Chinese procedural law only allows for recognition of foreign judgements if it is mutually warranted, therefore mutual recognition must first be ascertained according to this Chinese perception, before foreign judgements may be recognised. While there was no endeavour of obtaining recognition of a Chinese judgement prior to the Berlin Court's finding, its purpose was rather to encourage such a practice of mutual recognition. Since the Chinese judicature at that time was averse to recognition of arbitral awards rendered in Germany, in fact repudiation would have been indicated.[398]

In conclusion, the Higher Regional Court of Berlin found with the Chinese vacatur being flawless in respect of Chinese law, the judgement was to be recognised. The award on the contrary could not be recognised and enforced primarily by virtue of the Chinese judgement, but alternatively also due to the invalidity of the arbitration agreement pursuant to Chinese law.

d) Higher Regional Court of Dresden (2007)[399]

After the claimant, a U.S. company, had commenced an arbitration proceeding under the Arbitration Rules of the International Chamber of Commerce in Minsk, against the respondent, a Belarus state-owned enterprise, claiming due payments for the delivery of wheels and rims for the respondent's tractors, it obtained an award in its favour adjudicating payments amounting to US$ 2.1 million. However, on appeal from the respondent, the Belarus Supreme Commercial Court found that "(i) the arbitration agreement was not valid because the branch office of the claimant in Minsk had not been properly registered and had therefore not been legally competent to conclude the arbitration agreement, (ii) that the arbitral tribunal had not followed the proper procedure by issuing an award signed only by two arbitrators, (iii) that the claimant had not been properly represented in the proceedings and (iv) that the arbitral tribunal had ignored a payment and set-off prohibition", and thus decided to nullify the award.[400] As the respondent had a German-based affiliate, the claimant applied for exequatur in Germany, which the respondent in turn attempted to defend by referring to the Belarusian vacatur of the award. However, the claimant demanded that the court ignore such a judgement, since Belarus was a dictatorship, with the mere purpose of the court's annulment

---

398 For the court's detailed considerations on the warranty of reciprocity see 102 et seq. of the decision.

399 Higher Regional Court of Dresden, decision of 31 January 2007 – 11 Sch 18/05, SchiedsVZ 2007, 327 et seq.; Kröll, Die schiedsrechtliche Rechtsprechung 2007 (part 2), SchiedsVZ 2007, 119.

400 Higher Regional Court of Dresden (2007), *op. cit.*, 327.

of the award against a state-owned enterprise being to secure Belarus' financial interests, rather than securing a fair and just result.

As a legal basis for a leave for enforcement, the Higher Regional Court of Dresden considered the German Code of Civil Procedure, Section 1061 involving reference to the New York Convention in connection with the European Convention. The court assumed:

> *"U.S. and Belarus are both contracting states to the New York Convention, but that does not hinder the applicability of the European Convention, which provides in Article IX a limitation of the valid grounds for vacatur of an award pursuant to Article V(1)(e) New York Convention to those listed in Article IX European Convention. The European Convention is applicable, since in relation between the U.S. and Belarus the 'more favourable law' command is in effect."*[401]

In its further considerations, the court first clarified that it would not presume the incorrectness of the Belarusian judgements merely because the president is a dictator, as even in dictatorships court rulings may be lawful, before examining the grounds for nullification set out in Article IX(1) of the European Convention, which constitute a justification to refuse enforcement of the thus vacated award. In the course of this examination the Dresden Court found two of the listed Article IX grounds to be met: first, the award was vacated, since the Belarusian court had determined the invalidity of the arbitration clause,[402] in addition, it was ascertained that the arbitral procedure, especially the decision-making process of the tribunal was not in accordance with the agreed Arbitration Rules of the International Chamber of Commerce in Minsk, which required the outcome of the arbitration to be resolved by all the arbitrators constituting the tribunal, while in the present case only two out of the three finalised the award.[403]

As two of the grounds on which the Belarusian vacatur was based, constituted justifications to refuse enforcement in accordance with the European Convention, Article IX(1)(a),(d), the Court decided to reject Y's request for exequatur, without further evaluation of other grounds advanced by the Belarus Supreme Commercial Court for the setting aside of the award. While the Dresden Higher Regional Court did not clarify, whether or not vacating judgments of a court in the home state of the arbitral award are to be recognised without detailed examination,[404] or rather have to qualify for enforcement in accordance with the general prerequisites for

401 This is no official translation, but the authoress' personal translation of Higher Regional Court of Dresden (2007), *op. cit.*, 328.

402 European Convention, Article IX(1)(a).

403 European Convention, Article IX(1)(d).

404 With reference to Schwab/Walter (2005), *op. cit.*, Ch. 30, para. 14.

recognising foreign judgements set out in German Code of Civil Procedure, Section 328,[405] it did however indicate its appreciation of the first approach.[406]

e) Conclusions on the German Approach

Basically, German courts tend to deny enforcement of set aside awards.[407] Like courts in other states, German courts basically apply enforcement regimes outlined by the Conventions and German national law correctly. In fact, the European Convention applied twice, and the concerned courts properly approved the European Convention's precedence over the New York Convention, Article V(1)(e) on enforcement of a set aside award. In the matter of Radenska the Higher Regional Court of Munich duly recognised the award in absence of a justifiable annulment ground, whereas in the second European Convention case (Dresden Higher Regional Court) the foreign annulment was based on two recognised Article IX grounds permitting the German courts to deny enforcement. The New York Convention provision for refusal of enforcement was only once on its own relevant to determine the enforcement decisions. In that case the German court (Higher Regional Court of Rostock) construed Article V(1)(e) as mandatorily requiring a refusal to enforce set aside awards, holding that enforcement "must be denied".

Besides, the Berlin court evidenced that German courts place emphasis on international comity towards foreign court decisions annulling an award, rather than on maintaining the finality of international arbitral awards. This approach is tempting under a political point of view. Enforcing an arbitral award notwithstanding its previous nullification by a foreign – here Chinese – court inheres a manifest disrespect of the foreign adjudication, which may be perceived as a political affront. But international arbitration is primarily an institution of private law that with regard to party autonomy such an overemphasis on international comity is not tenable. Enforcement of awards rendered in international arbitration is not about intergovernmental relations, but only about the parties' agreement to arbitration under private law. As long as giving effect to the award in question is valid under German law, enforcement should not be refused solely for international comity reasons without giving any consideration to the parties consent agreement

405 With reference to Schütze, Die Bedeutung eines ausländischen Urteils über die Wirksamkeit eines Schiedsspruchs für dessen Exequierung im Inland, in: Jahrbuch für die Praxis der Schiedsgerichtsbarkeit, Glossner (ed.), (1989), 121.

406 The Court noted: *"The present proceeding, however, shows, that the position of Schwab/Walter inheres wisdom"*, Higher Regional Court of Dresden, Versagung der Anerkennung eines ausländischen Schiedsspruchs, SchiedsVZ 2007, 329.

407 Park (2006), *op. cit.*, 185, 186.

on arbitration. Admittedly, political as well as economic relations between the concerned states may be adversely affected, but not as a cogent consequence. A general deterioration of inter-state relations with regard to the rare occurrence of such events is not to be feared. In summary, international comity should not be used as a categorical argument to refuse enforcement of previously annulled awards. Indeed, international comity may justify such refusal in particular cases, but always requires a careful case-by-case approach, taking all circumstances of the case into consideration.

5. *Dutch Case Law*

In 1984 the District Court of Amsterdam had to take a stand on the issue of giving effect to a set aside award.

The Southern Pacific Properties (SPP) (Middle East) Limited, the Minister of Tourism of Egypt and the Egyptian General Organisation for Tourism and Hotels (EGOTH) concluded a "Heads of Agreement" (without arbitration clause) for the construction of two tourist complexes, one on the Pyramids Plateau, the other on the Mediterranean coast. In the following, a second contract specifying project matters was concluded between SPP and EGOTH, which contained a supplement stating "approved, agreed and ratified by the Minister of Tourism" and the Minister's signature, and an arbitration clause for ICC arbitration. In a later arisen dispute SPP initiated an ICC arbitration in Paris alleging that the Egyptian Minister of Tourism had violated its obligations and duties in respect to SPP both according to the terms of Egyptian law (Law No. 43) and according to the "Heads of Agreement". Although the Egyptian government objected to the tribunal's jurisdiction due to an invalid arbitration agreement, the ICC tribunal awarded SPP damages amounting to US$ 12,5 mio. While the Egyptian government subsequently aimed to challenge the award at the Paris Court of Appeal because it did not enter into the arbitration agreement, SPP sought to enforce the award in the Netherlands. The Paris Court of Appeal set aside the award, arguing the Egyptian government had not become a party to the arbitration agreement, since it had never entered into it, but rather merely "approved" it. The District Court of Amsterdam, in contrast, allowed for enforcement of the ICC award, assuming that the Egyptian government had entered into the arbitration agreement and the ICC therefore had personal jurisdiction over Egypt:

"With reference to Art. V para. 1 under a, of the Convention, respondent has in the first place contended that no valid arbitration agreement exists because it was not a party to the agreement of December 12, 1974, in which the arbitration clause is included. Respondent made the same contention in the arbitral proceedings. This issue is dealt with extensively

in the arbitral award. We hold that the aforementioned contention of respondent is not proven, having regard to what the arbitrators have considered about the contention and in particular the fact that the following words are mentioned at the bottom of the agreement of December 12, 1974 (...)".

As to Egypt's alternative objection that the ICC had not yet become binding in the light of the pending annulment proceeding in France, the Dutch judge countered:

"It results from both the legislative history of the Convention and the text of Arts. V, para. 1 under e, and VI, that the mere initiation of an action for setting aside, to which the initiated recours en annulation must be deemed to belong, does not have as consequence that the arbitral award must be considered as not binding. An arbitral award is not binding if it is open to appeal on the merits before a judge or an appeal arbitral tribunal. If this were otherwise, the words 'has been set aside or suspended' in Art. V, para. 1 under e, to which reference is made in Art. VI, would have no meaning. The drafters of the Convention chose the word 'binding' in order to abolish the requirement of the double exequatur, which was the result of the word 'final' in the Geneva Convention of 1927. Having regard to the system of Arts. 1504 and 1490 NCCP,(3) the view expounded by respondent would result into a reintroduction of the double exequatur."

Finally, the Egyptian government requested adjournment of the enforcement proceeding while the challenge of the award was pending in the French courts, but the request was denied by the District Court of Amsterdam, arguing that the New York Convention's pro-enforcement bias *"subjecting the recognition and enforcement to a minimum number of conditions, the recours en annulation initiated by respondent is no reason for us to adjourn the decision on enforcement."* Additionally, Egypt's refusal of giving suitable security contributed to the finding of the Dutch court.

However, on the very same day when SPP was granted enforcement, the Paris Court of Appeal set aside the ICC award, encouraging SPP to appeal against that decision at the French Cour de Cassation, while Egypt challenged the leave for enforcement within the Netherlands. Lastly, the French Court upheld the setting aside of the arbitral award, whereupon the Dutch court revoked its leave for enforcement.[408]

408 District Court of Amsterdam, decision of 12 July 1984, translated in 24 I.L.M. (1985), 1040; Court of Appeals of Paris, decision of 12 July 1984; the French Supreme Court, decision of 6 January 1987, 2 Mealey's Int Arb Rep (1987), 17.

In the matter of Société Nationale pour la Recherche, le Transport et la Commercialisation des Hydrocarbures (Sonatrach) v. Ford, Bacon and Davis Inc., the Brussels Court of First Instance was asked to grant enforcement to an award previously annulled by Algerian courts.[409]

The Belgian Court denied the applicability of both the New York Convention and the European Convention. Indeed, Belgium ratified both international conventions, but as to the New York Convention it made use of the reservation of reciprocity, and Algeria adhered to the New York Convention, but only in 1988. Hence, Algeria was not a Signatory at the time the award or its preliminary acts were performed, nor when the Court annulled the award, or when the Belgian Court of First Instance granted enforcement. Furthermore, the Belgian Court denied a retroactive applicability of the New York Convention, in particular as it was not alleged by the applicant. With regard to the European Convention, Algeria is not a member at all.

Finally, the Belgian Court allowed for enforcement notwithstanding the annulment, solely based on Belgian law (Part Six of the Belgian Judicial Code, Articles 1719-1723). Since no reason for refusal of enforcement as listed in Article 1723 of the Judicial Code was apparent, no ground for annulment as listed in Article 1704 of the Judicial Code had been invoked, and the Belgian court did not recognise the Algerian annulment decision as *res judicata*, it granted enforcement of the set aside award.

As there is today only one request for enforcement of a set aside award in Belgium, the Belgian courts did not have a chance to develop a categorical approach. However, it has been held that granting enforcement to annulled awards would be even easier under Belgian law than under French law, as "the delocalization under Belgian law is complete and consistent", while under French law all awards rendered in international arbitration are principally subject to appeals for annulment. Therefore the Brussels court's disrespect of the Algerian judgement is said to be "in conformity with" the allowance for a waiver of review or annulment proceedings provided under Belgian arbitration law.[410]

409 Brussels Court of First Instance, decision of 6 December 1988, Société Nationale pour la Recherche, le Transport et la Commercialisation des Hydrocarbures (Soantrach) v. Ford, Bacon and Davis, unreported, but excerpt in an English translation in XV Y. B. Com. Arb. (1990), 370.

410 Gharavi (2002), *op. cit.*, 89.

V. Conclusion on the Inconsistent Case Laws

The adduced court decisions on applications for enforcement of awards, previously set aside by a competent authority within their forum state, show that most national courts exercise what they perceive as their "residual discretion" in the light of the various national and international enforcement regimes, while some courts have also taken into consideration the principles of international comity.[411] As long as the foreign setting aside of the arbitral award is not affected by violations of due process or public policy, and does not contradict another *res judicata*, enforcement courts have been inclined to recognise such foreign adjudication and have therefore denied enforcement of the set aside award.[412]

Courts in Austria, the Netherlands and Belgium have had only isolated encounters with requests for enforcements of vacated awards, not sufficient enough to develop the aforementioned "bright lined rules". Generally speaking, four distinct approaches may be distinguished: (i) courts generally deny enforcement of annulled awards due to the recognised *res judicata* effect of the foreign annulment decisions either in the light of international comity, or due to a mandatory interpretation of Article V(1)(e) of the New York Convention – this approach has primarily been taken by German courts; (ii) some courts have only recognised the foreign annulment as *res judicata* if it was based on internationally recognised grounds, or they were under the obligation of Article IX of the European Convention to enforce the award notwithstanding the foreign annulment – this was equally the case in German decisions, but also in U.S. decisions; (iii) other courts have only decided for enforcement, if the foreign annulment violated the public policy in favour of the maintenance of arbitration as an effective and autonomous means of dispute resolution; or if the annulment disregarded the parties' agreement on a *final* award, e.g. by virtue of a "no recourse" clause – this approach has basically been taken by U.S. courts; (iv) finally, courts may also generally allow for enforcement by disregarding the foreign annulment decision either based on a permissive understanding of Article V(1)(e) of the New York Convention, or based on Article VII of the New York Convention in connection with more favourable national laws – this approach has primarily been taken by French courts.

German and French court decisions reflect a mandatory interpretation of Article V(1) of the New York Convention, actually requiring courts in both countries to refuse enforcement of set aside awards, but French courts feel equally bound by Article VII of the New York Convention to apply their more favourable national law allowing, or rather requiring enforcement notwithstanding a foreign annul-

411 Sampliner (1997), *op. cit.*, 150.
412 Abascal (2008), *op. cit.*, 173 et seq.

ment decision. German courts, in contrast, have consequently denied enforcement, unless they were obliged to grant enforcement by virtue of Article IX(1) of the European Convention, which is also duly recognised by Austrian courts. U.S. courts lastly incline to enforcing set aside awards, mainly if the annulment is in violation of a "no recourse" clause – which is however maintained in most arbitration rules. Austrian courts have demonstrated a judicious approach by properly considering the relevant legislative regimes and their distinct interaction in form and content, reasonably inferring that the European Convention, Article IX in fact requires enforcement of the Slovenian, though vacated, award. As subsequently prudently administered by the Bavarian court, such leave for enforcement was the only valid conclusion for each party to the European Convention. Denying enforcement would have been adverse to and a breach of the European Convention. However, French courts have occasionally failed to consider the currently applicable European Convention regime.

However, regarding enforcement decisions on non-European Convention awards, parties are not directed by such confined guidelines and tend to refuse enforcement as demonstrated by the German courts. This ambiguity has been criticised as being fundamentally ambivalent, disregarding annulment decisions of certain nations, while respecting those of others merely based on a multilateral agreement. However, this is exactly the objective of such international agreements: to achieve an amicable resolution based on reciprocal preferential treatment on certain issues as compared to the usual process. Wherever no such arbitration-friendly agreement exists, treatment might be less favourable or at least less predictable and consistent. Due to the European Convention on International Commercial Arbitration, its parties are "living incontrovertible proof of the fact that" sovereign adjudication of a foreign court on the validity of an arbitral award is not automatically given *erga omnes* effect.[413] Beyond the confined European Convention regime, German courts tend rather to recognise the foreign setting aside of an award, particularly if the international comity in favour of recognition of foreign judgements is either manifested by an international treaty, or evidenced between Germany and the forum state by a trend of mutual show of respect towards each other's decisions, equally extending their legal effect throughout both jurisdictions. Besides, German courts have not only been willing to follow such practice of mutual recognition and enforcement, but are in absence also ready to initiate such a trend in order to encourage henceforth international comity in favour of corresponding court decisions. This is mainly because any decision on the (non) enforcement of an award passes a judging on the foreign court decision setting

413 Paulsson, Delocalisation of International Commercial Arbitration: when and why it matters, 32 I.C.L.Q. (1982), 61.

aside the award, which is actually adverse to the principles of international comity and reciprocity. Non-enforcement of a set aside foreign award would necessarily involve recognition of the foreign (possibly ambiguous) foreign court decision, whereas enforcement would necessarily mean non-recognition of the foreign court decision and thus involves "a measure of disrespect".[414]

But particularly beyond the scope of the European Convention, when solely Article V(1)(e) and Article VII of the New York Convention and the constraints imposed by their interaction are relevant, opinions differ: French courts have manifested a fairly distinct approach, based on their national procedural laws by virtue of the New York Convention's 'more favourable law' clause, while the practice of U.S. courts appears less distinct concerning this matter and driven by their ambition of achieving in each particular case a result reconcilable not only with a common sense of justice, but also with the principles of international comity and the respect of foreign states' sovereign judiciary power.

Generally speaking, signatories to the New York Convention can either exercise their "residual discretion", granted by the permissive language of Article V(1)(e), allowing the enforcing court to be more receptive as to enforcement of annulled awards than the "minimum standard" set out by the Convention, or rely on their domestic procedural law, provided it is more favourable than the New York Convention regime in the sense of Article VII.[415] This ambivalent regime enabled courts to decide inconsistently on enforcement of nullified awards – though courts, in particular, appear unanimous about the nature of guidance of such provisions: whether courts are compellingly bound to refuse enforcement of nullified awards under Article V(1)(e) and/or whether Article VII necessarily requires the application of more favourable national law.

While French courts in the light of the French text presume that Article V(1)(e) demands a denial of enforcement for nullified awards, they equally consider Article VII to mandate by all means the application of more enforcement-friendly national law,[416] which has provoked the remark that "[a] quick reading of both rulings of the French Supreme Court could lead to hasty conclusions: French law ought to change its rules on res judicata or, even better, its rules on the confirma-

414 Sampliner (1997), *op. cit.*, 157.

415 Webster (2006), *op. cit.*, 203 et seq. at fn. 14: *"Logically"* not limited to Article V(1)(e) but also for a-d; *"difficult to see how this could result in unacceptable enforcement of awards as it would in any event be at the discretion of the enforcing court. This interpretation may be relevant in case of countries that do not permit enforcement of an annulled award under their national law, such as the Netherland or Italy"*; See Goode, The Role of the Lex Loci Arbitri in International Commercial Arbitration, 17 Arb. Int'l (2001), 19-40.

416 Koch (2009), *op. cit.*, 269 et seq.

tion and recognition of annulled awards, to avoid the potentially dramatic practical consequences for the losing party of an award who subsequently becomes the winning party."[417] U.S. courts on the contrary, have concluded that enforcement of an award vacated in its forum state must not necessarily be refused by virtue of Article V(1)(e).[418] However, they have tended especially since the more recent decisions to construe Article VII more restrictively than their French colleagues, arguing "the mechanical application of domestic arbitral law to foreign awards under the Convention would seriously undermine finality and regularly produce conflicting judgements."[419]

Such diverging interpretations of the constraints and interaction of Article V(1)(e) and Article VII provide the main source of contradictory approaches to applications for enforcement of nullified awards, which became particularly apparent in the inconsistent U.S. decisions in 'Chromalloy' as compared to the 'Baker Marine' and 'Spier' cases, where U.S. courts increasingly refrained from relying on their domestic law by virtue of Article VII.[420] Though, in the light of the New York Convention's major purpose of facilitating and promoting enforcement of arbitral awards beyond their forum state, it is nothing but consistent to maintain provisions *in favour* of enforcement like Article VII, allowing for enforcement under the most favourable arbitration regime, in a *mandatory* language, in order to achieve the widest scope of application, while provisions capable of *affecting* enforcement are maintained in a rather *permissive* language like Article V(1)(e) in order to emphasise the remaining option to neglect the affecting alternative. Therefore, the French courts were, in fact, by virtue of Article VII under the obligation of granting enforcement to nullified awards passing muster under Article 1502 of the French New Code of Civil Procedure,[421] and their approach is consistent with the text of the New York Convention, particularly Articles V(1)(e) and VII. Based on their local law and enforcement standard, French courts are not required to give considerations to the foreign annulment decision, even if such a decision is deemed to be valid, as evidenced in the matter of Chromalloy, where the French

---

417 Haravon (2007), *op. cit.*, 33.

418 A detailed examination of U.S. and foreign courts' decisions as well as scholarly contributions took place in Yusuf Ahmed Alghanim v. Toys "R" Us and Baker Marine v. Chevron; *See* Freyer (2000), *op. cit.*, 5 with reference to Baker Marine, 191 F.3d (2d Cir. 1999) at 196, n.2, quoting van den Berg (1981), *op. cit.*, and Yusuf, 126 F.3d at 18-20, 24-25.

419 Court of Appeals for the Second circuit in XXIVa Y. B. Com. Arb. (1999), 914.

420 Freyer (2000), *op. cit.*, 1 et seq.

421 Paulsson (1996), *op. cit.,* 107 with further information in fn. 19.

court recognised the arbitral award, thereby ignoring the Egyptian decision, though assuming it as proper under the applicable Egyptian law.[422]

However, it has been argued the French approach would – despite its textual coherency – run contrary to the New York Convention's purpose of international harmonisation of recognition and enforcement of arbitration awards. But this concern is to be objected to, as the authors of the New York Convention primarily aimed to facilitate enforcement, rather than harmonising it – especially with particular respect to the strong tradition of nationalised legal systems in the past when states did not seriously consider ceding their sovereign legislative competences to a supranational Convention, thus depriving themselves of autonomous regulations at their discretion. If harmonisation had been one of the superior targets of the New York Convention, the drafters would not have allowed for such a liberal more favourable law clause as Article VII.

However, by giving preference to the original, but set aside award over the second and valid award, as exercised in the Hilmarton and Putrabali decisions, French courts may incite a worldwide race of premature enforcement. Besides, it has been remarked that enforcement of vacated awards would also give rise to so-called 'floating awards', whose legal effect could not "be blocked with certainty", even though they are affected by serious defects, but the defending party would rather be obliged to object to enforcement in each single state, where the pursuing party submits an application.[423]

Nevertheless, the approach taken by French courts is in accordance with current legislation and actually would have been similarly valid under the Geneva Convention, which also allowed for the application of more favourable national laws.[424]

U.S. courts, in contrast, increasingly pay attention to international comity and therefore tend to respect foreign annulment decisions, which are due to the American perception rendered by the "primary jurisdiction", the only competent authority for annulment of arbitral awards, and are therefore to be respected by the country of enforcement, which is merely the "secondary jurisdiction". In this context, U.S. courts incline to interpret the New York Convention, Article V(1) as rather mandatory, holding that "a secondary Contracting State normally may not enforce an arbitration award that has been lawfully set aside by a 'competent

422 Indeed, the Court assumes that the decision of the Court of Appeal at Cairo is proper under applicable Egyptian law.

423 Gharavi (2002), *op. cit.*, 124 para. 297 et seq.; Gaillard (1998), *op. cit.*, 669.

424 Geneva Convention, Article 5: The provisions of the above Articles shall not deprive any interested party of the right of availing himself of an arbitral award in the manner and to the extent allowed by the law or the treaties of the country where such award is sought to be relied upon.

authority' in the primary Contracting State".[425] However, U.S. courts have neither satisfactorily justified their reversal interpretation of Article V(1)(e), nor their distinction between "primary" and "secondary" jurisdictions, which does not in that sense result from the New York Convention.[426]

The fundamental conflict involved in an application for enforcement of a vacated award is, on the one hand, the parties' choice of dispute resolution in terms of international arbitration issuing a final and binding award, which should be respected and therefore given effect through enforcement. On the other hand, there is the sovereignty of the forum state's judicial power, deciding for whatsoever reasons to abrogate the award's effectiveness, thus turning it into a legal nullum. By virtue of Article V, signatory states may at their own discretion opt for support of both, either for upholding the parties' autonomous choice or respecting state sovereignty in the light of international comity, and therefore also the principle of *ex nihilo nil fit*. Accordingly, the permissive nature of the New York Convention, Article V – though actually aimed at such intricacy – provides no denouement at all, which explains why judges, scholars and arbitration practitioners almost unanimously agree that the current international framework on recognition and enforcement of arbitral awards, particularly the New York Convention, has significant shortcomings in providing simplification, clarity and predictability. Therefore, the possibility of enforcing arbitral awards by virtue of national law (due to Article VII) is partially deemed to be an inadvertence of the New York Convention's drafters.[427] However, courts actually do not even need to rely on their progressive national laws to allow for enforcement of vacated awards, given the permissive nature of Article V(1)(e). As discussed before, it does not seem appropriate to dismiss the permissive language of Article V as an oversight; therefore enforcement of nullified awards is well in accordance with text and purpose of the Convention. Moreover, Article VII was adopted to enable parties to rely on even more liberal formal or procedural requirements on an application for enforcement, rather than for enhancing the already unlimited enforcement permission set out by the most liberal Article V. Therefore, national courts' references to their progressive domestic laws not listing the setting aside of an arbitral award as a justification to deny its enforcement are, in fact, redundant. All leave for enforcement issued by virtue of domestic law would have been

425 TermoRio S.A. E.S.P. and LeaseCo Group, LLC, v. Electrana S.P., et al., United States Court of Appeals, District of Columbia Circuit.

426 Gaillard (2007), *op. cit.*

427 *"Although the drafters (of the New York Convention) did not specify that this Article (VII) could be used as the basis for enforcing a nullified foreign award, they did not preclude this possibility"*, Sampliner (1996), *op. cit.*, 24.

equally valid in the light of the discretionary power provided for by the New York Convention, Article V(1)(e).[428]

With the New York and European Conventions providing for discretionary power on each application for enforcement (which is only limited for refusals, but never for admissions) depending only on the respective court's basic notions, the floodgates have opened for antithetical approaches, often even involving protection of local interests or the interest of nationals. Hence, French courts do not consider foreign awards rendered in international arbitration as being integrated into the legal system of their forum state, but have instead found that the award's validity may survive an annulment in such a state.[429] U.S. courts also have shown that enforcement could also be granted, assuming the choice of the substantial U.S. law also involves the applicability of its procedural law on the effectiveness of the arbitral award, while others presume annulled awards are legally null and void, and therefore lose protection of the New York Convention.[430]

Of all the peculiar decisions granting enforcement to currently vacated awards, the most remarkable is certainly the French *Hilmarton* decision, allowing for enforcement of the original but nullified award, whereas the subsequently rendered and in fact effective award was not given effect in France, due to the *res judicata* effect of the former recognition of the original award. Therefore, it may be criticised that enforcement of the original award "impliedly" characterised it as "existing" notwithstanding the sovereign annulment decision of a forum state court.[431] However, since the New York Convention abolished the need for *double exequatur*, a confirming decision on the award's enforceability by the forum state is no longer required, which may *e contrario* imply that decisions adverse to enforcement must not necessarily any longer be shown respect.[432] Besides, the French court did not primarily focus on recognising a court judgement on enforce-

428 Different Abascal (2008), *op. cit.*, 173: *"An award that was set aside in the place of arbitration may be enforced under the more favourable regime provided in Article VII of the New York Convention. This provision allows any party to rely on the domestic law of the place of enforcement. Thus if the law of the place of enforcement does not list the setting aside of an award as a ground to deny recognition and enforcement, the court may enforce it."*

429 Gaillard (1998), *op. cit.*, 654.

430 Gaillard/Goldmann (eds.) (1999), *op. cit.*, para. 1688; *see also* van den Berg (1981), *op. cit.*, 331-58.

431 Haravon (2007), *op. cit.*, 36; Park (2006), *op. cit.*, 185.

432 *"Si la décision de cet Etat (du siège) doit automatiquement l'emporter sur les concepts de l'Etat d'accueil, le sursis à statuer s'impose. Toute exécution préalable `s l'existence d'une décision définitive dans l'Etat d'origine est de nature á créer des situations inextricables dans lesquelles un Etat doit revenir sur une décision d'exequatur qu'il estimait justifiée pour se conformer à une décision contraire rendue à l'étranger."*, Gaillard (1998), *op. cit.*, 662.

ability, while it neglected a court judgement on nullification. French courts rather simply decided for recognition and enforcement of the "international" award itself, without particular respect or intentional disregard to any judgements rendered by a foreign national court.

While the strong pro-enforcement bias of the New York Convention, – unlike the European Convention – can never at all be violated through enforcement,[433] the Hilmarton approach was principally feasible based on the international arbitration regimes, but might be affected, if states were also bound by a corresponding enforcement regime, providing for an internationally recognisable *erga omnes* effect of court judgements. The dilemma of Hilmarton might have been relieved, if either the French court had been obliged to recognise the foreign court judgement ruling the annulment of the original award, or the Swiss court had had to recognise the French enforcement decision as *res judicata* impeding a re-submission to arbitration of the same matter, or if at least the English court, finally granting enforcement of the second award, had been required to respect the former enforcement and therefore *res judicata* decision of the French courts, impeding enforcement of a contradictory award.

VI. The Council Regulation on Jurisdiction and the Recognition and Enforcement of Judgments in Civil and Commercial Matters (2001)

A regime providing for obligatory recognition and enforcement of judgements at least within Europe is the Council Regulation on Jurisdiction and the Recognition and Enforcement of Judgements in Civil and Commercial Matters (*Brussels I*).

1. Historical Development

While some states had already commenced in the 19th century to enter into bilateral agreements on mutual recognition and enforcement of judgements,[434] the multilateral Council Regulation on the Recognition and Enforcement of Foreign Arbitral Awards has its formal origins in Article 220 of the Treaty of Rome (today Article 293 EC Treaty), obligating the contracting states to simplify their for-

433 Paulsson (1996), *op. cit.,* 104.
434 Kleinknecht, Die verbraucherschützenden Gerichtsstände im deutschen und europäischen Zivilprozeßrecht (2007), 58.

malities required for recognition and enforcement of court judgements and arbitral awards.[435]

a) Brussels Convention (1968)

Subsequently, as from 1960 a committee of experts deliberated on an adequate treaty under the auspices of the Commission of the European Economic Community (*EEC*). On 27 September 1968 the states then members of the EEC[436] entered into the drafted "Brussels Convention on jurisdiction and the enforcement of judgments in civil and commercial matters" (*Brussels Convention*)[437], which came into force on 1 February 1973 in accordance with its Article 62.[438] The treaty's purpose was "to facilitate recognition and to introduce an expeditious procedure for securing the enforcement of judgments, authentic instruments and court settlements" in order to meet the pre-condition of Article 220 of Treaty of Rome.[439] While previous treaties merely attempted to facilitate recognition and enforcement, the Brussels Convention went further by forbidding its contracting states to question

435 Hascher, Recognition and Enforcement of Judgements on the Existence and Validity of an Arbitration Clause under the Brussels Convention, 13 Arb Int 1997, 33; Kropholler, Europäisches Zivilprozeßrecht, (2005), Art. 1 para. 41 with reference to the Jenard Report on Article 1 of the Brussels Convention at IV D.

436 Beglium, France, Germany, Italy, Luxembourg, Netherlands.

437 ABIEG No. L 299 of 1972.

438 Kleinknecht (2007), *op. cit.*, 58.

439 Preamble of the Brussels Convention on jurisdiction and the enforcement of judgments in civil and commercial matters: *"THE HIGH CONTRACTING PARTIES TO THE TREATY ESTABLISHING THE EUROPEAN ECONOMIC COMMUNITY, Desiring to implement the provisions of Article 220 of that Treaty by virtue of which they undertook to secure the simplification of formalities governing the reciprocal recognition and enforcement of judgments of courts or tribunals, Anxious to strengthen in the Community the legal protection of persons therein established, Considering that it is necessary for this purpose to determine the international jurisdiction of their courts, to facilitate recognition and to introduce an expeditious procedure for securing the enforcement of judgments, authentic instruments and court settlements, Have decided to conclude this Convention and to this end have designated as their Plenipotentiaries: HIS MAJESTY THE KING OF THE BELGIANS: Mr Pierre HARMEL, Minister for Foreign Affairs; THE PRESIDENT OF THE FEDERAL REPUBLIC OF GERMANY: Mr Willy BRANDT, ViceChancellor, Minister for Foreign Affairs; THE PRESIDENT OF THE FRENCH REPUBLIC: Mr Michel DEBRÉ, Minister for Foreign Affairs; THE PRESIDENT OF THE ITALIAN REPUBLIC: Mr Giuseppe MEDICI, Minister for Foreign Affairs; HIS ROYAL HIGHNESS THE GRAND DUKE OF LUXEMBOURG: Mr Pierre GRÉGOIRE, Minister for Foreign Affairs; HER MAJESTY THE QUEEN OF THE NETHERLANDS: Mr J.M.A.H. LUNS, Minister for Foreign Affairs; WHO, meeting within the Council, having exchanged their Full Powers, found in good and due form, HAVE AGREED AS FOLLOWS:"*

the original jurisdiction of another contracting state's court within the recognition and enforcement procedure of the judgement rendered by that court.[440] With its substantive regime on international jurisdiction and *lis pendens* the Brussels Convention contributed to preventing contradictory judgements on the very same dispute within its signatory states.[441]

b) Brussels I Regulation (2001)[442]

However, while the EEC was progressively growing, each accession involved changes not only in range but also in effect of the Brussels Convention.[443] Although the Brussels Convention significantly contributed to facilitation of recognition and enforcement of foreign judgements, and encouraged the contracting states to harmonise international jurisdiction in civil and commercial matters, it was deemed necessary to provide for jurisdiction, recognition and enforcement of judgments by way of a legal act of the ECC. In 1997, with the Treaty of Amsterdam establishing the autonomous legislative competence of the EC,[444] the European Council in Tampere[445] and the Council of the Ministers of Justice and of the Interior, resolved a set of measures[446] including the Council Regulation (EC) No 44/2001 on jurisdiction and the recognition and enforcement of judgments in civil and commercial matters coming into force on 2 March 2002.[447] Without the Treaty of Amsterdam it would have been impossible to enact a European Regulation providing for a common

440 Kleinknecht (2007), *op. cit.*, 59 with reference to the Reports of Jenard, 7 and de Bra, 125.

441 Haas, Der Ausschluß der Schiedsgerichtsbarkeit vom Anwendungsbereich des EuGVÜ, IPRax 1992, 292.

442 In the following it will be referred to the *Brussel Treaties* for the era before 2001.

443 For the accession of Danmark, Greatbritan and Ireland in 1978 see detailed explanations by Schlosser, ABIEG No. C 59, 71 of 5 March 1979; for the accession of Greece in 1983 see detailed explanations by Evrigenis/Karameus, ABIEG No. C 298, 1 of 24 November 1986; for the accession of Portugal and Spain in 1989 see detailed explanations by AlmeidaCruz/Desantes Real/Jenard, ABIEG No. C 189, 35 of 28 July 1990, the accession of Finland, Austria and Sweden in 1995 did not involve (objective) changes in the subject matter, see Schlosser, *EU-ZPR*, Introduction, Para. 9; Kropholler (2005), *op. cit.*, Introduction, para. 13.

444 Kleinknecht (2007), *op. cit.*, 60 with reference to the „Aktionsplan des Rates und der Kommission vom 3.12.1998", ABIEG Nr. C 19, 2, 23 January 1999; Posch, Vergemeinschaftung des Kollisionsrechts und die Verordnung Rom II, University of Graz, online publication available on: www.uni-graz.at/eurechtundpolitik/Rom_II_Prof. Posch.pdf.

445 Kleinknecht (2007), *op. cit.*, 61 with reference to 15./16 October 1999, NJW 2000, 1925.

446 *Ibid.*, 61 with reference to 24./30 November 2000, IPRax 2001, 163 et seq.

447 So provided by Article 76 Brussels I.

European civil procedure, but thus the former international treaty, the Brussels Convention was replaced by a regulation of the EEC pursuant to Article 249(1) EG. The legal nature of Brussels I is a regulation of secondary Community law.[448]

2. Core Provisions

Brussels I sets out rules for the three subject matters of international jurisdiction, recognition and enforcement, and further procedural provisions.[449] Brussels I, Article I identifies the scope of the regulation as involving "civil and commercial matters whatever the nature of the court or tribunal."

3. Exceptions

Despite the indication of a rather wide scope, both the Brussels Convention and Brussels I provide for the preclusion of some legal matters from their jurisdiction. Notwithstanding the previously established requirement of a European regime for recognition and enforcement, equally of judgements and arbitral awards, set out by Article 220 of the Treaty of Rome, Article I(2)(d) of Brussels I explicitly rules that the Regulation does not apply to arbitration.

a) Reasoning for the Exception

The necessity of a uniform regime for the free circulation of arbitral awards has so far been denied in the light of the numerous international treaties in the field of international arbitration, with particular regard to the EU-wide applicability of the New York Convention.[450] In fact, the expert report on the occasion of the Convention's elaboration stated: *"Arbitration, a form of proceedings encountered in civil, and in particular, commercial matters is excluded because of the existence of numerous multilateral international agreements in this area."*[451] Besides, the

448 Kleinknecht (2007), *op. cit.*, 61.

449 *Ibid.*, 64.

450 Kropholler (2005), *op. cit.*, Art. 1 para. 41 with reference to the *Federal Law Gazette* (BGBl) 1961 II 12; Schlosser, EU-Zivilprozessrecht: EuGVVO EuEheVO EuBVO EuZVO, (2003), Art. I EuGVO para. 23. The European Convention (1961), on the contrary, applies within the European Union merely to Austria, Belgium Denmark, France, Germany, Hungary, Italy, Latvia, Luxembourg, Poland, Slowakia, Slowenia and Spain.

451 Hascher (1997), *op. cit.*, 33 at fn. 2.

European Council had devised a European agreement on the implementation of a uniform law on arbitration amended by an Additional Protocol in order to facilitate recognition and enforcement of arbitral awards even further than the New York Convention.[452] As the aforementioned treaties on arbitration, in particular the New York Convention, involve provisions that are not directed to the arbitral authorities, but to the state courts concerned with recognition and enforcement of arbitral awards, the European Court of Justice concluded that the signatories to the Brussels Convention, when excluding arbitration from its applicability referring to the coverage of arbitration by international treaties, intended to exclude arbitration in its entirety, involving proceedings pending in national courts.[453]

b) Grievance of such Exclusion

However, this failed to recognise that court judgements involving arbitral awards are not yet granted unrestricted mobility, though with arbitration being widely used as an efficient mechanism for dispute resolution in inter-European economy, there is an exigency for international coverage of judgements as to arbitration matters.[454] Therefore it is questioned, whether court proceedings involving a review of the arbitration and its validity, and in particular the annulment of arbitral awards fall within the scope of 'arbitration' in terms of Brussels I, Article I(2)(d).[455] Also, the European Court of Justice was faced with the issue of identifying the scope of the exclusion of arbitration from the applicability of the Brussels I Regulation.

c) Classification of the Scope of Exclusion

The Official Report on the occasion of the first amendment to the Brussels Convention in the light of the accession of Denmark, Great Britain and Ireland in 1978 (see supra fn. 381) documents the authors' considerations as to such exclusion as follows:

"[I]t is contended that the literal meaning of the word arbitration itself implies that it cannot extent to every dispute affected by an arbitration agreement: that arbitration refers only to arbitration proceedings. Proceedings before national Courts would therefore be affected by Article 1, second paragraph, point (4) of the 1968 Convention only if they dealt

452 European Court of Justice, decision of 25 July 1991 – Rs. C 190/89, published in IPRax 1992, 313 no. 17 with reference to AblEG 1979 C 59, 1, NJW 1993, 189; Hascher (1997), *op. cit.*, 33.

453 European Court of Justice, decision of 25 July 1991 – Rs. C 190/89, published in IPRax 1992, 313 et seq., NJW 1993, 190.

454 Schlosser (2003), *op. cit.*, Art. I EuGVO para. 23.

455 *Ibid.*, Art. I EuGVO para. 23.

with arbitration as a main issue and did not have to consider the validity of an arbitration agreement merely as a matter incidental to an examination of the competence of the court of origin to assume jurisdiction."[456]

The drafters thus emphasized the exclusion applies only for court proceeding dealing with the arbitration itself as the main subject. The report of Schlosser instead distinguished the different qualities of impact such court proceedings have on arbitration.[457] It was assumed that the Brussels Convention would not apply to court proceedings aiming to *serve* realisation of an arbitration procedure. Such *serving* proceedings have been identified as proceedings being indispensible for the realisation of the arbitration – strictly speaking, proceedings, whose subject matter is arbitration as a 'field of law'. In contrast, court proceedings, which were merely intended to *support* the arbitration procedure, should fall within the scope of the Brussels Convention. Such *supporting* proceedings are primarily proceedings on the ruling of interim measures (on injunctions).

4. European Court of Justice in the matter of „Marc Rich"

In the matter of *Marc Rich* the European Court of Justice was requested to provide clarification on the preclusion of arbitration from Brussels I's field of application.[458]

The original dispute arose out of a purchase agreement for Iranian crude oil concluded between the Swiss company Marc Rich and Co. AG and the Italian company Societa Italiana P.A. by exclusive use of telex. Afterwards, Marc Rich sent a further telex on the terms of the contract, also providing for the following arbitration clause:

"Law and arbitration. Construction, validity and performance of this contract shall be construed in accordance with English law. Should any dispute arise between the buyer and the seller, the matter in dispute shall be referred to three persons in London. One to be appointed by each of the parties hereto and the third by the two chosen, their decision or that of any two of them should be final and binding on both parties."[459]

Impianti, however, did not reply to this last telex. Marc Rich intended to commence an arbitral proceeding while the defending party, Impianti asserted the invalidity

456 Hascher (1997), *op. cit.*, 33.
457 Schlosser Report.
458 European Court of Justice, Decision of 25 July 1991 – Rs. C 190/89 published in NJW 1993, 189 et seq.; English excerpt in Hascher (1997), *op. cit.*, fn. 6.
459 Hascher (1997), *op. cit.*, 36, fn. 16.

of the arbitration agreement and refused to participate in the arbitration, and contemporaneously initiated litigation in Italy. Marc Rich, subsequently sought an alternative nomination by the English courts, whereas Impianti aimed to continue the Italian litigation, holding that the Brussels Convention would apply in absence of a valid arbitration agreement – accordingly the Italian proceeding would have priority over the English litigation in the light of the Brussels Convention's *lis pendens* provisions.[460] The London Court of Appeal, where Marc Rich's request was pending, submitted the issue for a preliminary ruling to the European Court of Justice, which subsequently clarified:

"[t]he international agreements, and in particular, the...New York Convention on the recognition and enforcement of foreign arbitral awards...lay down rules which must be respected not by the arbitrators themselves but by the courts of the Contracting States. Those rules related, for example, to agreements whereby parties refer a dispute to arbitration and the recognition and enforcement of arbitral awards. It follows that, by excluding arbitration from the scope of the Convention on the ground that is was already covered by the international conventions, the Contracting Parties intended to exclude arbitration in its entirety, including a proceedings brought before a national court."[461]

The Court further clarified that only the subject matter of a dispute is relevant for the assessment of whether a court proceeding falls within the scope of the Brussels Convention.[462] Finally, the European Court of Justice concluded proceedings on the nomination of arbitrators do not fall within the scope of the Brussels Convention, thus the provisions aimed at the prevention of contradictory or parallel proceedings on the same dispute in different contracting states did not apply to the procedure pending in London.[463] The European Court of Justice's finding was widely appreci-

460 In concreto Impianti relied on Articles 21 and 22 of the Brussels Convention.

461 Hascher (1997), *op. cit.*, 36 fn. 17; European Court of Justice, Decision of 25 July 1991 – Rs. C 190/89 published in IPRax 1992, 313 no. 18 et seq.

462 European Court of Justice, Decision of 25 July 1991 – Rs. C 190/89 published in IPRax 1992, 314 no. 26.

463 In absence of a *lis pendens* rule between national courts and arbitration authorities, the London Court of Appeals was allowed to nominate an arbitrator on behalf of the declining party Impianti, enabling Marc Rich to initiate and conduct arbitration in Great Britain, while Impianti could continue its court proceeding on the same matter in Genoa, Italy. This inheres the risk of two contradictory findings on the same dispute in two divers contracting states, which at worst are both sought to be enforced in a third state. In light of such possible outcomes the Brussels treaties do not provide a remedy on the dilemma of enforcement of arbitral awards annulled by a judgement, but even worsens it by extending such dilemma to any kind of court judgement issued parallel to the arbitral award. *For further details and consequences see* Haas (1992), *op. cit.*, 292.

ated as being consistent with the text and intention of the Brussels Convention[464] and today it is deemed to apply equally to the Brussels I Regulation.

5. The Applicability of the Brussels I Regulation on judgments on the recognition and enforcement of arbitral awards

Although the European Court of Justice thus already fairly confined the scope of today's Brussels I Regulation, it remained unanswered, how to qualify proceedings that begin only after the arbitration was already concluded, like proceedings on recognition and enforcement of foreign arbitral awards.

While Schlosser in his report on the first Accession Convention to the Brussels Treaties precludes recognition as well as enforcement of arbitral awards from the field of applicability,[465] the European Court of Justice in its ad judgement on "Van Uden" merely deemed recognition as not covered by the Brussels Treaties. Accordingly, the European Court of Justice did not explicitly deny the applicability of the Convention on judgements on the enforcement of arbitral awards.

Since the approach of the European Court of Justice in 'Marc Rich' was also close to Schlosser's report, it may be assumed that the Brussels treaties do not cover a leave for enforcement in the forum state, which was to be recognised in the foreign state of enforcement, strictly speaking the double exequatur of arbitral awards.[466] Besides, as initially explained, enforcement of an arbitral award always entails its recognition. Within the meaning of the European Court of Justice's previous differentiation between serving and supporting proceedings, enforcement of an arbitral award is no 'parallel' proceeding, but rather a proceeding which is intended to implement the outcome of the arbitration by executing the arbitral award. Accordingly the judicial enforcement procedure serves the arbitral proceeding.[467]

6. Applicability of the Brussels I Regulation on Annulment Decisions

It remains to be clarified whether or not a court decision ruling on the nullification of an arbitral award falls under the scope of Brussels I.

---

464 Hascher (1997), *op. cit.*, 35.

465 Gomez, Internationale Schiedsgerichtsbarkeit und Binnenmarkt, IPRax 2005, 90 with reference to the Report of Schlosser on the Accession Convention of 9 October 1978 in ABl 1979 C 59/ 71 (117), 64-65.

466 Kropholler (2005), *op. cit.*, Art. 1 para. 43, Gomez (2005), *op. cit.*, 90.

467 Gomez (2005), *op. cit.*, 90; Kropholler (2005), *op. cit.*, Art. 1 para. 43.

The national courts of the contracting states have so far refused to recognise a foreign (non)annulment decision, based on Brussels I, Article I(2)(d) and Schlosser's report. Meanwhile, the European Court of Justice clarified that decisions on a request for nullification of an arbitral award are precluded from Brussels I.[468] Similarly, judgements that are deemed to incorporate arbitral awards – a view usually taken by courts in common law tradition based on the *merger doctrine* (*see above*) – are also excluded from applicability of the Brussels Treaties.[469]

7. Conclusions on the Impact of the Brussels I Regulation

For the purpose of a final conclusion some features need to be emphasised:

The field of arbitration, including preliminary questions, is deemed to *serve* arbitration and thus is excluded from the applicability of the Brussels I Regulation. Today, such judgements are not to be recognised or enforced within the E(E)C in accordance with the Brussels I Regulation, however, their recognition and enforcement abroad may still be granted by national law or bilateral treaties concluded between the forum state and the addressee.[470]

Court decisions, which are merely deemed to support arbitration, may fall under the scope of the Brussels I Regulation. The same is true for court decisions adjudicating the original dispute of a previously vacated award, as not being related to arbitration in terms of Article 1(2)(d) of the Brussels I Regulation.[471]

For the sake of completeness, it may be said that the enforceability of an award, which was not already left for enforcement, by no means falls within the scope of the Brussels I Regulation, but remains governed by the repeatedly referenced international treaties.

The Brussels I Regulation does not provide for recognition of foreign court decisions on the recognition, enforcement or annulment of arbitral awards. Accordingly, courts in the context of arbitral awards, are merely bound by the distinct arbitration regimes, such as the New York Convention on the Recognition and Enforcement of Foreign Arbitral Awards and the European Convention on International Commercial Arbitration.

---

468 Gomez (2005), *op. cit.*, 90 with reference to ECJ November 17, 1998 – Rs C-391(95), IPRax 1999, 240.

469 Kropholler (2005), *op. cit.*, Art. 1 para. 43.

470 Hascher (1997), *op. cit.*, 37.

471 Kropholler (2005), *op. cit.*, Art. 1 para. 43.

VII. Interim-Conclusion De Lege Lata

Neither the New York Convention nor the European Convention or Brussels I govern which state has international jurisdiction to review arbitral awards and decide on their effectiveness; neither provide for international recognition of such court decisions dealing with the award's effectiveness. While the New York and the European Conventions intentionally focus on matters of international arbitration, the Brussels I Convention covers jurisdiction and recognition for civil actions, but excludes arbitration in its entirety. In consequence, international arbitration treaties exhaustively cover arbitral awards themselves, but civil suits on arbitration matters (such as annulment and/or enforcement decisions) are excluded from both the scope of the Brussels Treaties and international arbitration treaties. Hence, the international framework on recognition of arbitral awards on the one hand, and recognition of judgements on the other hand involves a momentous regulatory gap concerning the recognition of judgments on arbitration matters.

Without a specific regulation giving an international *res judicata* effect to the forum states' annulment decisions, foreign courts may exercise their discretionary power provided by the International Arbitration Conventions. Accordingly they may give effect to either the arbitral award, by allowing for its enforcement, or to the foreign annulment decision, by refusing enforcement of the arbitral award. Both options are in accordance with the current international regimes, and may further adjudicate potential *res judicata* effects pursuant to their national procedural laws.[472]

Ever since the promulgation of the New York Convention some commentators feared Article V(1)(e) may enable courts to grant enforcement to annulled awards and could therefore ignore annulment decisions of other contracting states, other commentators were concerned that a local annulment decision could prevent enforcement for all other signatories.[473] Today, opinions still significantly differ on what is worse: the possible power of courts in forum states to prevent enforcement by vacating the arbitral award, usually based on local particularities,[474] or

472 Söderlund, (2005), *op. cit.*, 301: *"[T]he rules on lis pendens and res judicata are part of the domestic procedural arsenal of countries with reasonably well-developed legal traditions."*

473 Sampliner (1996), *op. cit.*, 28 et seq.

474 Freyer/Gharavi (1998), *op. cit.*, 103, and at fn. 7: *"This, at least, was presumed by the Convention's drafters to be the effect of an order setting aside an award unless the provisions of Article VII(1) of the Convention were applicable. As discussed below, however, this is not its effect under French law; nor was it recognized as a bar to enforcement in a recent U.S. case notwithstanding the absence of the Article VII(l) exception."*

the option for addressee states to grant enforcement notwithstanding an award's actual nullification.

During enforcement decisions courts have to take account of fundamental opposites: on the one hand the bargain of the parties in favour of final and binding arbitration, requiring recognition of the issued award; on the other hand the forum state's interest in respect of its sovereign annulment decision, therefore demanding to refuse enforcement of the award. The underlying issue is whether party autonomy in favour of final and binding arbitration, or states' interest of protecting their national legal order by ascertaining the award's legality, deserves preferential treatment. Further, on an international law level, the fundamental question is whether such order of priority may be bindingly assessed either by the forum state or rather by the enforcing state. Such dividedness is reflecting the contrasting notions of allotting the forum state or the enforcing state jurisdiction to decide on the effectiveness of the arbitral award, based on "the battle for supremacy between national law, ... and the independence or autonomy of the arbitration process system".[475]

In conclusion, the New York Convention does not address the issue of review of arbitral awards, nor does it allot jurisdiction on such matters to any state.[476] But also the European Convention, actually appreciated as a notable improvement on former shortcomings and said to provide a 'more balanced solution' than the New York Convention, neither allots nor restricts national jurisdiction on the review of arbitral awards.

475 Lew (2006), *op. cit.*, 179.
476 See also Gaillard (2003), *op. cit.*, 1106; Freyer/Gharavi (1998), *op. cit.*, 115.

D. Basic Concepts on Control Exercised in International Arbitration

In assessing which jurisdiction is competent to determine the effectiveness of an arbitral award, there are basically two opposing approaches: The traditional view attaches all relevant powers concerning the arbitration to the forum state and is therefore labelled as the 'territorial' approach. The more modern view aims to detach arbitration from almost any interference of national law or local courts, particularly at the seat of the arbitration, and is therefore identified as 'delocalised' or 'transnational'.

These views represent contradictory concepts on the nature of international arbitration viewing arbitration either as a dispute resolution mechanism, which is part of a national legal system, or as a co-existing, autonomous process. Such differentiation also involves diverging concepts as to the source and extent of the arbitrators' powers to adjudicate the issue presented to them and where such adjudication may be reviewed: in essence, the argument focuses on the distinct roles attributed to the seat of the arbitration and its *procedural* law.

Similarly, the issue of the applicable *substantive* law is highly controversial and almost omnipresent in international arbitration. It may arise at various moments of the arbitration and with regard to several (national) laws: Initially arbitrators have to consider the law governing the validity of the main contract and the stipulated matters (*lex contracti*), as well as the law applying to the arbitration agreement. Since the separability of the main contract and the arbitration agreement meanwhile is internationally recognised, they may be subjected to distinct national laws.[477]

477 Epping, Die Schiedsvereinbarung im internationalen privaten Rechtsverkehr nach der Reform des deutschen Schiedsverfahrensrechts (1999), 56 with reference to Fouchard, L'arbitrage commercial international, (1967), para. 127 et seq.; *"Die Frage, ob umgekehrt die Wahl des Schiedsortes eine stillschweigende Rechtswahl darstellt, kann offen bleiben, da der Schiedsort nach der Angleichung der nationalen an die internationalen Kollisionsnormen stets auch subsidiärer Anknüpfungspunkt für die Schiedsvereinbarung ist."*, *ibid.* at 57; *"It may be recalled that most arbitration laws adopt the doctrine of the separability of the arbitration agreement, that is, the invalidity of the main contract in which the arbitration agreement (clause) is included or to which the arbitration agreement relates does not affect the validity of the arbitration agreement (e.g., UNCITRAL Model Law, article 16(1)). A logical consequence of the separability doctrine is that the law applicable to the*

Also, in later stages several matters related to an arbitration proceeding may be affected by the *substantive* law of particular national legal systems: e.g. the capacity of the parties or the competence of the arbitrators by the laws at their domicile or seat (the *lex patriae* or *lex societatis*), matters related to the main contract by the laws of the place where such contract was concluded (the *lex loci contractus*) and/or the place where the performance has been/is to be accomplished (the *lex loci solutionis*). But also with regard to the applicable *procedural* law and the issue of jurisdiction for legal review of the arbitral award distinct national laws may be taken into consideration: the law governing the arbitration agreement, the law chosen by the parties to govern the arbitration, the law of the state of the seat of arbitration, the law of the (prospective) state of enforcement of the issued arbitral award – or at least their particular *ordre public*.[478]

Principally, parties may choose the law governing the substantive issues of their main contractual relation.[479] Equally, parties may also choose the law governing the arbitration procedure by stipulation in the arbitration agreements. While proponents of a delocalised, rather party-autonomy-oriented perception presume that the main contract, the arbitration agreement and the following arbitration procedure may be solely governed by the stipulated law, supporters of the territorial approach suggest that the conclusion of the arbitration agreement and the resulting arbitration proceeding itself are subjected to the law of the seat of the arbitration, the *lex fori*.[480]

I. Territorial Notion

The traditional notion of the territorial approach is characterised by giving greatest deference to the national law of the country at the seat of the arbitration. Basically it is held that the parties' agreement on arbitration is a kind of forum selection, therefore the choice of the arbitral seat involves a choice of the *lex loci arbitri* to govern the arbitration, and any subsequent appeals may be subjected to the national courts by virtue of the local procedural law.[481]

---

contract is not necessarily the same as the law governing the arbitration agreement (clause).", van den Berg, Explanatory Note on the Hypothetic Draft Convention on the International Enforcement of Arbitration Agreements and Awards, Sec. 39 available online at http://www.arbitration-icca.org/media/0/12133703697430/explanatory_note_ajb_rev06.pdf

478 Smit (1989), *op. cit.*, 634.

479 Thrope, A Question of Intent: Choice of Law and the International Arbitration Agreement, 54 Disp Res J (1999), 5.

480 *Ibid.*, 5, fn 35.

481 See also Lalive, Les règles de conflit de lois appliquées au fond du litige par l'arbitrage international siégant en Suisse, Rev. Arb. (1976), 159.

This approach was for a long time taken in England, where the seat of an international arbitration, is attached to the forum of a national court. F.A. Mann was one of the first proponents manifesting a territorial approach in his 1967 essay "Lex Facit Arbitrum".[482]

1. Principal Notions of 'International Arbitration'

Fundamentally, supporters of the territorial approach perceive 'international arbitration' as identified by the European Convention, as a "misnomer", misleadingly indicating arbitration detached from national law. Although, "even such an arbitration is a national arbitration", since the European Convention "applies only by reason of the fact that the State controlling the arbitration has become a party to it."[483] Arbitration could not be detached from national legal orders, but "like any other institution of municipal law, requires a firm legal basis, that can only be found in the recognition and implementation of the idea of *lex facit arbitrum*" (emphasis added).[484] Private persons can only act within the frames provided by national legal orders, as they have no rights beyond such national legal orders. All rights and duties private persons have, are rooted solely within positive law. Likewise, party autonomy enabling parties to choose arbitration or a particular law merely exists due to pertinent provisions set out by national legal orders. By no means do parties have the possibility to escape the constraints of national law by establishing "autonomous legal standards".[485] "When we say in conflict of laws: 'contracts are governed by the law chosen by the parties', we do so, and can do so, only by reason of the fact that the rule is part of a specific legal system". Accordingly, F.A. Mann concluded: "Lex facit arbitrum."[486] The *lex fori*, or more precisely the *lex arbitri* applicable to a particular arbitration is deemed to be the law of the country in which the arbitration is located, and thus determined by the parties' autonomous determination.[487] Taking the view that arbitration, like all

482 Mann, Lex Facit Arbitrum, in: International Arbitration: Liber Amicorum for Martin Domke, Sanders (ed.) (1967), 158.

483 *Ibid.*, 158.

484 *Ibid.*, 158 with regard to Philippe Fouchard's statement that international commercial arbitration would be *"un arbitration détaché de tous les cadres étatiques, soumis à tous égards à des norms et à des autorités véritablement internationals"*.

485 Thrope (1999), *op. cit.*, 6.

486 Mann (1967), *op. cit.*, 160: *"Every right or power a private person enjoys is inexorably conferred by or derived from a system of municipal law which may conveniently and in accordance with tradition be called the lex fori, though it would be more exact... to speak of the lex arbitri"*.

487 Mann (1967), *op. cit.*, 160/161.

legal relationships, can only arise if so provided by national law, a distinction is to be made between 'national' and 'foreign' arbitration, which depends on the perspective of a national court, while facilitating the determination of the applicable legal system.

2. Role of the Arbitrator

In light of the perception of the supporters of the territorial approach, arbitration cannot exist in a "legal vacuum", since all powers of the parties and likewise all powers of the arbitrators derive solely from national arbitration laws permitting party autonomy and arbitration. Arbitrators are, like national judges, inexorably subject to the "legislative jurisdiction" of the "local sovereign". Although arbitrators are "allowed and even ordered" to give credence to the directions of the parties, but only by virtue of and to the extent the local sovereign admits such liberties.[488]

3. Role of the Seat of the Arbitration

Strictly speaking, supporters of the territorialist approach not only presume that arbitrators and parties are necessarily bound by legal systems in general, but in particular emphasise that the arbitration is subject to the law of the country in which the arbitration has its seat.[489] According to this perception, it is principally the seat of the arbitration that 'anchors' the arbitration into the national legal order of that state,[490] which is similar to the differentiation between "primary" and "secondary" jurisdiction as proposed in literature and expressed in U.S. decisions, but also evidenced by German courts.[491]

The underlying perception is that the parties' choice to resolve their dispute by means of arbitration is nothing but "a specialised kind of forum-selection clause", providing not only for a particular seat but also the applicable procedure.[492] The law of the seat of the arbitration is deemed to form the statutory framework for

488 *Ibid.*, 161 and 162; Smit (1989), *op. cit.*, 630 et seq.

489 Mann (1967), *op. cit.*, 161.

490 Gaillard (1998), *op. cit.*, 647.

491 Webster (2006), *op. cit.*, 201/202: *"As regards the definition of the primary jurisdiction, the courts of both developing and developed countries, with rare exceptions, appear to focus soley on the place of arbitration rather than the law under which the awards has been rendered. ... The territorial approach thus prevailed, as is moreover reaffirmed when bilateral investment treaties enter the equation."*

492 Webster (2006), *op. cit.*, 207 with reference to Scherk v. Alberto-Culver Co., 417 U.S. 506 (1974) U.S. at 519.

all issues related to the arbitral procedure, including all rights and duties of the arbitrators and the parties.[493] Such an approach is assumed to be supported by the New York Convention, which attributes particularly within Article V(1)(e) ample significance to the country in which the parties laid the seat of their arbitration and where the arbitral award was made.[494] While the New York Convention alternatively refers to the law of the country in which or under the law of which (i.e. the particular procedural law chosen by the parties) the award was made, arbitration practitioners pointed out that a choice of law notwithstanding the law of the seat, is extremely seldom in practice.[495]

The country of the seat of the arbitration is said to have the most obvious and efficient suitability to control arbitrations held and awards rendered within its territory. More importantly, it would be "intolerable" if the country could not ensure the integrity of proceedings held within its territory and therefore be capable of overruling even an autonomous arbitration if its own protectable concerns are affected.[496] The local sovereign should have the right to ensure legality of all processes taking place within its territory, which are therefore deemed to be necessarily in their entirety subject to the local legal order. In this context, each legal order hosting arbitrations may at its own discretion determine the features of the arbitral procedure, including the role and power of the arbitrators.[497] Therefore, arbitral procedures are principally governed by the *lex arbitri* at the seat of the arbitration, which may provide for great latitude for the parties and arbitrators in determining the procedure at their own discretion. Owed to modern arbitration-friendly national laws this may become the new standard.[498] Arbitrators in support of the territorial view may deem the law of the seat as indispensible and tend to submit

493 Mann (1967), *op. cit.*, 161.

494 Webster (2006), *op. cit.*, 208.

495 Also referred to as "*exceptional*", "*almost unknown*", a "*purely academic invention*", a "*possibility more theoretical than real*", and as appearing "*once-in-a-blue moon*", see Webster (2006), *op. cit.*, 208 with reference to the Fith Circuit Court of Appeals in Karaha Bodas Co., LLC v. Perusahaan Pertambangan Minyak Dan Gas Bumi Negara, U.S. 482 (5th Cir. 2004), XXIX Y. B. Com. Arb. (2004), 1262; Paulsson (1996), *op. cit.*, 111 with further explanations in fn. 31.

496 Mann (1967), *op. cit.*, 161.

497 *Ibid,*, 162.

498 Thrope (1999), *op. cit.*, 6; Mann (1967), *op. cit.*, 164 and 167: "*Suppose a contract between and English and an Italian firm does not contrain a choice of law clause, but provides for arbitration under the auspices of the International Chamber of Commerce, which appoints a German arbitrator. He has to find the proper law of the contract, because the buyer's right of recession, so it is assumed, exists by English law, but is lost under Italian law. To ascertain the proper law the arbitrator plainly cannot proceed otherwise than by application of German conflict rules. No other system can help... locus regit actum*".

the dispute presented to them to the law of the country of the seat, even if they are actually asked to apply another national law – unless the conflict of law rules of their *lex fori* allows for application of foreign laws.[499]

Since the observance of national public policy at the seat of the arbitration is widely accepted, it is argued to be "both illogical and unrealistic" to approve disregard of the other provisions maintained by this legal order.[500] However, the scope of public policy is indeed vague and undefined, but certainly does not cover the entire national legislation. This is evidenced by foreign courts in context of enforcement decisions in favour of awards breaching public policy at the seat of the arbitration. Moreover, the European Convention, Article IX(1) lit. a-d allows for enforcement notwithstanding a violation of such public policy.

Supporters of the territorial approach not only find arbitration naturally emerging from and linked to national legal systems, but also assume that parties to international arbitration would not even intend to rule out national legal orders in its entirety.[501] Parties are said to "never provide for arbitration 'full stop'", but rather provide for arbitration taking place at a particular seat, thus indicating the parties' intention to hold an arbitration guided by a certain national law. In this context it was reasoned that parties would be less inclined "to arbitrate in Utopia under the rules of IUI (International Utopian Institution)".[502] Therefore, parties are deemed to 'directly or indirectly, expressly or impliedly' choose their applicable *lex arbitri* by choosing the seat of the arbitration. Such an approach was also appreciated as providing legal certainty and predictability, particularly in case of silent choices of law. In those cases fairly sophisticated requirements should be set out for (like the parties' awareness of any such declaration), but for avoidance of doubt it would by all means be advisable to presume a choice of the law of the stipulated seat of the arbitration.[503] Proponents further argue this connectedness of the choice of the seat and the choice of law would not preclude the parties' autonomy. The parties autonomously choose the seat of their arbitration and they may still subject their arbitration to any agreeable national law, provided that such stipulation is clearly expressed or accompanied by distinct indication.[504]

---

499 Gaillard (1998), *op. cit.*, 647.

500 Mann (1967), *op. cit.*, 165.

501 Brekoulakis (2007), *op. cit.*, 360.

502 *Ibid.*, 360.

503 Epping (1999), *op. cit.*, 54.

504 Mann (1967), *op. cit.*, 159 and 163, Epping (1999), *op. cit.*, 56 with reference to Fouchard (1967), *op. cit.*, para. 127 et seq., stating: *"Die Frage, ob umgekehrt die Wahl des Schiedsortes eine stillschweigende Rechtswahl darstellt, kann offen bleiben, da der Schiedsort nach der Angleichung der nationalen an die internationalen Kollisionsnormen stets auch subsidiärer Anknüpfungspunkt für die Schiedsvereinbarung ist."*

Another consideration is that losing parties must be given the chance to appeal against a burdensome award right after it was issued. This is only warranted, if the competent courts are those at the seat of the arbitration and if such binding adjudication is respected abroad. Otherwise the defending party would not only have to wait until the pursuing party requests for enforcement in another state in order to defend such a request, but also would have to defend enforcement in every single country in which assets are located and enforcement is sought.[505] However, under the present international framework, enforcement could still be quickly achieved, when the annulment proceeding is still pending in the forum state. Therefore, even the territorial perception may not impede the evident risk of the race for enforcement.[506]

4. Appreciation of Enforcement of Annulled Awards

The concept of the territorial approach of arbitration is not necessarily solely traditional, but also concerned with international arbitration within globalised economies and increasingly concerted legal frameworks. In this context it is argued that the evidenced negligence of national courts towards annulment decisions of another national court would be "incoherent and a threat to the harmony and development of international relations", and would bring back principles of "absolute territorialism" in light of which "[c]hacun pour soi"[507] pay deference to nothing but its own laws and concepts.[508] Moreover, such an attitude is also considered as "harmful" on the maintenance of international arbitration as an effective means of dispute resolution by evoking inconsistent arbitral awards. For instance, countries that are in fact increasingly supporting arbitration provided their national courts may control the issued awards, might be discouraged if other countries at the same time adopt arbitration laws, which allow a general disrespect for foreign decisions on the validity of arbitral awards.[509]

505 Van den Berg (1981), *op. cit.*, 355.

506 Haravon (2007), *op. cit.*, 36.

507 Gharavi (2002), *op. cit.*, 123 with reference to Oppetit, B., case commentary of the Supreme Court's decision of 23 March 1994, Rev. Crit. DIP (1995), 359-360.

508 Gharavi (2002), *op. cit.*, 123 with reference to Mayer, *L'Etat et le droit international privé*, 16 Droits (1993), 39.

509 Sampliner (1997), *op. cit.*, 157; Gharavi (2002), *op. cit.*, 132 at para 314: *"The practice of enforcement of annulled awards seems somewhat arrogant and condescending. Arrogant for wanting to reach harmonization through a dictatorial method, i.e. by command and force. Condescending for its overall disregard of foreign annulment decisions and the intent of the parties. This attitude could very well reduce general enthusiasm for international arbitration."*

Arbitration laws allowing for disregard of annulment decisions in the forum state, like the French New Code of Civil Procedure, are blamed for disrespecting the parties' choice for a particular national law. These laws allow for enforcement of arbitral awards notwithstanding a valid annulment based on the chosen law, which makes it entirely unpredictable whether the remedies of the law validly stipulated by the parties will be effective.[510] These arbitral awards incapable of *erga omnes* annulments though suffering genuine defects have also been identified as "sentences flottantes".[511] To counter these negative effects, supporters of the territorial approach acknowledge and respect the validity of awards rendered by courts at the seat of the arbitration, and deny enforcement of awards set aside by that competent authority.[512]

II. Delocalised Notion

As a counter conception to the localised notion of international arbitration, Prof. Fragistas was evidently the first to assume parties who chose arbitration in fact "détacher l'arbitrage de tout ordre juridique et lui donner un caractère supranational."[513] Therefore, this conception has been identified as delocalised, also labelled as de-national, a-national, transnational notion of international arbitration generating floating, drifting or, as critics say limping awards.[514]

1. Principal Notions of 'International Arbitration'

The basic notion of the delocalised approach is that the arbitral award is "a private act, signed by private parties, that is the product of a procedure decided and determined by the agreement of the parties to the arbitration to solve their dispute through arbitration."[515] Accordingly, arbitration is perceived as an autonomous instrument of dispute resolution without tedious subjection to particularities of

510 Sampliner (1997), *op. cit.*, 158.
511 Gaillard (1998), *op. cit.*
512 Gaillard (2007), *op. cit.*
513 Mann (1967), *op. cit.*, 159.
514 Haas (2002), *op. cit.*, Article I para. 25; Smit (1989), op. cit., 629; Lew (2006), *op. cit.*, 196; Gaillard (1998), op. cit., 670; Solomon, Die Verbindlichkeit von Schiedssprüchen in der internationalen privaten Schiedsgerichtsbarkeit, (2007), 182.
515 Lastenouse, Why setting aside an arbitral award is not enough to remove it from the international scene, 16 J Int'l Arb (1999), 25; Jan Paulsson even criticises Francis A. Mann as making *"occasionally... entirely unsupported statement which appear on analysis to be but a whim or an idée fixe, irresistibly recalling a line from Le*

national legal systems and supported by the New Convention's major purpose of freeing "the international arbitral process from domination by the law of the place of arbitration."[516] If no particular legal system applies to arbitration it may be appropriately identified as 'international' arbitration. The regime of the New York Convention is accepted as establishing the first "cornerstones" towards internationalised arbitration by recognising that the effectiveness of arbitration agreements, proceedings and awards may be determined by various jurisdictions with particular focus on removing the need for double exequatur.[517] Beyond the New York Convention, the autonomy of international arbitration is deemed to be established by all significant arbitration rules not referring to any national arbitration laws at all, neither that of the parties, nor of the arbitrators or of the arbitral seat.[518]

Given that the New York Convention allows for the country in which (or according to the law of which) the arbitration took place may set aside or annul the award, the country where the pursuing party seeks enforcement is allowed to decide, to its own discretion, on enforcement of such award. Accordingly, the Convention empowers both the forum state and the addressee state to autonomously decide on the effectiveness they consider appropriate to give to the arbitral award. Hence, proponents of the delocalised perception find it unsustainable to assume international arbitrations would "derive their legitimacy solely from the national law of the *situs* country."[519]

2. *Role of the Arbitrator*

Principally, it is argued that the effectiveness of rendered awards under international arbitration do not necessarily emerge from the legal systems of the locus at which the award "happened to be rendered".[520] Arbitrators, unlike judges, are

Mariage de Figaro: Prouver que j'ai raison serait accorder que je puis avoir tort", Paulsson (1996), *op. cit.*, 110 with reference to Act I, Scene I, Suzanne (Figaro).

516 *Ibid.*, 104; Lew (2006), *op. cit.*, 179.

517 Lew (2006), *op. cit.*, 183 et seq.

518 *Ibid.*, 195.

519 Sampliner (1997), *op. cit.*, 151; Gaillard (1998), *op. cit.*, 674: *"Il reste vrai que 'lex facit arbitrum' mais cette lois est celle d'une communauté d'Etats et non celle d'un seule d'entre eux, fût-il celui du siège de l'arbitrage. On n'ira pas jusqu'à dire, ce qui serait une provocation, 'lex mercatoria facit arbitrum' mais certainement que le droit de différents Etats, pour ne pas dire les règles transnationales, font la juridicité de la sentence arbitrale."*

520 Paulsson (1982), *op. cit.*, 53 about its publication Arbitration Unbound: Award Detached From the Law of its Country of Origin, I.C.L.Q. (1981), 358.

not a judicial body of a particular state because their powers do not derive from a national legal order. Therefore, arbitrators have no forum.[521] While supporters of the territorial approach claim that proponents of delocalisation perceive arbitrators as acting in a "legal vacuum", Transnationalists admit that arbitration could not "exist outside of a legal context", but rather deem that the effectiveness of international arbitration is not necessarily bound by national legislation, and can be attributed to "international agreements"[522] or even to the "collectivity" of jurisdictions approving international arbitration.[523] Accordingly, the role of the arbitrator is construed as an "organ of the international community",[524] although others also tend to perceive the arbitrator as "a sui generis source of rights and obligations".[525] In opposition to the territorial approach, Transnationalists strictly dismiss any empowerance of the arbitrator by the local law of the arbitral venue,[526] blaming it as "rather artificial" to presume the arbitrator's authorisation would stem "very indirectly" from "a tolerance of the State" where the arbitration takes place.[527] Accordingly, arbitrators have no forum and are not obliged to apply the procedural law or the conflict of law rules of the state where the arbitration takes place.[528]

Parties, usually businessmen, would choose arbitration as "a one-shot"-instrument of dispute resolution aimed at avoidance of "the sequence of appeals and retrials frequent in litigation" in ordinary courts. Particularly, as there would be no warranty that the subsequent national courts' decisions are more lawful than the original award.[529] Arbitration intends to avoid the procedural and substantive "technicalities" set out by national laws (less for commercial matters), without actually intending to generally escape from the scope of mandatory provisions.[530] Arbitration agreements are deemed to be of "exceptional character" by rebutting, at least for international business relations, the assumption that national courts con-

521 Mann (1967), *op. cit.*, 169.

522 Smit (1989), *op. cit.*, 630 et seq.

523 Gaillard (2007), *op. cit.*: *"international arbitration in anchored in all legal systems that accept, according to their respective standards, to recognize the arbitral award, and not in a single legal system assimilating the arbitrators to its judges and integrating their awards into the judicial product of its courts."*; Gaillard (1998), *op. cit.*, 648.

524 Lalive, Transnational (or Truly International) Public Policy and International Arbitration, in Comparative Arbitration Practice and Public Policy in Arbitration, 3 ICCA Congress Series (1998), para. 44; Lew (2006), *op. cit.*, 196.

525 Pryles (2007), *op. cit.*, 7; Lew (2006), *op. cit.*, 179.

526 Paulsson (1996), *op. cit.*, 109.

527 Lalive (1976), *op. cit.*, 159.

528 Gaillard (1998), *op. cit.*, 648.

529 Mourre/di Brozolo (2006), *op. cit.*, 171.

530 *Ibid.*, 171.

stitute the "natural forum."[531] A major advantage of arbitration – opposed to usual means of litigation – lies in the parties' "unique" power to define their procedure. This autonomy constitutes a considerable improvement as regards "certainty, predictability, and uniformity" of their dispute settlement procedure.[532] Accordingly, party autonomy enables the parties to meet their "reasonable expectations" (fn. 30) and is deemed to restrict, at least partially, the jurisdiction of national courts by commanding deference of the parties' choice of law *(fn. 31).* "[533] Parties active in today's globalised economy would principally seek a "neutral and independent forum" that is less imperilled by bias or "political pressure", encouraging continuance of their economic relations. Therefore, interference of national courts in the arbitral process would be minimised to "truly exceptional circumstances",[534] as there would be "no justification for national courts to intercede in the arbitration process or second guess the determinations and analysis of an international arbitration tribunal… [ignoring] the intention and expectation of the parties and the autonomy of international arbitration.[535]

3. Role of the Seat of the Arbitration

Transnationalists tend to criticise the term 'seat of the arbitration' as "ill-chosen" and an "abus de langage" (misuse of language), because it implies international arbitration is confined to territorial borders and not emerged from private autonomy, as is the case.[536]

Rendering the parties' choice of the seat of their arbitration as an implied choice of law would contravene the parties' intention of choosing the seat for practical convenience like geographical proximity and economic advantages such as conference rooms, accommodations, flights or for tax reasons.[537] Instead of ensuring predictability such presumption would instead leave parties "exposed for an indefinite period of time to the risk that any change in the laws of the country chosen as seat of the arbitration, or in the attitude of the courts of such country

531 Brekoulakis, The Notion of the Superiority of Arbitration Agreements over Jurisdiction Agreements: Time to Abandon it?, 24 J Int'l Arb (2007), 359.
532 Thrope (1999), *op. cit.*, 5 and 16.
533 Thrope (1999), *op. cit.*, 5.
534 Mourre/di Brozolo (2006), *op. cit.* 171.
535 Lew (2006), *op. cit.*, 179.
536 Gharavi (2002), *op. cit.*, 107 et seq. with reference to Aubert, 37 Rev Crit DIP (1958), 372.
537 Gaillard (1998), *op. cit.*, 673; Paulsson (1982), *op. cit.*, 53 about its publication Arbitration Unbound: Award Detached From the Law of its Country of Origin, ICLQ (1981), 358.

towards arbitration".[538] A consequence could be an annulment of the award due to the local law preventing world-wide enforcement, even though the award was well in accordance with the parties' agreements. In such cases it is worth emphasising that "parties have agreed on international arbitration and not on jurisdiction of the local courts."[539]

Party autonomy would not only embrace the freedom of determining substantive contractual obligations, but also the right to select an adequate forum for the settlement of disputes arising out of the main contract. When parties agree on international arbitration they prefer a forum detached from territorial or juridical connectedness to their main contract and the national forum.[540] In arbitration agreements it is therefore often stipulated that the resolution of the dispute should be solely subject to the procedural autonomy of the parties, although the courts of the state of the arbitral seat actually are the default forum.[541] Therefore, the claim for the jurisdiction of local courts to control the arbitral procedure has been labelled as *'judicial jealousy'* towards alternative means of dispute resolution such as arbitration.[542] Disregarding the choice of the parties to resolve their dispute by means of international arbitration is regarded as violation of "party autonomy, which is part of the ordre public international."(Emphasis added)[543]

However, parties not only dismiss the jurisdiction of national courts by opting for international arbitration, but may, from the delocalised point of view, also neglect application of the local arbitration law, the *lex loci arbitri*. This is because, any kind of interference of national laws and courts should be removed, since the parties are said to have chosen a dispute resolution on a "non-national or transnational level", which is deemed to be supported by the international arbitration conventions, as well as institutional arbitration rules and particular national arbitration laws.[544] In particular, the New York Convention, Article V(1)(e) seems to support

538 Paulsson (1982), *op. cit.*, 53.

539 Webster (2006), *op. cit.*, 224; Brekoulakis (2007), *op. cit.*, 342: Arbitration agreements, like jurisdiction agreements, *"constitute…plausible alternatives to the default jurisdiction of the national courts"*.

540 *Ibid.*, 342.

541 *Ibid.*, 359.

542 Lew (2006), *op. cit.*, 179, fn. 17.

543 Berger, International Economic Arbitration (Studies in Transnational Economic Law), (1993), 682.

544 Lew (2006), *op. cit.*, 196: *"[International Arbitration] exists in its own space – a non – national or transnational or, if you prefer, an international domain. Admittedly international arbitration must coexist with national laws. There are rules of private international law that regulate the interaction of different or conflicting national laws. There are also rules to regulate the relations between national laws and international arbitration. These rules have their origin in public international l aw, private inter-*

such notion, by allowing for disregard of the legal positions taken on the award's effectiveness in its forum state.[545] However, strict observance of the territorial approach would fail to respect the permissive language of Article V(1)(e), requiring denial of enforcement of any set aside award.[546] Transnationalists perceive the New York Convention's body of rules and regulations as attributing greatest deference to arbitral awards as "primary product" of the arbitration, rather than to adjudications of local laws at the seat of the arbitration.[547]

The inherent (possible) disregard of local adjudications is not considered as inappropriate, as neither the parties nor the subject matter of international arbitration proceedings are usually in anyway associated with the local sovereign in whose territory the arbitration takes place. Therefore there would be no linking factor for national jurisdiction. A state merely hosting international arbitration is said to have no "intrinsic interest" in controlling a process with which it has nothing in common but the geographical position. Besides, Transnationalists fear local courts would be unable to live up to the parties' expectations as to the settlement of their dispute involving considerations of their particular business relation, their distinct cultural backgrounds and legal traditions. Thus it would be unreasonable to let local particularities affect this individual procedure.[548] Therefore, the emanating rationale is that arbitral awards are by no means integrated into the national legal system of the host state, instead this state's legal assessments as to the effectiveness of the delocalised award are irrelevant.[549] It is considered as inappropriate to recognise a decision nullifying the legal effect of an award based on mere local standards, even though the award is the valid result of an arbitration proceeding complying with the terms of the parties' arbitration agreement.[550]

However, while its aim is to avoid impact of local particularities of the laws and courts at the seat of the arbitration, emphasising that it seeks to "escape" legal systems in its entirety "would be misguided", because the organisation of international arbitration is reliant on national court assistance, particularly in terms

---

national l aw and intergovernmental and non-government instruments which have developed procedures and practices that have wide international acceptance."

545 Gaillard (2007), *op. cit.*

546 Sampliner (1997), *op. cit.*, 159 et seq.

547 Gaillard (2007), *op. cit.*; Sampliner (1997), *op. cit.*, 159 et seq.

548 Paulsson (1996), *op. cit.*, 109; Lalive (1976), *op. cit.*, 159.

549 Goldman, Une bataille judiciare autour de la lex mercatoria, Rev Arb (1983), 391; Gaillard (1998), *op. cit.*, 660: *"Seules les sentences rendue dans des situations purement internes à un Etat donné, entre parties relevant de cet Etat et sur on objet affectant exclusivement le commerce dans cet Etat, pourraient se voir opposer le fait que leur annulation dans l'Etat d'origine les prive de toute existence légale en raison de leur 'integration' exclusive dans l'ordre juridique de cet Etat."*

550 Freyer/Gharavi (1998), *op. cit.*, 109.

of recognition and enforcement of arbitral awards.[551] Therefore, awards under the delocalised perception are not considered to be independent of any kind of legal basis, but primarily based on a "minimum norms of transnational currency such as those reflected in the major international conventions".[552]

4. Role of the Enforcing State

The delocalised perception, which was in principle also shown by French courts, is based on the presumption that the law of the venue is not exclusively competent to determine an award's validity, but the law of the enforcement state should be "equally well positioned" to determine the validity in context of the enforcement decision,[553] and therefore "[e]ach court should have discretion to recognize and enforce a foreign arbitral award regardless of any foreign court decisions on the validity of such award"[554]

Another aspect relativising the impact of the country where the award was made is that parties to international arbitration usually stem from different countries. This means their assets are presumably often located all over the world, which necessitates that the issued award may easily be transported into the respective legal systems. Transnationalists, therefore, do not approve that the court's view in the state of arbitration should be authorative over the states in which enforcement is sought, but an award's effectiveness should be assessed where it will be in fact given effect. While the venue of the arbitration is deemed to be chosen for rather practical considerations, and its connection to the arbitration would therefore be limited to the furnishing of accommodations and conference rooms, and customary service delivery, the states of enforcement in contrast host the assets of the parties, thus having a stronger economical and legal connection to the parties and their capital.[555]

For these considerations Transnationalists reject the territorial notion that the choice of the seat of arbitration would likewise infer a choice of the applicable law.

---

551 Paulsson (1982), *op. cit.*, 54.

552 *Ibid.*, 58/59: "There is no a priori reason to criticise the law of country A" but why does the annulment decision rendered there necessarily have erga omnes effect? Country B should be allowed to consider the award properly in light of its own national law. "Might not country A in fact be relieved that whilst it has been able to uphold its local law…?"

553 Gaillard (2003), *op. cit.*, 1105: *"each court should have discrection to recognize and enforce a foreign arbitral award regardless of any foreign court decisions on the validity of such award."*

554 *Ibid.*, 1105.

555 Gaillard (1998), *op. cit.*, 673.

They emphasise that a silent agreement on the choice of law requires awareness of the parties as to such declaration and may only be assumed if the parties' interests can be established "with sufficient certainty" from the matters of the dispute.[556] However, when entering into a business contract, parties indeed might consider adequate mechanisms for resolving possible future disputes, but would not go so far to consider possible remedies against the results emanating from such a mechanism.[557] Likewise, various U.S. court decisions demonstrated that the choice of the locus where the arbitration takes place is a mere "'venue clause', not a choice-of-law clause."[558]

Even the regime of the New York Convention gives great discretionary power to the courts in the state of enforcement, explicitly allowing for disregard of a foreign annulment decision, thereby stressing that the *lex loci arbitri* is not necessarily the sole jurisdiction to determine whether the award should be given effect.[559] Instead, "the arbitral procedure is predominantly governed by the arbitration agreement and thus by party autonomy, because the drafters of the Convention did not consider it necessary to subject the arbitration to the national procedural law in the host state unless such agreement was made. Basically, the judicial control of arbitral awards is therefore confined to the review of the court in the state where enforcement is sought. Only if the arbitral award is challenged, the court that asked in the state where the arbitration took place is competent, whilst the court asked for enforcement may stay or decline the enforcement.[560] Courts in enforcing states are concerned that annulment decisions are not only based on local particularities but also intended to protect local interests, therefore they decide for enforcement assuming to uphold the bargain of the parties.[561] However, if parties intend to anchor such "floating awards" they merely need to postulate that their award be subjected to the national law at the seat of the arbitration.[562]

However, the New York Convention's "two-pronged definition" of capable awards, based on the territorial and the procedural theory and therefore differentiating between foreign and non-domestic awards dependent on the *situs* respectively

556 Epping (1999), *op. cit.*, 51.

557 Gaillard (1998), *op. cit.*, 672: *"Il est réaliste de penser qu'au moment de la signature du contrat, les parties se préoccupent certainement de l'exécution de leur contrat, parfois du contentieux de leur contrat (l'arbitrage) et rarement du contentieux du contentieux de leur contrat (le recours contre la sentence arbitrale)."*

558 Haravon (2007), *op. cit.*, 35.

559 Smit (1989), *op. cit.*, 639 et seq: *"In a real sense therefore, the Convention provides potent support for the view that the applicable law is not necessarily the lex loci arbitri."*

560 *Ibid.*, 42.

561 *Ibid.*, 630 et seq.

562 Paulsson (1982), *op. cit.*, 61.

the *lex arbitri*, has been criticised as "far from felicitous". The territorial approach was deemed to be too "mechanical", as the seat of the arbitration would not automatically identify its "character", whereas the procedural approach was considered as too "conceptual", making the award's enforceability dependent on whether the addressee state considers it as "non-domestic". Accordingly, these distinct territorial respectively procedural links were considered to have enabled inconsistent enforcement decisions, but could be corrected, if courts generally enforced arbitral awards that were apparently in accordance with their applicable law.[563] However, such an approach would not only fail to respect the discretionary powers of enforcing courts provided by Article V(1), but would also remarkably extend the scope and impact of the *lex loci arbitri*, because the addressee states may not be expected to enforce arbitral awards without at least a summary examination ensuring the maintenance of at least their national public policy.

5. Appreciation of Enforcement of Annulled Awards

National court decisions granting enforcement of arbitral awards notwithstanding their previous annulment at the arbitral seat have been considered to be "a major victory for supporters of binding international arbitration".[564] Particularly French courts and laws assiduously put forward the ambition of minimising the obstacles of local particularities.[565]

While most courts did not follow a distinct concept, but simply obeyed the rules set out by their national law in accordance with the international regimes on recognition and enforcement, French courts clearly emphasised their notion of arbitral awards as "not anchored in any national legal order at all" though noting that this would "not mean that the award is not attached to any legal system." Rather, French courts identify arbitral awards as a "decision of international justice"[566], because each state has autonomous discretionary power to determine its sovereign territory and its own standards, whether or not it is inclined to grant legal effect. A court's adjudication allowing for enforcement of a nullified award is argued not to generate "a new decision from thin air", but would solely enforce the finding of the arbitrators, which is, in turn, a result of the parties' agreed procedure.[567]

563 Smit (1989), *op. cit.*, 639 et seq.
564 Sampliner (1996), *op. cit.*, 28 et seq.
565 Gaillard (1998), *op. cit.*, 649.
566 See supra Putrabali v. Rena.
567 Webster (2006), *op. cit.*, 224.

In light of the delocalised approach such a decision is not intended to have impact on the award's objective existence as an unattached international decision.[568] Though another effect of such enforcement decisions is that courts would refrain from annulling arbitral awards in order to protect mere local interest, knowing that such annulment could not impede enforcement abroad.[569]

As to the territorial allegation that the practice of disregarding foreign annulment decisions contravenes the aimed harmonisation of international arbitration and virtually evokes inconsistent awards,[570] Transnationalists counter that the New York Convention was not aimed at harmonisation, but at facilitation of enforcement.[571]

Due to the transnational approach, enforcement decisions rather warrant the parties' bargain in favour of arbitration and a final and binding decision by the nominated arbitral panel.[572] This original bargain of the parties should not be affected by an interfering decision of a local court at the arbitral venue.[573] Such court interference would restrict the parties' freedom to select and determine a particular dispute resolution procedure and implies that "parties must be protected from their own folly".[574]

---

568 Gaillard (2007), *op. cit.*.

569 Freyer/Gharavi (1998), *op. cit.*, 109.

570 *"The conduct to which Mr. Paulsson refers is totally at odds with the Convention's purpose of facilitating the enforcement of foreign arbitral awards."* found Freyer/Gharavi (1998), *op. cit.*, 109 with reference to Paulsson, J., *Rediscovering the N.Y. Convention: Further Reflections on Chromalloy,* 12 Mealey's Int'l Arb. Rep. 20 (April 1997).

571 Paulsson (1996), *op. cit.,* 104.

572 Haravon (2007), *op. cit.*, 36.

573 Gaillard (2003), *op. cit.*, 1106: *"ne donner effet, dans un etat tiers, à la sentence annulée au siège que lorsque cette reconnaissance peut se prevaloir de la volonté supposée des parties en ce sens revient donc à introduire des distinctions byzantines et injustes".*

574 Paulsson, *Delocalisation of International Commercial Arbritration: when and why it matters*, 32 I.C.L.Q. (1982), 56: *"...and will be asked whether their resistance is based in much on genuine concern for potential future victims of failure of due process as on their desire to protect professional prerogatives"*; and 60; Webster (2006), *op. cit.*, 223 et seq. with reference to Swiss and Belgian law allowing for opt out of annulment proceedings.

III. Conclusions on the Distinct Approaches

1. Considerations on the territorial and delocalised approach

Generally, as maintained in the New York Convention, the law applicable to an arbitration proceeding can be determined based either on an objective territorial approach referring to the seat of the arbitration, or on a rather subjective procedural approach related to the stipulation of the parties.[575]

While the territorial approach is deemed to be too mechanical, the procedural approach is deemed not so easy to track, because the parties often do not clearly stipulate or preclude a particular law. Some courts and arbitration practitioners favour a strict application of the *lex loci arbitri* for the sake of clarity and predictability. Others rely on the concept of transnational arbitration in favour of the initial bargain of the parties by avoiding undue court interference at the seat of the arbitration and facilitating enforcement abroad. But it remains questionable what exactly this bargain was, since at least one party aimed to have the award set aside by resorting to the local courts, rather than longing for enforcement. Besides, an award sufficiently defective (under the territorial approach) to be set-aside in the state of the seat might be just as little acceptable (under the transnational approach) for enforcement in the addressee state.

Proponents of a transnational arbitration actually intend to detach arbitration proceedings from local laws and subject them to a rather inter- or transnational law, whilst still claiming assistance of national courts during the proceeding itself, such as a possible nomination of an arbitrator, and especially subsequent to the proceeding in terms of state recognition and enforcement. Admittedly arbitration cannot exist, however, beyond national legislations merely on a higher transnational level – cherry-picking assisting mechanism, while neglecting confining conditions. Moreover, the delocalised conception does not support predictability and legal certainty – at least for the defending party. In order to challenge the legal effect of the onerous arbitral award, the defending party would have to wait until the pursuing party initiates an enforcement proceeding, which can be objected. Consequently, the defending party would have to take action against every request in any state the pursuing party seeks for enforcement. Even if the number of potential enforcement states is limited by the allocation of the defending party's assets, each party must be given the right to challenge an unlawful, burdensome decision. Predictability and legal warranties are instead provided by the territorial approach. However, the flaw of the territorial approach is that parties might be subjected to

575 Kaufmann-Kohler, Globalization of Arbitral Procedure, 36 Vand. J. Transnat'l L. (2003), 1315.

the national law and local court interference that they did not even consider when choosing the seat of the arbitration only for reasons of convenience.

2. Conciliating Approach

Article V(1)(e) of the New York Convention maintains a conflict of law provision admitting an arbitration may be governed either by the laws "of the country in which" the award was made, i.e. the law of the seat, or alternatively by the law under which the parties submitted their arbitration, provided the law of the seat of the arbitration and the law chosen by the parties permits the choice of a foreign law, or rather the applicability abroad.[576] This New York Convention regime was actually intended to provide for predictability and legal certainty.[577] Therefore, parties are free to submit their arbitration to any law they deem appropriate to govern their proceedings. In absence of such postulation, the New York Convention provides for a subsidiary application of the law at the chosen seat of the arbitration that is aimed at ensuring the parties' (assumed) characteristic interests, easing the identification of the applicable law by avoiding intricate determination of the focus of the parties' contractual relation and promoting harmonisation of the legal connection of the arbitration agreement to a particular law.[578] Therefore, the traditional territorialist approach neglects the parties' ascertained right of choosing a law different to that of the seat of their arbitration. In practice, however, parties seldom stipulate a favoured applicable law in their arbitration agreement, or, if they do, classically agree on application of the law at the seat of their arbitration.[579] Likewise in practice, it has meanwhile been acknowledged that the actual arbitration proceeding, such as the hearings, does not necessarily need to take place at the stipulated seat of the arbitration.[580]

Parties may choose Vienna as their *locus arbitri* and nevertheless hold their meetings in Frankfurt for geostrategic reasons such as allround reachability because of the international airport. Whilst the actual venue of the arbitration is not necessarily bound to its formal seat, parties no longer have to choose their seat randomly, but for practical reasons. Consequently, the only residual determinant

576 Turner/Paulsson, Grounds for Refusal of Recognition and Enforcement Under the New York Convention: A Comparative Approach, Contribution to the OECD Experts Group Meeting on Dispute Resolution and Corporate Governance on 25 June 2003 at the UNCITRAL Secretariat, Vienna International Centre, 4.

577 Epping (1999), *op. cit.*, 54.

578 Fouchard (1967), *op. cit.*, para. 126.

579 Freyer (2000), *op. cit.*, 8.

580 Redfern/Hunter (2004), *op. cit.*, paras. 2-14 et seq.; Webster (2006), *op. cit.*, 205.

for a proper choice of seat is the *lex fori* or rather the *lex arbitri*. Therefore, it has been held that the seat of the arbitration has become a mere "legal fiction".[581] In contrast to the transnational assumption, the seat is no longer dedicated to determine the most convenient venue for both the parties and the arbitrators to hold their arbitral proceedings, but should be chosen only in order to determine an accommodating national law. The genuine purpose of denationalisation is directed at the prevention of "unintended effects of certain arbitration-hostile features" of the legislation at the seat of the arbitration, which can be equally achieved by choosing an appropriate "arbitration-friendly fictional seat," thereby meeting the Transnationalists' objective and therefore making delocalisation redundant.[582] The reference to the laws at such a fictional seat offers the greatest extent of predictability and legal certainty, and complies with many arbitration laws, which in any case provide for their application when arbitration is seated within their territory.[583] Though invariably, linking the applicable law to the seat of the arbitration, leaving no option for a deviating choice of law, might be said to curtail the scope of the New York Convention by referring not only to the law at the seat of the arbitration but also to the law under which parties subjected their arbitration. However, if the choice of a fictional seat solely serves as the choice of the applicable law, the law at the seat of the arbitration is similarly the law under which parties deliberately submitted their arbitration.[584]

Parties and their counsel can properly consider which national law best suits their individual expectations, concepts and legal relations, and accordingly choose their seat – remaining free to hold their meetings wherever considered as convenient. As today's national arbitration laws are increasingly favouring international arbitration as an autonomous instrument of dispute resolution, in order to promote their country as an attractive host state, parties could choose to have their arbitration seated in such modern arbitration venues that provide supportive assistance, while deterring their courts from undue interference. In case a party considers the award to be defective, legal remedies at reliable and competent courts are at

581 Kaufmann-Kohler (2003), *op. cit.*, 1315; van den Berg, Explanatory Note on the Hypothetic Draft Convention on the International Enforcement of Arbitration Agreements and Awards, Sec. 37: *"Unlike 50 years ago, parties are now well aware of the legal significance of choosing the place of arbitration, being that it entails the applicability of the arbitration law of the place of arbitration, and that it is not to be confused with the place of arbitration in the physical sense (cf. UNCITRAL Model Law, articles 1(2) and 20(2); see also § 94 below)."*

582 Kaufmann-Kohler (2003), *op. cit.*, 1319 et seq.

583 German Code of Civil Procedure, Sec. 1025; Swiss Private International Law Act, Ch. 12; English Arbitration Act 1996, §§ 2(1), 3; Netherlands Arbitration Act, 1986, Art. 1073(1); Swedish Arbitration Act 1999 Art. 46.

584 See also Freyer/Gharavi (1998), *op. cit.*, 115.

hand. While this conception appears to provide the most pertinent solution within the present legal framework, it is essential that parties, counsel, arbitrators and arbitration institutions give adequate consideration to the seat and the choice of seat of the arbitration.[585]

3. National Approaches De Lege Lata

Generally speaking, parties favouring a delocalised conception as their arbitration proceeding have plenty of options in choosing an appropriate seat.

Since the adoption of the 1996 Arbitration Act that intended to encourage arbitration as "one-stop adjudication", courts in Great Britain principally follow a restrictive "hands off policy". This policy perceives arbitration as a "freestanding system" that enables parties to determine their own procedure, whilst permitting the arbitrators to apply substantive laws they consider appropriate.[586]

Belgian and Swiss laws go even further by allowing for a waiver of any kind of judicial review on the arbitral award and hence, de facto, take account of the Transnationalists' notions, but also involve serious risks as to the rectification of any defects of the award or the arbitral procedure.[587]

(The frequently cited French law also provides for great freedom for the parties in determining their arbitration procedure.[588]) The French New Code of Civil Procedure maintains jurisdiction of national courts at least as to requests for setting aside of an award rendered within French territory. In this case the competent court may examine the award's compliance with substantive laws of the French legal order even if a foreign *lex arbitri* applied to the arbitration.[589]

U.S. courts were principally discordant whether a law chosen by the parties is not only intended to govern procedural issues but also substantive matters related to the performance of the main contract.[590] On the other hand, the Supreme Court

585 Paulsson (1982), *op. cit.*, 54, 55: ICC choses the seat of the arbitration for *"its geographic appropriateness given the context of a particular case"* and not due to *"its degree of confidence in the local legal system's proven compatibility with the ICC Rules of Arbitration"*.

586 Mourre/di Brozolo (2006), *op. cit.*, 178/179 with reference to Lesotho Highlands Development Authority v. Impregilo S.p.A. and others, [2005] U.K.H.L. 43.

587 See supra; Freyer/Gharavi (1998), *op. cit.*, 114.

588 The former French Code of Civil Procedure, Article 1494(1) permits the parties to *"define the procedure to be followed in the arbitral proceedings" and the determination of "a given procedural law."*

589 Kaufmann-Kohler (2003), *op. cit.*, 1317 with reference to Article 1504(1) of the French New Code of Civil Procedure.

590 Thrope (1999), *op. cit.*, 4.

found that "a broad choice of law clause" would not necessarily signify that the parties deliberately submitted "both the substantive and procedural" matters of their dispute to the stipulated law.[591]

III. Exercise of Enforcement Discretion

While a step towards predictability and conformity of outcomes may be reached by accepting the choice of the fictional seat as a choice of the applicable law, inconsistency may still occur due to the discretion given to enforcement courts by virtue of the international Conventions, particularly when facing a request for enforcement of an award annulled at the seat of the arbitration. Even if the enforcing court acknowledges the foreign annulment decision as in accordance with and in effect arising from the parties' choice of the respective national law, the enforcing court could still feel bound by its national laws to allow for enforcement. An arbitral award issued in an arbitration proceeding held in Vienna, which was deliberately chosen to open recourse actions to Austrian courts, was validly set aside in course of such action, but subsequently sought to be enforced in France. As evidenced before, French courts feel obliged to principally enforce arbitral awards in accordance with their national law pursuant to the New York Convention, Article VII, unless a reason to refuse enforcement analogous to Article 1502 of the New Code of Civil Procedure is apparent.

Another aspect in enforcement decisions is the appreciation of the foreign court's legal standards and the quality of its adjudication. The tendency is to recognise decisions of well-developed Western countries, while being more hesitant accepting adjudications from jurisdictions of non-Western cultural areas or less-sophisticated legal systems. Other criteria may be whether the judgement was rendered "in good faith" and complies with "fundamental notions of justice", which may be negated in case of bias, fraud, undue court interference, violation of due process or international public policy.[592] In contrast it is noted that "the deference" given to the adjudication of courts at the seat of an arbitration could not "justifiably depend on the degree of admiration one holds for the relevant national legal system".[593] Whilst one can speak of "Local Standard Annulments" based on

591 *Ibid.*, 4 with reference to Mastrobuono v. Shearson Lehman Hutton, Inc., No. 94-18, 514 U.S. 52 (1995); Haravon (2007), *op. cit.*, 35 with reference to Mastrobuono v. Shearson Lehman Hutton, Inc., 514 U.S. 52 (1995), XXI Y. B. Com. Arb. (1996), 181–192.

592 Park (2006), *op. cit.*, 204.

593 Paulsson (1982), *op. cit.*, 57: *"To accept delocalisation of awards rendered in developing countries, whilst rejecting it when the situs is in an industrialised country*

improper local particularities at the seat of the arbitration that ought to be rejected by enforcing courts, one may also speak of "Local Standard Enforcement" based on notions that are just as little universally valid. Not only may annulment decisions be biased, aimed at protection of local interests or deficient of due process, but also enforcement decisions may favour the interests of the corresponding nationals (in Norsolor the English court finally granted enforcement of the award in favour of its national, while French courts denied to do so; but also French courts decided half of the enforcement requests in favour of domestic parties).

There is no assurance that adjudications by enforcement courts are invariably more prudent and valuable than adjudications by courts at the forum state, nor are arbitrators principally more Solomonic than judges. National courts at the *situs* reviewing an arbitral award, and enforcing states 'reviewing' a foreign annulment both aim to revise possible mistakes of the previous decision by only questioning the discernment and sagacity of the other, but never their own.

However, it might be true that "[a]ny such thing as the 'right' solution to a legal issue is obviously a myth".[594] Therefore, the effectiveness of international arbitration on the one hand, and the avoidance of inconsistent outcomes on the other hand, may proportionally enhance "the willingness of national courts to let go of matters" they used to ascribe to their own jurisdictions.[595]

---

smacks of the distinction between civilised and uncivilised nations which we surely better had leave behind."

594 Mourre/di Brozolo (2006), op. cit., 179 with reference to di Brozolo, Antitrust: A Paradigm of the Relation between Arbitration and Mandatory Rules: A Fresh Look at the "Second Look", 23 Int'l Arb L Rev (2004), 28; di Brozolo, L'illicéité "qui crève les yeux": critère de contrôle des sentences au regard de l'ordre public international, Rev. Arb. (2005), 540-541.

595 Haravon (2007), *op. cit.*, 35 with reference to Mitsubishi Motors Corp. v. Soler Chrysler-Plymouth, Inc., 473 U.S. 614 (1985)

E. Conclusion

There is much commotion to do with enforcing arbitral awards that were previously set-aside in their forum state. Basically parties to international arbitration aim to obtain a final and binding award. Also the general trend in international arbitration conventions and many national arbitration laws is to promote the validity of arbitral awards in order to maintain arbitration as an effective instrument of autonomous dispute resolution.[596] This trend is fundamentally based on and supported by the New York and the European Conventions. However, neither Convention warrants a full protection of the parties' major goal of obtaining an effective award. The award's effectiveness is, therefore, still under threat by annulment or non-enforcement. Though some courts allow for enforcement to the greatest possible extent either based on arbitration-friendly national law, Article V(1)(e) of the New York Convention or Article IX(1) lit. a-d; other courts demonstrated their readiness to abrogate the legal effect of arbitral awards by either nullification based on the national law governing the arbitration or by refusing enforcement based on Article V(1)(e) New York Convention.

This is because neither of the Conventions provides guidance, but leaves much room for national discretion on decisive issues like jurisdiction and/or criteria for review and particularly annulment of arbitral awards. The current legal framework is therefore naturally predestined to cause inconsistent results in different countries. Even though the New York Convention contributed substantially to the facilitation of recognition and enforcement of foreign arbitral awards, its well-intentioned enforcement-friendly regime using permissive language causes much controversy and uncertainty. Even if the European Convention intended to revise certain shortcomings of the New York Convention, and indeed improved the enforceability of arbitral awards by limiting the valid reasons for enforcement refusals, it actually failed to allot jurisdiction for review of arbitral awards and set out an internationally recognised standardised catalogue of sole reasons for vacatur of an arbitral award. This would have avoided strange situations in which

596 See also Abascal (2008), op. cit., 171 et seq. with reference to van den Berg, Annulment of Awards in International Arbitration, in International Arbitration in the 21st century: Towards 'Judicalization' and Uniformity?, Lillich/Browner (eds) (1994), 135.

an award may be enforced notwithstanding its previous valid annulment in its forum state. This lack of jurisdiction is also a major oversight of the drafters of Brussels I, who, though appropriately regulating the recognition and enforcement of arbitral awards, ignored the absence of any international convention predictably conferring jurisdictional powers for binding decisions on the validity of these awards.

In light of the present legal framework concerning the arbitration, national courts may follow their own conviction as to aligning the maintenance of arbitration as an autonomous process with the co-existent need of warranting its lawfulness. Whilst some courts and national laws favour party autonomy, therefore leaving much room for party direction while reducing court interference, if at all to serious defects, other jurisdictions concentrate on warranting the observance of its national laws and are rather inclined to confine party autonomy. Similar approaches are taken to enforcement decisions, particularly as to annulled awards: some courts are satisfied and willing to grant enforcement only if the arbitral award complies with their public policy (though even among these courts inconsistencies arise as to the canon of public policy), other courts exercise their discretion on a case by case basis by taking into consideration the particularities of the foreign adjudication and its valuation, while again other courts (mainly in Germany, but also in the U.S., Belgium and the Netherlands) principally refuse to enforce annulled awards in light of international comity, disrespecting their admitted discretion.

Even though the different approaches taken by national courts when faced with a request for enforcement of an annulled award were in accordance with the *lex lata*, this does not counterbalance the emerging uncertainty and lack of predictability for parties entering into arbitration. Instead the inconsistent adjudications gave rise to the drawbacks of (i) a race and chase for enforcement and (ii) endless attempts of enforcement – in order to obtain satisfaction of the awarded claims and/or *res judicata* effect of the award. "The possibility of obtaining enforcement of a vacated award might encourage pursuing parties to apply for enforcement, rather than recommencing an arbitration proceeding at the original seat".[597] However, even if the losing party initiates a second arbitration and in fact obtains an award in his favour, it is less likely that the second, though valid award will be given effect, at least in the primary enforcement state. Even if enforcement is granted in another state (as in the Hilmarton-saga in England), such enforcement will never be able to completely undo the effects of the previous adverse enforcement. The summation of two contradictory awards is not necessarily a 'zero-sum game'.

597 Gaillard (1998), *op. cit.*, 655.

The "overarching goal" of parties choosing arbitration is to obtain a binding adjudication of their dispute in terms of an enforceable award.[598] Since parties of international arbitrations usually stem from – and more importantly have their assets located in – various countries, it is essential for the value of their adjudicated claims that their award is 'transportable', i.e. recognisable and enforceable in all asset-hosting states. In order to achieve this, the applicable enforcement standards should be similar. In respect of the present case law and legislation, such harmonisation is not yet accomplished. Even though losing parties frequently perform the awarded obligations voluntarily due to the high certitude that enforcement could anyway and anytime be obtained by assistance of national courts. This effect could be diminished if the certitude of enforceability decreases. Similarly, the reputation of arbitrators may depend on their award's capability for enforcement, and also several institutional rules and national laws require their arbitrators to issue an enforceable award.[599]

Although the significance of enforcement decisions that disregards a previous annulment is small in numbers, its indicative effect is much more sizable, and its frequency is "at risk of increasing".[600]

598 Lew (2000), *op. cit.*, 585.

599 *Ibid.*, 585 with reference to the 1998 ICC Rules of Arbitration, Article 35 and 1998 London Court of International Arbitration Rules, Article 32.2.

600 Abascal (2008), *op. cit.*, 167.

F. Recommendations

In light of the obvious gaps of the current interaction of international regimes it has often been criticised and suggested for revision.[601] The latest added multilateral act was the Brussels I Regulation, but lacking essential impact on matters of arbitration, this Regulation was not capable of reaching a legislative improvement, consistent interpretation or uniform conception to the open issues. There is still disunity on internationally acknowledged grounds for nullification of awards or uniform standards on the exercise of discretionary power on enforcement decisions. Not only do the parties principally expect their award to be final, such finality is also essential for maintaining and promoting international arbitration as a feasible instrument to settle disputes in international business matters.[602] Besides, "[p]articipants in international transactions should play according to the same rules."[603] These "rules" however, need to balance the tension between the parties' equal interest in the finality and the fairness of the issued award.

I. Recommendations De Lege Ferenda

The controversial and intensely debated decisions in favour of enforcement of vacated awards basically emerged, because not only courts (and laws) of the forum state, but also courts (and laws) of the enforcing state are equally permitted to determine the validity of arbitral awards.[604] Therefore, it is of vital importance to define the interaction of forum states and enforcing states when assessing the legal effectiveness of arbitral awards.

---

601 Freyer/Gharavi (1998), *op. cit.*, 113; Webster (2006), *op. cit.*, 201.
602 Mourre/di Brozolo (2006), *op. cit.*, 171.
603 Paulsson (1996), *op. cit.*, 114.
604 See also Gaillard (1998), *op. cit.*, 645.

1. Harmonisation of National Laws

A first improvement enforceable on a national level could be to promote harmonisation of national arbitration law, either by implementing the New York Convention or, even better, the UNCITRAL Model Law.[605] This would at least override more favourable national laws like the French arbitration law, which basically always allows for enforcement.[606] However, regarding recognition and enforcement of foreign awards the UNCITRAL Model Law reproduces *verbatim* the permissive and discretionary wording of the New York Convention ("Recognition or enforcement of an arbitral award (…) may be refused only (…)"), which is the major source of uncertainty and inconsistent interpretation.[607] Besides, such harmonisation would not only still be burdened by the complexities as to enforcement discretion, and ambiguities as to jurisdiction as currently maintained on the international level, but also be dependent on the commitment of the various countries and would therefore in any case be unlikely to achieve success.

2. Specifications on Annulment Decisions

A more feasible solution would be to determine bindingly which country has the exclusive jurisdiction to annul an arbitral award, or to establish an internationally binding set of exhaustive grounds justifying an annulment by each national court.

Admittedly, parties must be given the opportunity to challenge burdensome awards, even if arbitration should be principally maintained as a "one-shot" dispute

605 Harmonisation of national arbitration laws was recently suggested by Emmanuel Gaillard at the ICC Conference in Dublin on June, 11th 2008 by promoting that *"national arbitration laws can be amended to offer a more efficient regime that goes beyond the baseline set by the New York Convention"*. – As France did.

606 Abascal (2008), *op. cit.*, 174 with reference to the General Assemby Documents, A/54/17 Report of UNCITRAL on the work of its 32nd session, para. 376, 396: *"In 1999, the UNCITRAL decided that the topic of enforcement of awards annulled on the place of arbitration 'should be accorded high priority'"*. But already in 2000 in *"the Plenary 'the view was expressed that the issue was not expected to raise many problems and that the case law that gave rise to the issue should not be regarded as a trend'"*.

607 Paulsson (1996), *op. cit.*, 109: *"Like the NYC itself, the Model Law is a great achievement in many other way but in this particular score perpetuates exactly the same half-hearted thinking, because Article 36 simply repeats all five paragraphs of NYC Article V(1), and thereby proposes a national law on the enforcement of awards which contains the same discretionary hesitation with respect to paragraph (e)."*; see also van den Berg, Explanatory Note on the Hypothetic Draft Convention on the International Enforcement of Arbitration Agreements and Awards, Sec. 3.

resolution. There should still be a safety net on the scene,[608] but in an universally recognised mode. As evidenced in Belgium where parties, after the 1985 amendment of the Judicial Code, which principally precluded annulment actions for non-Belgian parties in international arbitrations seated within Belgium, were rather reluctant to arbitrate within Belgium, parties prefer having the opportunity to challenge utterly undue awards by means of annulment in national courts. Such annulment decisions should then be recognised as *rei judicatae.*

a) Definition of annulment standard

It may be advisable to adopt an internationally binding agreement setting out an exhaustive list of grounds serious enough to justify an annulment of the relevant award. These grounds should be limited, intending to ensure only fundamental legal principles of private procedural law, in particular due process, and are essentially to be construed restrictively, and only an annulment pursuant to such standard may be given *res judicata* effect. Among the distinct decisions in case law the following generally "accepted grounds for setting aside an award [have already been] summarised as exclusive ones: (i) nullity of the arbitration agreement; (ii) breach of the arbitration agreement; (iii) lack of due process of law; (iv) *ultra* or *infra petitia*; (v) non-arbitrability and violation of public policy. Corruption and gross offenses of a similar nature may be considered to be included as a violation of public policy."[609] A comparable set of rules of core justifications for annulments is set out by Article 34 of the UNCITRAL Model Law,[610] and should be adopted on an international law basis and become binding for all signatories, precluding any

---

608 Paulsson criticised the *"prudential argument has surface appeal"*, as he finds it *"specious"*: *"It is not obvious that we cannot live with occasional situations of inconsistent decisions"*. However it was objected: *"as the trend, during the globalization era, is towards harmonization and coordination among States, and not the nationalism symbolized by the practice of enforcement of annulled awards. The statement is audacious as it turns around the situation, seeking clumsily to justify a practice which, in reality and at best, only substitutes one evil with another evil, and which can be stricken by the same fatalist philosophy on which it attempts to rely: the international community can live with occasional archaic and/or biased judicial annulment decisions, particularly where the alleged misadventures are largely self-induced."* See Paulsson (1996), *op. cit.*, 110; Gharavi (2002), *op. cit.*, 133 at para. 318.

609 Abascal (2008), *op. cit.*, 171 et seq. with reference to van den Berg (1994), *op. cit.*, 135.

610 UNCITRAL Model Law, Article 34 – Application for setting aside as exclusive recourse against arbitral award: …
(2) An arbitral award may be set aside by the court specified in article 6 only if:
(a) the party making the application furnishes proof that:

disregard by foreign national courts.[611] The standard manifested within Article 34 of the Model Law corresponds closely to the grounds listed in Article V(1) a-d of the New York Convention, and which are also reflected in Article IX(1) lit. a-d of the European Convention. Limiting the grounds for the setting aside of arbitral awards to the grounds enumerated in Article 34 of the Model Law is therefore similar to the approach taken by Article IX(1) lit. a-d of the European Convention, which also only permits denying enforcement of set aside awards, if the setting aside is based on one such listed grounds. But unlike the European Convention's enforcement standard taking into account the annulment grounds, an international annulment standard would apply already to the recourse against the award, and would not put the defending party off to the enforcement proceeding.

If the set of rules set out in the UNCITRAL Model Law, Article 34 were necessarily to allow for annulment in case of public policy violations, the international agreement should also define a limited international standard of public policy, referring to fundamental values and strictly precluding a *révision au fond*.[612] Additionally, a claim for annulment could be precluded if the claiming party did not contest the issue before or during the arbitration proceeding, e.g. if a party got engaged in the arbitration without contradiction, the party could not claim annulment

---

(i) a party to the arbitration agreement referred to in article 7 was under some incapacity; or the said agreement is not valid under the law to which the parties have subjected it or, failing any indication thereon, under the law of this State; or
(ii) the party making the application was not given proper notice of the appointment of an arbitrator or of the arbitral proceedings or was otherwise unable to present his case; or
(iii)the award deals with a dispute not contemplated by or not falling within the terms of the submission to arbitration, or contains decisions on matters beyond the scope of the submission to arbitration, provided that, if the decisions on matters submitted to arbitration can be separated from those not so submitted, only that part of the award which contains decisions on matters not submitted to arbitration may be set aside; or
(iv)the composition of the arbitral tribunal or the arbitral procedure was not in accordance with the agreement of the parties, unless such agreement was in conflict with a provision of this Law from which the parties cannot derogate, or, failing such agreement, was not in accordance with this Law; or
(b)the court finds that:
(i) the subject-matter of the dispute is not capable of settlement by arbitration under the law of this State; or
(ii) the award is in conflict with the public policy of this State.
(3) An application for setting aside may not be made after three months have elapsed from the date on which the party making that application had received that award or, if a request had been made under article 33, from the date on which that request had been disposed of by the arbitral tribunal. …

611 See also Freyer/Gharavi (1998), *op. cit.*, 115.

612 Mourre/di Brozolo (2006), *op. cit.*, 188.

of the resulting award by asserting the invalidity of the arbitration agreement.[613] Even if the local *lex arbitri* were to preclude any review of arbitral awards, the enforcement court could be authorised to either set aside the award once and for all, or at least be bound to refuse enforcement in presence of one such listed ground. An international standard of annulment grounds would make annulment decisions predictable and traceable, although this might also be achieved through a proper choice of seat. On the other hand, an international standard would also protect parties against unforeseeable changes in legislations, whilst a considerable amount of time passes between conclusion of an arbitration agreement and the initiation of an arbitration proceeding, and even more until a possible appeal against the issued award.

However, even though an exclusive international set of rules of serious grounds would be an essential contribution on harmonising case law on validity of arbitral awards, it would not provide sufficient predictability for parties seeking a remedy. This is because especially courts in the forum states could deny jurisdiction abandoning the defending party until the pursuing party applies for enforcement and therefore enabling the defending party to object enforcement of a claim for nullification.

613 See also Mallmann (2004), *op. cit.*, 157;
Such a preclusion is available under the Dutch Arbitration Law:
Article 1065: (4) The ground mentioned in paragraph (1)(c) above shall not constitute a ground for setting aside if the party who invokes this ground has participated in the arbitral proceedings without invoking such ground, although it was known to him that the arbitral tribunal did not comply with its mandate;
(7) Notwithstanding the provisions of the second sentence of article 1064(3), the time limit for making an application for setting aside mentioned in the preceding paragraph shall be three months from the date of deposit of the additional award or the copy of the notification mentioned in article 1061(5) with the Registry ofthe District Court.
Art. 1064: (3) An application for setting aside may be made as soon as the award has acquired the force of res judicata. The right to make an application shall be extinguished three months after the date of deposit of the award with the Registry of the District Court. However, if the award together with leave for enforcement is officially served on the other party, that party may make an application for setting aside within three months after the said service, irrespective of whether the period of three months mentioned in the preceding sentence has lapsed.
Also van den Berg forsees in its Hypothetical Draft Convention on International Enforcement of Arbitration Agreements and Awards, Article 5 para. 5: "The party against whom the award is invoked cannot rely on grounds (a) to (e) of paragraph 3 if that party has not raised them in the arbitration without undue delay after the moment when the existence of the ground became known to that party."

b) Allocation of Exclusive Jurisdiction

For the sake of greater predictability an international convention could additionally be adopted, defining the exclusive competent jurisdiction for decisions on the validity of arbitral awards. Adjudications rendered by such an authority based on the defined international annulment standard should be recognised by all foreign national courts.

Adhering to the afore-discussed delocalisation concept, such jurisdiction, if any, should be deferred to the enforcing state. While the arbitral award is not integrated into the legal system of its forum state, making any interference by the local courts inappropriate and undue, arbitral awards may well be 'anchored' by application for enforcement within a particular country. This country, or rather the courts of this country, are considered to have original interest in ascertaining the legal validity of an award, because they are asked to grant its legal effect throughout their territory. The courts of enforcement might also be granted exclusive jurisdiction for nullification, so that not even another country would be allowed to enforce the nullified award. However, even if the defending party could thus achieve a binding decision that was internationally recognised, it would still be harmful being obliged to wait until the pursuing party applies for enforcement in order to initiate an appeal against an onerous award.

It might be more appropriate to grant the country where the arbitration takes place the jurisdiction to vacate the rendered award. As discussed before, there are in fact considerable reasons arguing for jurisdiction of the forum state. Not only because then the seat and thus the forum state is (or at least could be) deliberately chosen by the parties, but in contrast to the enforcing courts, forum state courts are even during the arbitration proceeding near and prepared to support a smooth functioning of the arbitration, e.g. by appointment of arbitrators or issuance of interim measures. Soon after the closing of the proceedings, the burdened party may challenge the award without an undue waiting period. Admitting the forum state's exclusive jurisdiction to bindingly define the validity of an arbitral award would provide the greatest possible predictability and legal certainty. If Transnationalists again fear undue court interference or arbitration-adverse national laws, they should carefully choose their prospective seat, considering in particular the applicable procedural laws.

For maintaining international arbitration as a self-sustaining system, which is deliberately chosen by the parties it has been suggested empowering arbitral panels either to „declare whether its award exists or not", though this solution confuses primary instance and review for remedy, or alternatively the arbitrators could be capable of determining the consequences a potential annulment would involve for the issued award.[614] However, future appeals or the continuation of an award's validity is rather in the interest of the parties than the arbitrators (although arbitrators' reputation may be connected to the enforceability of the awards), so if at all, such determination could only be made by the parties. Though a preclusion of post-annulment consequences has, except for additional litigation costs, similar effect as a pre-annulment waiver of legal remedies, which appears more elaborated and prevalent.

Nevertheless establishing an inner-arbitral review is a perspicacious notion, which might become feasible through the creation of a permanent international, independent authority for the review of arbitral awards, possibly staffed with "an elite corps of international arbitrators",[615] providing an efficient and absolute authority deciding on the validity of awards rendered in international arbitration.[616] "International Arbitration would thus become a sort of transnational "Supreme Court" with arbitrators acting as judges vested with (i) a mission equivalent to the one of Supreme Court judges but at a global level and (ii) the power then to render not just ordinary arbitral awards but quasi-divine judgements quasi-incontestable on Earth."[617] However, creating such an institution intensive in staff, administration and costs is a very complex challenge, and as the adjudication of arbitrators is not invariably wiser than civil court adjudication, one may as well consider a review of arbitral awards by the International Court of Justice. However, reviewing arbitral awards would assumably exceed the ICJ's capacity, and international arbitration practitioners may be more proficient in assessing intricacies arising out of their specialised field of activity – which is a general advantage, also opposed to a review by national courts. But still, constituting a permanent international board of arbitrators reviewing all kinds of international awards is presumably unfeasible in the foreseeable future.

Finally, it appears most appropriate for the parties if they are given the opportunity to initiate annulment proceedings in courts at the seat of the arbitration,[618] as already indicated by Article V(1)(e) of the New York Convention.[619] But also the forum state itself has a due interest in controlling the legal findings produced within its territory. Ceding some of its original prerogatives to the arbitral panel,

614 See Haravon (2007), *op. cit.*, 33.
615 Paulsson, Ethics, Elitism, Eligibility, 14 J Int. Arb. (1997), 20.
616 Freyer/Gharavi (1998), *op. cit.*, 113.
617 Gharavi (2002), *op. cit.*, 136 at para. 328.
618 See also Freyer (2000), *op. cit.*, 8.
619 XXXII Y. B. Com. Arb. (2007), 662: *"Art. V(1)(e) reflects the generally accepted rule that (...) the setting aside of an arbitral award pertains to the exclusive jurisdiction of the courts in the country of origin and is to be adjudicated on the basis of the arbitration law of that country."*

the forum state retains the right and the duty of executing a kind of "risk management" by controlling its output, i.e. awards rendered within its sovereign territory. However, awards may only be validly set aside if based on an international canon of justifications as contained in UNCITRAL Model Law, Article 34. Hence, parties would not only be granted a sophisticated, internationally recognised standard for the review of their awards, but also immediate access to national courts without undue procrastination. Also, the features or requirements for litigation (like the court system, official language or accredited/local lawyers) would not be unforeseeable, because the parties may deliberately chose the seat of their arbitration and thus the competent forum for a possible review. Attributing the courts of the forum state the jurisdiction for annulment proceedings guided by an international standard, would best balance the coexisting interests of finality of the arbitral award. For all these reasons it should be determined at an international level to grant the courts at the seat of an arbitration the exclusive jurisdiction to decide on applications for annulment of an arbitral award.

3. Definition of Enforcement Discretion

However, even if jurisdiction over annulments was bindingly determined and actually recognised, countries could still enforce arbitral awards notwithstanding their valid annulment in the forum state by virtue of their discretionary power established in New York Convention, Article V(1)(e).

Since there is no defined guidance,[620] today courts exercise their discretion in different ways, especially when they are asked for enforcement of an annulled award: while some national courts never give *res judicata* effect to foreign annulment decisions, primarily based on national law, others exercise their discretionary power and will only do so, if the annulment is based on internationally recognised grounds and/or does not violate the public policy in favour of maintaining the effectiveness of international arbitration. Lastly, a third type of court, never uses its discretion, but generally recognises foreign annulment decisions as *res judicata.*

The risk of biased decisions in favour of national interests or a lack of due process not only occurs with appeals at forum state courts, but also at courts of the enforcing state. But, while the risk of undue annulment proceedings may be avoided through a careful choice of the seat, the enforcing courts may neither be chosen nor prevented.[621]

620 See also Sampliner (1996), *op. cit.*, 23.
621 See also Gharavi (2002), *op. cit.*, 128 at para. 307.

In light of the wide-ranging discretion given to enforcing courts, it is to be determined "whether and when it is wise – or indeed obligatory on another [maybe international comity] basis" to decide for (non)enforcement of previously nullified awards.[622] Most attempts to define the courts' discretion have been identified as "cryptic or conclusory", basically requiring a denial of enforcement, if the annulment decision was "corrupt or biased".[623] Others still suggest that each sovereign country should autonomously identify the "conditions" for recognition and enforcement of arbitral awards through their courts. This might naturally involve a "qualitative evaluation of other countries' court decisions" which is actually to be avoided in light of international comity.[624] Further, it has been suggested exercising the enforcement discretion as to annulled awards involving either a recognition or disregard of the foreign annulment adjudication on the "same standard… as is used generally for other foreign judgements," indicating a refusal of enforcement if the adjudication lacked jurisdiction, violated the principles of due process and public policy, or was affected by corruption or bias. Besides, it was adduced that enforcement courts should consider that a foreign judgment annulling a finding of an arbitral authority deliberately chosen by the parties may "effectuate the intent of the contracting parties to have a forum of their choice resolve their disputes".[625] In this context, it was suggested recognising only those foreign annulment decisions that meet an "International Annulment Standard" establishing the Article V(1) lit. a-d grounds as justifications to annul arbitral awards.[626]

However, defining only the discretionary power of enforcing courts without likewise defining jurisdiction and conditions of annulment decisions is only half-way towards predictability and harmonisation. Defining the enforcement discretion as to annulment decisions according to the general standards of recognition of foreign judgements would ensure only the legal consequences of annulment decisions but not necessarily their emergence. Parties could still at first either be denied access to local courts in the forum state (e.g. as the local courts deny jurisdiction for international arbitration matters without particular links to the national legal order, but the venue of the arbitration proceedings) or obtain an annulment decision based on exceptional particularities, including even bias in favour of national interests.

For the sake of harmonisation of case law and legal certainty for parties it appears essential to establish an internationally binding set of conditions for

622 Paulsson (1996), *op. cit.,* 104.

623 Sampliner (1997), *op. cit.*, 159 et seq.

624 Gaillard (2007), *op. cit.*; Gaillard (2003), *op. cit.*, 1112; Sampliner (1997), *op. cit.*, 162.

625 Sampliner (1997), *op. cit.*, 161.

626 *Ibid.*, 162.

recognising and enforcing foreign arbitral awards, defining the discretion provided by the New York Convention, Article V(1). Likewise, it is necessarily to preclude the applicability of the 'more favourable law' clause of Article VII for enforcement decisions, since courts could thus undermine the novel enforcement barrier by recourse to their national laws.[627] Otherwise, courts would still be free to second-guess annulment decisions issued by the determined jurisdiction based on internationally agreed standards, at least with respect to their compliance with local laws. Therefore, it is additionally required to standardise annulment conditions to establish a standardised international approach towards exertion of enforcement discretion, providing for obligatory recognition of internationally accepted valid annulment decisions, and for refusal of enforcement of such annulled awards.[628] Hence, parties would be granted legal certainty and predictability as well as prevention of undue national court interference, be it by forum state courts or enforcement state courts. Similarly, the risks of ' a race for exequatur' could be diminished, as pursuing parties could no longer "chase a nullified award around the world, attempting to find a court to enforce it".[629]

4. Legal Framework

The most feasible approach to clarity and consistency involves the establishment of an international agreement allocating jurisdiction for annulment decisions to courts at forum states while likewise defining an exhaustive list of exclusive annulment grounds, whereas at the same time the discretionary power of enforcing courts is confined to recognising corresponding foreign annulment decisions. However, it is questionable if such a stipulation should be made in terms of a new agreement or as an amendment to one of the existing Conventions.

a) Brussels I Regulation

As the question of competency for annulment decisions is to be allocated to national courts, it is natural to think of an endorsement of Brussels I Regulation, revising its displayed shortcoming as to jurisdiction in arbitral matters. Due to the obvious lack of ascertained and binding jurisdiction on issues related to arbitration, and as the Brussels I Regulation has actually been drafted to provide a clear allocation of judicial competency rendering binding and recognisable adjudication, it appears

627 See also Goode (2001), *op. cit.*, 19-40.
628 See also Freyer/Gharavi (1998), *op. cit.*, 115.
629 Sampliner (1997), *op. cit.*, 162.

absolutely appropriate to amend corresponding provisions for arbitral matters in Brussels I. Such an amendment would contribute considerably to legal certainty, harmonisation and the effectiveness of international arbitration, at least within European countries. As for the non-European parties to the New York Convention, such an amendment would naturally provide no direct improvement, but might encourage adoption of a similar regime on a more international basis. Besides, it was already suggested to extend the applicability of the Brussels I Regulation to judgements that are indeed related to arbitration.[630] However it has been countered not only that Brussels I would cause more novel problems rather then solving the present one, but also that the ultimate ambition in international arbitration should be to avoid interference of national courts, i.e. an exception, not a standard.[631]

b) European Convention

Likewise the European Convention failed to define the control of arbitral awards, though Article IX(1) indicates a kind of "International Annulment Standard". However, as previously mentioned, such a standard defining only enforcement decisions does not suffice in providing appropriate guidance in annulment matters. But just like the Brussels I Regulation the European Convention's range is quite limited, thus an amendment would not have a significant impact on the globalised world of international arbitration. However, the European Convention remains adverse to any change in favour of a *res judicata* effect of foreign annulment decisions or a definition of (non)enforcement decisions with Article IX requiring parties in most instances (except for lit. a-d) to grant enforcement of nullified awards.

c) New York Convention

As all parties to the European Convention are equally subject to the New York Convention, an amendment of the latter would be wide reaching and probably provide the greatest endorsement for the harmonisation of international arbitration.

630 Poudret, Quelle Solution pour finir avec l'affaire Hilmarton?, Rev. Arb. (1998), 7.

631 Fouchard, *Suggestions pour accroitre l'effacitité internationale des sentences arbitrales,* Rev. Arb. (1998), 653: *"L'interférence des Conventions de Bruxelles et de Lugano a jusqu'ici été heureusement évitée. Si l'on venait à les appliquer, elles apprêteraient inévitablement des difficultés et des conflits de juridictions qui nous sont épargnés aujourd'hui. Plus généralement, l'intervention des juges étatiques dans l'arbitrage international doit être considérée comme anormale (sauf pour l'exécution forcée de la sentence et, en case de besoin, pour l'appui à la constitution du tribunal arbitral)."*

Besides, not only Brussels I, but also the New York Convention failed to adopt "a complete and harmonious system of control of arbitral awards".[632] Though the New York Convention is highly appreciated and a great benefit to international arbitration, as was noted before, its particular provisions have ever since been debated, and even the risk of (non)enforcement of awards annulled in the forum state was envisaged and amendments have been suggested for the revision of the language of Article V(1), eliminating the 'more favourable law' clause, or defining the 'binding' requirement.[633]

In June 2008 at the ICC Conference in Dublin on the occasion of the 50th anniversary of the New York Convention the most recent proposal as to a reform or even replacement was made by Prof. van den Berg asking "[a]re we too complacent with a text and structure now 50 years old?", emphasising that some provisions would need to be added, others would need to be revised and some would need to be clarified.[634] Van den Berg's draft is addressed to the "International Enforcement of Arbitration Agreements and Awards" and focuses on modernising the enforcement regime, while keeping it "clear and simple".[635] Primarily the discretionary 'may' of Article V was replaced by a mandatory "shall be refused" for avoidance of inconsistent interpretations, and the list of limitative enforcement refusals applies "in manifest cases only",[636] while enforcement of annulled awards may only be refused in a similar manner to the European Convention, Article IX(1) if the annulment decision is based on one of the enumerated grounds.[637] Besides, the debated 'binding' requirement of New York Convention, Article III was effaced.[638] Van den Berg also aimed to abolish the 'procedural approach' as to the determination of the applicable law, holding "the reference to the law under which the award was made" "outdated" and emphasising that the choice of the

632 Gharavi (2002), *op. cit.*, 124 para. 295.

633 Paulsson (1996), *op. cit.*, 99 with reference to van den Berg (1981), *op. cit.*, 355; Webster (2006), *op. cit.*, 223 and at fn. 82; Freyer/Gharavi (1998), *op. cit.*, 114 and fn. 62.

634 Van den Berg (2007), *op. cit.*, 49: *"The cracks of the Convention are already visible. It is not a question of whether it is revised, but when"*. Copies of van den Berg's draft convention and his explanatory note thereto are available on the ICCA website: *http://www.arbitration-icca.org/articles.html?author=Albert_Jan_van_den_Berg&sort=author*

635 Van den Berg (2008), *op. cit.*, para. 2.

636 *Ibid.*, para. 72, 75.

637 *Ibid.*, para. 89, 92, the valid annulment grounds correspond closely to the generally recognised grounds set forth in UNCITRAL Model Law, Article 34(2)(a), and are intended to conciliate the opposite positions of New York Convention, Article V(1)(e) allowing for refusal of annulled awards regardless of the underlying grounds, while French arbitration law does not allow for refusal of enforcement of annulled awards at all.

638 *Ibid.*, para. 48.

arbitral seat implies a choice of the applicable law.[639] This focus on the law of the seat for all matters concerning the validity of the arbitral procedure and award[640] provides clarity and is a considerable improvement. But it does not suffice (for the afore-noted reasons) with regard to annulment standards and still subjects the parties to local particularities and potential changes in law. A further textual indication for a continued promotion of arbitration as an autonomous system is the intended shift in terminology, no longer confined to "foreign" arbitral awards, but rather on "international enforcement".[641]

However, the evaluation of the draft, as generally of the New York Convention, varied; while some welcomed its "elegant simplicity", others objected that there was "no need to reinvent the wheel", for one thing due to the low number of today's refusals of enforcement, and also because inconsistencies in enforcement would not genuinely arise from the Convention's regime, but from its "misapplication by judiciaries and the state organs", including bias in favour of state owned entities, which might be better diminished by "education programmes for judges",[642] an international index identifying the objective enforcement risk in different countries and an obligation for courts to disclose their reasons for enforcement decisions. Besides, it was noted that even a revised New York Convention would still necessarily provide for a public policy exception, reopening a backdoor for local concepts.[643]

While it is essential to preclude enforcement of annulled awards, it is important as a counterbalance that enforcement is not necessarily precluded or adjourned, if an annulment proceeding is being initiated in the forum state, which would enable the defending party to easily obstruct enforcement.[644]

However, putting up the New York Convention for rediscussion might encourage states to opt out by declining signature of the new draft. Anyway, achieving a concordant draft is an intricate challenge requiring a consensus among all current 142 parties to the New York Convention, and could even backfire as some signatories might rather claim provisions for standardised recognition of foreign

639 *Ibid.,* para. 1(e), 35 et seq.

640 See also *ibid.*, para. 18, 88: *"The competence to consider and decide on the setting aside of an arbitral award belongs exclusively to the courts of the country where the award was made. ... Setting aside ... can be considered and decided by courts of any country insofar as it concerns the courts' (territorial) jurisdiction."*

641 *Ibid.*, para. 7 and 8.

642 Education programs were already suggested by Freyer/Gharavi (1998), *op. cit.*, 114 and fn. 62.

643 Jan Paulsson stated that he remains *"relentlessly neutral"* on the issue.

644 See also Jan Paulsson (1996), *op. cit.,* 112.

annulment decisions.[645] Nevertheless, the New York Convention provides the most suitable framework (either in the form of amendment or endorsement) for adopting both an international annulment standard for forum states and a limitation of the enforcement discretion granting *res judicata* effect to foreign annulment decisions.

As all parties to the European Convention are also subject to the New York Convention, the amendment/endorsement should for the avoidance of doubt expressly provide for its priority over the European Convention, Article IX(1)lit. a-d, even though the adoption of a new enforcement regime has precedence due to *lex posterior derogat legi priori*.

II. Recommendations De Lege Lata

1. Choice of Seat

As long as the New York Convention is not officially reformed, it is advisable for parties, counsels and arbitrators in international arbitrations to consider the choice of the arbitral seat as a choice of the *lex loci arbitri*. Parties can secure for themselves a certain degree of predictability by properly drafting their arbitration agreement and carefully choosing the seat of the arbitration, not only by looking for a neutral venue, but by also taking into account any distinctions of local law, particularly with focus on the grounds for annulment and the functionality of the court system. Subsequently, not only the law of the forum state applies to the arbitral procedure, but the local courts are also available for assistance while the proceeding, or legal remedies against the award, providing the parties a sound legal protection and stability.

2. Waiver of Review

In case parties intend to avoid any court engagement at all, they might also either stipulate an explicit waiver of review, or postulate that their award should be final and binding. However, the validity or effectiveness of such clauses is debated. Several national arbitration laws provide for a waiver of review,[646] or provide like

645 See also Jan Paulsson und Peter Turner at the ICCA Conference in Dublin, and Freyer/ Gharavi (1998), *op. cit.*, 114 and fn. 62.

646 English Arbitration Act, Section 69; Netherlands Arbitration Act, Article 1065(1)(c),(e); Swiss Private International Law Act, Article 192.

many institutional rules for "final and binding" awards,[647] while others like the U.S. Arbitration Act and the corresponding case law deny the validity of such a waiver,[648] though in *Chromalloy* enforcement of the annulled award was granted only because the court found the foreign annulment to contravene the parties' initial agreement on a "final and binding" award. A principal interpretation of "final and binding" clauses as an exhaustive waiver of all means of judicial review would therefore be of remarkable impact. [649]

Proponents argue that parties having full faith in the integrity of private dispute resolution or merely aiming to prevent "the delay, expense and publicity of a post-award court challenge, should be given the right to subject their dispute ultimately to "the mercy of private arbitrators".[650] On the opposite side, it was assumed as "relatively clear" that an entire waiver of judicial review is not valid under the New York Convention[651] and would preclude legal remedies "even in cases involving fraud, procedural irregularities, or exertion of improper influences upon arbitrators".[652] For avoidance of such disadvantages waivers of judicial review, if even valid, are frequently said to be construed as solely precluding a review on the merits, but not "as barring applications to enforce or to set aside awards on the limited grounds set forth in the New York Convention" and in several arbitration—friendly national laws.[653]

The conciliating and prevailing notion is apparently to determine the validity and scope of waivers of judicial recourse accordant to the applicable law of the

---

647 Art. 28(6) of the ICC Rules of Arbitration (1998): *"Every award shall be binding on the parties. By submitting the dispute to arbitration under these Rules, the parties undertake to carry out any award without delay and shall be deemed to have waived their right to any form of recourse insofar as such waiver can validly be made."*; Art. 26(9) of the London Court of International Arbitration Rules (1998): *"awards shall be final and binding... the parties... waive irrevocably their right to any form of appeal, review or recourse... insofar as such waiver may be validly made."*; Art. 32(2) of the UNCITRAL Rules: *"The award shall be made in writing and shall be final and binding on the parties."*; Art. 27(1) of the American Arbitration Association International Arbitration Rules (1997): *"Awards shall be made in writing, promptly by the tribunal, and shall be binding and final on the parties."*

648 Hamlin (1998), *op. cit.*, 55 et seq; see also Lew (2000), *op. cit.*, 587, and Freyer (2000), *op. cit.*, 6 at fn. 25.

649 Freyer (2000), *op. cit.*, 7 with further references.

650 Hamlin (1998), *op. cit.*, 56.

651 *Ibid.*, 60.

652 *Ibid.*, 60 with reference to the U.S. Sixth Circuit Court of Appeals in M&C Corp v. Erwin Behr GmbH, 87 F.3d at 847.

653 Freyer (2000), *op. cit.*, 6; Freyer/Gharavi (1998), *op. cit.*, 101 at 114-115 and note 44, King, Enforcing Annulled Awards: U.S. Courts Chart Their Own Course, 15 Mealey's Int Arb Rep (2000), at 15, 19, 21, note 25.

forum state.[654] Thus, if parties aim to eliminate all forms of review this option is needs to be taken into account when choosing the arbitral seat, but parties should also carefully consider whether they actually intend to preclude recourse even for violations of fundamental notions like due process, and be aware that enforcing courts might construe that awards precluded from all means of national review are not capable of enforcement under the New York Convention.[655] The most practical approach is, therefore, to choose a seat where the applicable arbitration law indeed provides for a preclusion of judicial review, but not for grounds corresponding to New York Convention, Article V(1).[656]

3. Courts of Enforcement

Enforcing courts should principally aim to respect foreign annulment decisions for the sake of consistency and international comity, even though they are given greater discretion under the current enforcement regime and an automatic *erga omnes* effect of the foreign judgement might add up to an undue intervention in terms of public international law. However, whenever the European Convention, Article IX(1) applies, enforcing states could be obliged to enforce an arbitral award even though the court review resulting in the annulment was initially involved in the parties' considerations and subsequent stipulation.

4. Concluding Remarks

At first glance enforcement of annulled awards may appear cynical. However, thorough analysis reveals not only a valid legal basis for such decisions, but also legitimate considerations of national and international legislation, international comity and party autonomy.

Still, in light of the current legal framework there is too much latitude for both annulment decisions and enforcement decisions, likewise entailing a sizeable degree of unpredictability and a lack of clarity. Even though parties can conduce to legal certainty by detailed and diligently stipulated arbitration agreements, includ-

654 Freyer (2000), *op. cit.*, 6 and 7.

655 Gaillard (1998), *op. cit.*, 663: *"S'il est vrai qu'une sentence annulée dans l'Etat d'origine n'a plus aucune existence légale et, que, de ce fait, elle ne peut être exécutée ailleurs, il devrait en aller de même des sentences qui, faute de pouvoir trouver dans l'ordre juridique du siège la justification de leur juridicité, ne correspondraient pas davantage à la philosophie de la Convention."*

656 Freyer (2000), *op. cit.*, 8 et seq.

ing a studied choice of their arbitral seat, as can arbitrators, by paying sufficient attention to the *lex loci arbitri* and possibly even to distinct laws in prospective enforcement states, but some factors linked to the 'overarching goal' of enforcement still remain within the remit of the sovereign states and may only be harmonised on international law basis.[657] Though it may be said each particular transborder business transaction involves certain risks which cannot be completely relieved on a legal basis,[658] the present risks related to undue annulment and (non)enforcement could very well be diminished by means of an international treaty confining the relevant conditions for adjudications by national courts.

In total, it may be concluded that since the adoption of the first Geneva Treaties back in the 1920's, international arbitration has undergone a remarkable development towards a recognised and popular means of neutral and flexible dispute resolution, particularly for international business transactions, which is largely due to the trend-setting New York Convention as well as the modernisation of national arbitration laws. In comparison with enforcement of court judgments, the enforcement quota of arbitral awards is still encouraging, approximately 90 per cent of all arbitral awards are either voluntarily performed or enforced, out of which in fact only a small number will ever by set aside.[659] The issue of enforcement of annulled awards is not quotidian, but rather occurs once in a while. Yet, whenever it occurs it causes quite a stir and much debate among arbitrators, judges and scholars, and is particularly surprising for the concerned parties. Therefore, it remains important to close the floodgates for unpredictable and inconsistent (non)enforcement decisions.

Nevertheless arbitration is legitimately expected "to remain the common method" of dispute resolution in border-crossing commercial matters and investments,[660] which will be the case all the more if the discussed ambiguities are revised. On that score, it was proposed that increasingly harmonised arbitration laws might one day become "truly interchangeable" making it negligible which law is to apply.[661] Should this occur, arbitration will be genuinely harmonised.

---

657 As Prof. van den Berg once stated: *"'[T]he unfortunate few' simply constitute a collection of lessons to be learned by parties, arbitrators, arbitral institutions and national courts on order to ensure the efficacy and enforceability of awards."* van den Berg, *Refusals of Enforcement under the New York Convention of 1958: The Unfortunate Few*, 10 ICC Bulletin (1999), 75 (Special Supplement), 94; Tannock (2005), *op. cit.*, 75.

658 Haravon (2007), *op. cit.*, 36; Paulsson (1998), *op. cit.*, 14.

659 Webster (2006), *op. cit.*, 201; Tannock (2005), *op. cit.*, 84 with reference to van den Berg, Refusals of Enforcement under the New York Convention of 1958: The Unfortunate Few, 10 ICC Bulletin (1999) (Special Supplement), at 75.

660 Tannock (2005), *op. cit.*, 72.

661 Kaufmann-Kohler (2003), *op. cit.*, 1320.

United Nations Convention on the Recognition and Enforcement of Foreign Arbitral Awards (New York, 10 June 1958)

Article I

1. This Convention shall apply to the recognition and enforcement of arbitral awards made in the territory of a State other than the State where the recognition and enforcement of such awards are sought, and arising out of differences between persons, whether physical or legal. It shall also apply to arbitral awards not considered as domestic awards in the State where their recognition and enforcement are sought.

2. The term "arbitral awards" shall include not only awards made by arbitrators appointed for each case but also those made by permanent arbitral bodies to which the parties have submitted.

3. When signing, ratifying or acceding to this Convention, or notifying extension under article X hereof, any State may on the basis of reciprocity declare that it will apply the Convention to the recognition and enforcement of awards made only in the territory of another Contracting State. It may also declare that it will apply the Convention only to differences arising out of legal relationships, whether contractual or not, which are considered as commercial under the national law of the State making such declaration.

Article II

1. Each Contracting State shall recognize an agreement in writing under which the parties undertake to submit to arbitration all or any differences which have arisen or which may arise between them in respect of a defined legal relationship, whether contractual or not, concerning a subject matter capable of settlement by arbitration.

2. The term “agreement in writing” shall include an arbitral clause in a contract or an arbitration agreement, signed by the parties or contained in an exchange of letters or telegrams.

3. The court of a Contracting State, when seized of an action in a matter in respect of which the parties have made an agreement within the meaning of this article, at the request of one of the parties, refer the parties to arbitration, unless it finds that the said agreement is null and void, inoperative or incapable of being performed.

Article III

Each Contracting State shall recognize arbitral awards as binding and enforce them in accordance with the rules of procedure of the territory where the award is relied upon, under the conditions laid down in the following articles. There shall not be imposed substantially more onerous conditions or higher fees or charges on the recognition or enforcement of arbitral awards to which this Convention applies than are imposed on the recognition or enforcement of domestic arbitral awards.

Article IV

1. To obtain the recognition and enforcement mentioned in the preceding article, the party applying for recognition and enforcement shall, at the time of the application, supply:

(a) The duly authenticated original award or a duly certified copy thereof;

(b) The original agreement referred to in article II or a duly certified copy thereof.

2. If the said award or agreement is not made in an official language of the country in which the award is relied upon, the party applying for recognition and enforcement of the award shall produce a translation of these documents into such language. The translation shall be certified by an official or sworn translator or by a diplomatic or consular agent.

Article V

1. Recognition and enforcement of the award may be refused, at the request of the party against whom it is invoked, only if that party furnishes to the competent authority where the recognition and enforcement is sought, proof that:

(a) The parties to the agreement referred to in article II were, under the law applicable to them, under some incapacity, or the said agreement is not valid under the law to which the parties have subjected it or, failing any indication thereon, under the law of the country where the award was made; or

(b) The party against whom the award is invoked was not given proper notice of the appointment of the arbitrator or of the arbitration proceedings or was otherwise unable to present his case; or

(c) The award deals with a difference not contemplated by or not falling within the terms of the submission to arbitration, or it contains decisions on matters beyond the scope of the submission to arbitration, provided that, if the decisions on matters submitted to arbitration can be separated from those not so submitted, that part of the award which contains decisions on matters submitted to arbitration may be recognized and enforced; or

(d) The composition of the arbitral authority or the arbitral procedure was not in accordance with the agreement of the parties, or, failing such agreement, was not in accordance with the law of the country where the arbitration took place; or

(e) The award has not yet become binding on the parties, or has been set aside or suspended by a competent authority of the country in which, or under the law of which, that award was made.

2. Recognition and enforcement of an arbitral award may also be refused if the competent authority in the country where recognition and enforcement is sought finds that:

(a) The subject matter of the difference is not capable of settlement by arbitration under the law of that country; or

(b) The recognition or enforcement of the award would be contrary to the public policy of that country.

Article VI

If an application for the setting aside or suspension of the award has been made to a competent authority referred to in article V (1) (e), the authority before which the award is sought to be relied upon may, if it considers it proper, adjourn the decision on the enforcement of the award and may also, on the application of the party claiming enforcement of the award, order the other party to give suitable security.

Article VII

1. The provisions of the present Convention shall not affect the validity of multilateral or bilateral agreements concerning the recognition and enforcement of arbitral awards entered into by the Contracting States nor deprive any interested party of any right he may have to avail himself of an arbitral award in the manner and to the extent allowed by the law or the treaties of the country where such award is sought to be relied upon.

2. The Geneva Protocol on Arbitration Clauses of 1923 and the Geneva Convention on the Execution of Foreign Arbitral Awards of 1927 shall cease to have effect between Contracting States on their becoming bound and to the extent that they become bound, by this Convention.

Article VIII

1. This Convention shall be open until 31 December 1958 for signature on behalf of any Member of the United Nations and also on behalf of any other State which is or hereafter becomes a member of any specialized agency of the United Nations, or which is or hereafter becomes a party to the Statute of the International Court of Justice, or any other State to which an invitation has been addressed by the General Assembly of the United Nations.

2. This Convention shall be ratified and the instrument of ratification shall be deposited with the Secretary-General of the United Nations.

Article IX

1. This Convention shall be open for accession to all States referred to in article VIII.

2. Accession shall be effected by the deposit of an instrument of accession with the Secretary-General of the United Nations.

Article X

1. Any State may, at the time of signature, ratification or accession, declare that this Convention shall extend to all or any of the territories for the international relations of which it is responsible. Such a declaration shall take effect when the Convention enters into force for the State concerned.

2. At any time thereafter any such extension shall be made by notification addressed to the Secretary-General of the United Nations and shall take effect as from the ninetieth day after the day of receipt by the Secretary-General of the United Nations of this notification, or as from the date of entry into force of the Convention for the State concerned, whichever is the later.

3. With respect to those territories to which this Convention is not extended at the time of signature, ratification or accession, each State concerned shall consider the possibility of taking the necessary steps in order to extend the application of this Convention to such territories, subject, where necessary for constitutional reasons, to the consent of the Governments of such territories.

Article XI

In the case of a federal or non-unitary State, the following provisions shall apply:

(a) With respect to those articles of this Convention that come within the legislative jurisdiction of the federal authority, the obligations of the federal Government shall to this extent be the same as those of Contracting States which are not federal States;

(b) With respect to those articles of this Convention that come within the legislative jurisdiction of constituent states or provinces which are not, under the constitutional system of the federation, bound to take legislative action, the federal Government shall bring such articles with a favourable recommendation to the notice of the appropriate authorities of constituent states or provinces at the earliest possible moment;

(c) A federal State Party to this Convention shall, at the request of any other Contracting State transmitted through the Secretary-General of the United Nations, supply a statement of the law and practice of the federation and its constituent units in regard to any particular provision of this Convention, showing the extent to which effect has been given to that provision by legislative or other action.

Article XII

1. This Convention shall come into force on the ninetieth day following the date of deposit of the third instrument of ratification or accession.

2. For each State ratifying or acceding to this Convention after the deposit of the third instrument of ratification or accession, this Convention shall enter into force on the ninetieth day after deposit by such State of its instrument of ratification or accession.

Article XIII

1. Any Contracting State may denounce this Convention by a written notification to the Secretary-General of the United Nations. Denunciation shall take effect one year after the date of receipt of the notification by the Secretary-General.

2. Any State which has made a declaration or notification under article X may, at any time thereafter, by notification to the Secretary-General of the United Nations, declare that this Convention shall cease to extend to the territory concerned one year after the date of the receipt of the notification by the Secretary-General.

3. This Convention shall continue to be applicable to arbitral awards in respect of which recognition and enforcement proceedings have been instituted before the denunciation takes effect.

Article XIV

A Contracting State shall not be entitled to avail itself of the present Convention against other Contracting States except to the extent that it is itself bound to apply the Convention.

Article XV

The Secretary-General of the United Nations shall notify the States contemplated in article VIII of the following:

(a) Signatures and ratifications in accordance with article VIII;

(b) Accessions in accordance with article IX;

(c) Declarations and notifications under articles I, X and XI;

(d) The date upon which this Convention enters into force in accordance with article XII;

(e) Denunciations and notifications in accordance with article XIII.

Article XVI

1. This Convention, of which the Chinese, English, French, Russian and Spanish texts shall be equally authentic, shall be deposited in the archives of the United Nations.

2. The Secretary-General of the United Nations shall transmit a certified copy of this Convention to the States contemplated in article VIII.

European Convention on International Commercial Arbitration

Preamble

The undersigned, duly authorized, Convened under the auspices of the Economic Commission for Europe of the United Nations, Having noted that on 10th June 1958 at the United Nations Conference on International Commercial Arbitration has been signed in New York a Convention on the Recognition and Enforcement of Foreign Arbitral Awards, Desirous of promoting the development of European trade by, as far as possible, removing certain difficulties that may impede the organization and operation of international commercial arbitration in relations between physical or legal persons of different European countries, Have agreed on the following provisions:

Article I – Scope of the Convention

(1) This Convention shall apply:

(a) to arbitration agreements concluded for the purpose of settling disputes arising from international trade between physical or legal persons having, when concluding the agreement, their habitual place of residence or their seat in different Contracting States;

(b) to arbitral procedures and awards based on agreements referred to in paragraph 1(a) above.

For the purpose of this Convention,

(a) the term "arbitration agreement" shall mean either an arbitral clause in a contract or an arbitration agreement being signed by the parties, or contained in an exchange of letters, telegrams, or in a communication by teleprinter and, in relations between States whose laws do not require that an arbitration agreement be made in writing, any arbitration agreement concluded in the form authorized by these laws;

(b) the term "arbitration" shall mean not only settlement by arbitrators appointed for each case (ad hoc arbitration) but also by permanent arbitral institutions;

(c) the term "seat" shall mean the place of the situation of the establishment that has made the arbitration agreement.

Article II – Right of legal persons of public law to resort to arbitration

(1) In the cases referred to in Article I, paragraph 1, of this Convention, legal persons considered by the law which is applicable to them as "legal persons of public law" have the right to conclude valid arbitration agreements.

(2) On signing, ratifying or acceding to this Convention any State shall be entitled to declare that it limits the above faculty to such conditions as may be stated in its declaration.

Article III – Right of foreign nationals to be designated as arbitrators

In arbitration covered by this Convention, foreign nationals may be designated as arbitrators.

Article IV – Organization of the arbitration

(1) The parties to an arbitration agreement shall be free to submit their disputes:

(a) to a permanent arbitral institution; in this case, the arbitration proceedings shall be held in conformity with the rules of the said institution;

(b) to an ad hoc arbitral procedure; in this case, they shall be free inter alia

(i) to appoint arbitrators or to establish means for their appointment in the event of an actual dispute;

(ii) to determine the place of arbitration; and

(iii) to lay down the procedure to be followed by the arbitrators.

(2) Where the parties have agreed to submit any disputes to an ad hoc arbitration, and where within thirty days of the notification of the request for arbitration to the respondent one of the parties fails to appoint his arbitrator, the latter shall, unless otherwise provided, be appointed at the request of the other party by the President of the competent Chamber of Commerce of the country of the defaulting party's habitual place of residence or seat at the time of the introduction of the request for arbitration. This paragraph shall also apply to the replacement of the arbitrator(s)

appointed by one of the parties or by the President of the Chamber of Commerce above referred to.

(3) Where the parties have agreed to submit any disputes to an ad hoc arbitration by one or more arbitrators and the arbitration agreement contains no indication regarding the organization of the arbitration, as mentioned in paragraph 1 of this article, the necessary steps shall be taken by the arbitrator(s) already appointed, unless the parties are able to agree thereon and without prejudice to the case referred to in paragraph 2 above. Where the parties cannot agree on the appointment of the sole arbitrator or where the arbitrators appointed cannot agree on the measures to be taken, the claimant shall apply for the necessary action, where the place of arbitration has been agreed upon by the parties, at his option to the President of the Chamber of Commerce of the place of arbitration agreed upon or to the President of the competent Chamber of Commerce of the respondent's habitual place of residence or seat at the time of the introduction of the request for arbitration. Where such a place has not been agreed upon, the claimant shall be entitled at his option to apply for the necessary action either to the President of the competent Chamber of Commerce of the country of the respondent's habitual place of residence or seat at the time of the introduction of the request for arbitration, or to the Special Committee whose composition and procedure are specified in the Annex to this Convention. Where the claimant fails to exercise the rights given to him under this paragraph the respondent or the arbitrator(s) shall be entitled to do so.
(4) When seized of a request the President or the Special Committee shall be entitled as need be:

(a) to appoint the sole arbitrator, presiding arbitrator, umpire, or referee;

(b) to replace the arbitrator(s) appointed under any procedure other than that referred to in paragraph 2 above;

(c) to determine the place of arbitration, provided that the arbitrator(s) may fix another place of arbitration;

(d) to establish directly or by reference to the rules and statutes of a permanent arbitral institution the rules of procedure to be followed by the arbitrator(s), provided that the arbitrators have not established these rules themselves in the absence of any agreement thereon between the parties.

(5) Where the parties have agreed to submit their disputes to a permanent arbitral institution without determining the institution in question and cannot agree ther-

eon, the claimant may request the determination of such institution in conformity with the procedure referred to in paragraph 3 above.

(6) Where the arbitration agreement does not specify the mode of arbitration (arbitration by a permanent arbitral institution or an ad hoc arbitration) to which the parties have agreed to submit their dispute, and where the parties cannot agree thereon, the claimant shall be entitled to have recourse in this case to the procedure referred to in paragraph 3 above to determine the question. The President of the competent Chamber of Commerce or the Special Committee, shall be entitled either to refer the parties to a permanent arbitral institution or to request the parties to appoint their arbitrators within such time-limits as the President of the competent Chamber of Commerce or the Special Committee may have fixed and to agree within such time-limits on the necessary measures for the functioning of the arbitration. In the latter case, the provisions of paragraphs 2, 3 and 4 of this Article shall apply.

(7) Where within a period of sixty days from the moment when he was requested to fulfil one of the functions set out in paragraphs 2, 3, 4, 5 and 6 of this Article, the President of the Chamber of Commerce designated by virtue of these paragraphs has not fulfilled one of these functions, the party requesting shall be entitled to ask the Special Committee to do so.

Article V – Plea as to arbitral jurisdiction

(1) The party which intends to raise a plea as to the arbitrator's jurisdiction based on the fact that the arbitration agreement was either non-existent or null and void or had lapsed shall do so during the arbitration proceedings, not later than the delivery of its statement of claim or defence relating to the substance of the dispute; those based on the fact that an arbitrator has exceeded his terms of reference shall be raised during the arbitration proceedings as soon as the question on which the arbitrator is alleged to have no jurisdiction is raised during the arbitral procedure. Where the delay in raising the plea is due to a cause which the arbitrator deems justified, the arbitrator shall declare the plea admissible.

(2) Pleas to the jurisdiction referred to in paragraph 1 above that have not been raised during the time-limits there referred to, may not be entered either during a subsequent stage of the arbitral proceedings where they are pleas left to the sole discretion of the parties under the law applicable by the arbitrator, or during subsequent court proceedings concerning the substance or the enforcement of the

award where such pleas are left to the discretion of the parties under the rule of conflict of the court seized of the substance of the dispute or the enforcement of the award. The arbitrator's decision on the delay in raising the plea, will, however, be subject to judicial control.

(3) Subject to any subsequent judicial control provided for under the lex fori, the arbitrator whose jurisdiction is called in question shall be entitled to proceed with the arbitration, to rule on his own jurisdiction and to decide upon the existence or the validity of the arbitration agreement or of the contract of which the agreement forms part.

Article VI – Jurisdiction of courts of law

(1) A plea as to the jurisdiction of the court made before the court seized by either party to the arbitration agreement, on the basis of the fact that an arbitration agreement exists shall, under penalty of estoppel, be presented by the respondent before or at the same time as the presentation of his substantial defence, depending upon whether the law of the court seized regards this plea as one of procedure or of substance.

(2) In taking a decision concerning the existence or the validity of an arbitration agreement, courts of Contracting States shall examine the validity of such agreement with reference to the capacity of the parties, under the law applicable to them, and with reference to other questions

(a) under the law to which the parties have subjected their arbitration agreement;

(b) failing any indication thereon, under the law of the country in which the award is to be made;

(c) failing any indication as to the law to which the parties have subjected the agreement, and where at the time when the question is raised in court the country in which the award is to be made cannot be determined, under the competent law by virtue of the rules of conflict of the court seized of the dispute.

The courts may also refuse recognition of the arbitration agreement if under the law of their country the dispute is not capable of settlement by arbitration.

(3) Where either party to an arbitration agreement has initiated arbitration proceedings before any resort is had to a court, courts of Contracting States subsequently asked to deal with the same subject-matter between the same parties or with the question whether the arbitration agreement was non-existent or null and void or had lapsed, shall stay their ruling on the arbitrator's jurisdiction until the arbitral award is made, unless they have good and substantial reasons to the contrary.

(4) A request for interim measures or measures of conservation addressed to a judicial authority shall not be deemed incompatible with the arbitration agreement, or regarded as a submission of the substance of the case to the court.

Article VII – Applicable law

(1) The parties shall be free to determine, by agreement, the law to be applied by the arbitrators to the substance of the dispute. Failing any indication by the parties as to the applicable law, the arbitrators shall apply the proper law under the rule of conflict that the arbitrators deem applicable. In both cases the arbitrators shall take account of the terms of the contract and trade usages.

(2) The arbitrators shall act as amiables compositeurs if the parties so decide and if they may do so under the law applicable to the arbitration.

Article VIII – Reasons for the award

The parties shall be presumed to have agreed that reasons shall be given for the award unless they

(a) either expressly declare that reasons shall not be given; or

(b) have assented to an arbitral procedure under which it is not customary to give reasons for awards, provided that in this case neither party requests before the end of the hearing, or if there has not been a hearing then before the making of the award, that reasons be given.

Article IX – Setting aside of the arbitral award

(1) The setting aside in a Contracting State of an arbitral award covered by this Convention shall only constitute a ground for the refusal of recognition or enforcement in another Contracting State where such setting aside took place in a State in which, or under the law of which, the award has been made and for one of the following reasons:

(a) the parties to the arbitration agreement were under the law applicable to them, under some incapacity or the said agreement is not valid under the law to which the parties have subjected it or, failing any indication thereon, under the law of the country where the award was made, or

(b) the party requesting the setting aside of the award was not given proper notice of the appointment of the arbitrator or of the arbitration proceedings or was otherwise unable to present his case; or

(c) the award deals with a difference not contemplated by or not falling within the terms of the submission to arbitration, or it contains decisions on matters beyond the scope of the submission to arbitration, provided that, if the decisions on matters submitted to arbitration can be separated from those not so submitted, that part of the award which contains decisions on matters submitted to arbitration need not be set aside;

(d) the composition of the arbitral authority or the arbitral procedure was not in accordance with the agreement of the parties, or failing such agreement, with the provisions of Article IV of this Convention.

(2) In relations between Contracting States that are also parties to the New York Convention on the Recognition and Enforcement of Foreign Arbitral Awards of 10th June 1958, paragraph 1 of this Article limits the application of Article V(1)(e) of the New York Convention solely to the cases of setting aside set out under paragraph 1 above.

Article X – Final clauses

(1) This Convention is open for signature or accession by countries members of the Economic Commission for Europe and countries admitted to the Commission in a consultative capacity under paragraph 8 of the Commission's terms of reference.

(2) Such countries as may participate in certain activities of the Economic Commission for Europe in accordance with paragraph 11 of the Commission's terms of reference may become Contracting Parties to this Convention by acceding thereto after its entry into force.

(3) The Convention shall be open for signature until 31 December 1961 inclusive. Thereafter, it shall be open for accession.

(4) This Convention shall be ratified.

(5) Ratification or accession shall be effected by the deposit of an instrument with the Secretary-General of the United Nations.

(6) When signing, ratifying or acceding to this Convention, the Contracting Parties shall communicate to the Secretary-General of the United Nations a list of the Chambers of Commerce or other institutions in their country who will exercise the functions conferred by virtue of Article IV of this Convention on Presidents of the competent Chambers of Commerce.

(7) The provisions of the present Convention shall not affect the validity of multilateral or bilateral agreements concerning arbitration entered into by Contracting States.

(8) This Convention shall come into force on the ninetieth day after five of the countries referred to in paragraph 1 above have deposited their instruments of ratification or accession. For any country ratifying or acceding to it later this Convention shall enter into force on the ninetieth day after the said country has deposited its instrument of ratification or accession.

(9) Any Contracting Party may denounce this Convention by so notifying the Secretary-General of the United Nations. Denunciation shall take effect twelve months after the date of receipt by the Secretary-General of the notification of denunciation.

(10) If, after the entry into force of this Convention, the number of Contracting Parties is reduced, as a result of denunciations, to less than five, the Convention shall cease to be in force from the date on which the last of such denunciations takes effect.

(11) The Secretary-General of the United Nations shall notify the countries referred to in paragraph 1, and the countries which have become Contracting Parties under paragraph 2 above, of

(a) declarations made under Article II, paragraph 2;

(b) ratifications and accessions under paragraphs 1 and 2 above;

(c) communications received in pursuance of paragraph 6 above;

(d) the dates of entry into force of this Convention in accordance with paragraph 8 above;

(e) denunciations under paragraph 9 above;

(f) the termination of this Convention in accordance with paragraph 10 above.

(12) After 31 December 1961, the original of this Convention shall be deposited with the Secretary-General of the United Nations, who shall transmit certified true copies to each of the countries mentioned in paragraphs 1 and 2 above.

Bibliography

Books

Berger, K.	*International Economic Arbitration (Studies in Transnational Economic Law)*, Springer Verlag, Vienna 1993.
Bollée, S.	*Les methodes du droit international privé à l'épreuve des sentences arbitrales N° 8*, Economica (2004).
Epping, M.	*Die Schiedsvereinbarung im internationalen Rechtsverkehr nach der Reform des deutschen Schiedsverfahrensrechts*, C.H. Beck Verlagsbuchhandlung, Munich 1999.
Fasching, H. W.	*Kommentar zu den Zivilprozeßgesetzen*, Manzsche Verlags- und Universitätsbuchhandlung, Wien 2007.
Fouchard, Ph.	*L'arbitrage commercial international*, Librairie Balloz, Paris 1967.
Fouchard, Ph. Gaillard, E. Savage, J.	*Fouchard Gaillard Goldmann On International Commercial Arbitration*, Aspen Publishers, New York 1999.
Gharavi, H.	*The International Effectiveness of the Annulment of an Arbitral Award*, Kluwer Law International, The Hague 2002.
Greimer, R.	*Internationales Zivilprozeßrecht*, Verlag Dr. Otto Schmid, Köln 2001.
Haas, U.	*Convention on the Recognition and Enforcement of Foreign Arbitral Awards, New York, June 10, 1958*, in Weigand, F.-B. (ed.), *Practioner's Handbook on International Arbitration*, C.H. Beck Verlag, Munich 2002.

Heller, L., Berger, F., Stix, L. — *Die Exekutionsordnung*, Angst, P., Jakusch, W. (eds.), Manz'sche Verlagsbuchhandlung, Vienna 1988.

Lew, J.D.M. — *Proof of Applicable Law in International Commercial Arbitration*, in: Festschrift Otto Sandrock zum 70. Geburtstag, K. Berger, W. Epke, S. Elsing (eds.), Recht und Wirtschaft, Frankfurt 2000, p. 581.

Kleinknecht, A. — *Die verbraucherschützenden Gerichtsstände im deutschen und europäischen Zivilprozeßrecht*, LIT Verlag, Berlin 2007.

Kropholler, J. — *Europäisches Zivilprozeßrecht: Kommentar zu EuGVO, Lugano-Übereinkommen und Europäischem Vollstreckungstitel*, Recht und Wirtschaft, Frankfurt 2005.

Menzel, J., Pierlings, T., Hoffmann, J. — *Völkerrechtssprechung, Ausgewählte Entscheidungen zum Völkerrecht in Retrospektive*, Mohr Siebeck, 2004.

Park, W. — *Arbitration of International Business Disputes: Studies in Law and Practice*, Oxford University Press 2006.

Paulsson, J. — *International Handbook on Commercial Arbitration: National Reports and Basic Legal Texts*, Looseleaf, Suppl. 26, Kluwer Law International, The Hague 1998.

Rauscher, Th., Wax, P., Wenzel, J. — *Münchener Kommentar zur Zivilprozeßordnung,* Vol. 3, C. H. Beck Verlag, Munich 2008.

Redfern, A., Hunter M. — *Law and Practice of International Commercial Arbitration*, Sweet & Maxwell Limited, Bath Press, London 2004.

Sanders, P.	IX Y. B. Com. Arb., Kluwer International Law, The Hague 1984.
	X Y. B. Com. Arb., Kluwer International Law, The Hague 1985.
Schlosser, P.	*Das Recht der internationalen privaten Schiedsgerichtsbarkeit*, Mohr Siebeck Verlag, Tübingen 1989.
	Rechtsverfolgung im Ausland: Prozessführung vor ausländischen Gerichten und Schiedsgerichten, Recht und Wirtschaft, Heidelberg 1998.
	Die Bedeutung eines ausländischen Urteils über die Wirksamkeit eines Schiedsspruchs für dessen Exequierung im Inland, in: *Jahrbuch für die Praxis der Schiedsgerichtsbarkeit,* Vol. 3, Ottoarndt Glossner (ed.), Verlag Recht und Wirtschaft GmbH, Heidelberg 1989.
Schütze, R.A. Tschernig, D. Wais, W.	*Handbuch des Schiedsverfahrens – Praxis der deutschen und internationalen Schiedsgerichtsbarkeit*, Walter de Gruyter, Berlin 1985.
Schwab, K. H. Walter, G.	*Schiedsgerichtsbarkeit*, Verlag C. H. Beck, München 2005.
Schwind, F.	*Handbuch des Internationalen Österreichischen Privatrechts*, Springer, Wien 1975.
Siehr, K.	*Internationales Privatrecht, Deutsches und Europäisches Kollisionsrecht für Studium und Praxis*, C.F. Müller Verlag, 2001.
Smit, H. Pechota, V.	*International Arbitration Treaties*, Juris Publishing, Inc., New York 2005.
Solomon, D.	*Die Verbindlichkeit von Schiedssprüchen in der internationalen privaten Schiedsgerichtsbarkeit*, Selier European Law Publishers, Munich 2007.

van den Berg, A. *The New York Convention of 1958: Towards a Uniform Judicial Interpretation*, Kluwer Law and Taxation, Boston 1981.

XV Y. B. Com. Arb., A. van den Berg (ed.), Kluwer Law International, The Hague 1990.

XIX Y. B. Com. Arb., A. van den Berg (ed.), Kluwer Law International, The Hague 1994.

XX Y. B. Com. Arb., A. van den Berg (ed.), Kluwer Law International, The Hague 1995.

XXI Y. B. Com. Arb., A. van den Berg (ed.), Kluwer Law International, The Hague 1996.

XXII Y. B. Com. Arb., A. van den Berg (ed.), Kluwer Law International, The Hague 1997.

XXIVa Y. B. Com. Arb., A. van den Berg (ed.), Kluwer Law International, The Hague 1999.

XXIII Y. B. Com. Arb., A. van den Berg (ed.), Kluwer Law International, The Hague 2003.

XXX Y. B. Com. Arb., A. van den Berg (ed.), Kluwer Law International, The Hague 2005.

XXXII Y. B. Com. Arb., A. van den Berg (ed.), Kluwer Law International, The Hague 2007.

XXXIII Y. B. Com. Arb., A. van den Berg (ed.), Kluwer Law International, The Hague 2008.

The New York Arbitration Convention of 1958, Informationsveranstaltung Internationale Vollstreckung von ausländischen Schiedssprüchen, Wien 08 June 1989.

The New York Arbitration Convention of 1958: Towards a Uniform Judicial Interpretation, Kluwer Law International, The Hague 1994.

Essays

Abascal, J. M. — Effects of Annulment, Dispute Resolution International (2008), 171.

Alvarez, H. — *The Enforcement of Arbitral Awards*, Commercial Arbitration (Continuing Legal Education, June 1996) at 1.1.19.

Braumüller, G. — *Das Schicksal im ehemaligen Jugoslawien ergangener „internationaler" Schiedssprüche*, WBL 1996, 99 .

Brekoulakis, S. — *The Notion of the Superiority of Arbitration Agreements over Jurisdiction Agreements: Time to Abandon It?*, 24 J. Int'l Arb (2007), 341.

Delaume, G. — *Enforcement Against a Foreign State of an Arbitral Award Annulled in the Foreign State*, RDAI 1997, 253.

Reflections on the Effectiveness of International Arbitral Awards, 12 J. Int'l Arb (1995), 5.

Derains, Y. Goodman-Everard, R. — France, Annex I-II, Suppl. 26, February 1998, in *International Handbook on Commercial Arbitration*, Paulsson (ed.), 1998.

Dubarry, J. C., Loquin, E. — Note sous Hilmarton, RTD com. 1994, 702.

Erecinski, T. — *Die Aufhebung eines in der internationalen Handelsschiedsgerichtsbarkeit getroffenen Schiedsspruchs durch ein staatliches Gericht*, Jahrbuch der Schiedsgerichtsbarkeit (1989), 14.

Fouchard, Ph. — *Suggestions pour accroitre l'effacitité internationale des sentences arbitrales*, Rev. Arb. 1998, 653.

Freyer, D. H. — *The Enforcement of Awards Affected by Judicial Orders of Annulment at the Place of Arbitration*, in May, Cameron (ed.), Enforcement of Arbitration Agreements and International Arbitral Awards the New York Convention in Practice, 757.

United States Recognition and Enforcement of Annulled Foreign Arbitral Awards – The Aftermath of the Chromalloy Case, 17 J. Int'l Arb (2000), 1.

Freyer, D. H.
Gharavi, H. G. — *Finality and Enforceability of Foreign Arbitral Awards: From "Double Exequatur" to the Enforcement of Annulled Awards: A Suggested Path of Uniformity Admist Diversity*, 13 ICSID Review – Foreign Investment Law Journal (1998), 101.

Gaillard, E. — *Anti-suit injunctions et reconnaissance des sentence annulées au siège, une évolution remarquable de la jurisprudence américaine*, J. D. I. (2003), 45.

The Representations of International Arbitration, New York Law Journal, October 4, 2007.

Enforcement of Nullified Foreign Award, New York Law Journal, October 2, 1997.

Gharavi, H. — *Chromalloy: Another View*, Mealey's Int. Arb. Rep. 1997, 21.

The Legal Inconsistencies of Chromalloy, Mealey's Int. Arb. Rep 1997.

Gomez, M. — *Internationale Schiedsgerichtsbarkeit und Binnenmarkt*, IPRax 2005, 84.

Goode, R. — *The Role of Lex Loci Arbitri in International Commercial Arbitration*, 17 Arb. Int. 2001, 32.

Goldmann, B. — *Une bataille judiciare autour de la lex mercatoria*, Rev. Arb. 1983, 379.

Gómez, M. — *Internationale Schiedsgerichtsbarkeit und Binnenmarkt*, IPRax 2005, 84.

Haas, U. — *Der Ausschluß der Schiedsgerichtsbarkeit vom Anwendungsbereich des EuGVÜ*, IPRax 1992, 292.

Hamlin, J. B. — *Contractual Alteration of the Scope of Judicial Review: The US Experience*, 15 J. Int'l Arb 1998, 47.

Haravon, M. — *Enforcement of Annulled Foreign Arbitral Awards : The French Supreme Court Confirms the Hilmarton Trend*, 22 Mealey's Int. Arb. Rep. 2007, 32.

Hascher, D. — *Principe et pratique de procédure dans l'arbitrage commcercial international*, 279 RCADI (1999), 51.

Recognition and Enforcement of Judgements on the Existence and Validity of an Arbitration Clause under the Brussels Convention, 13 Arb. Int. (1997), 33.

Horvath, G. — *What weight should be given to the Annulment of an Award under the Lex Arbitri? – The Austrian and German Perspectives*, 26 J. Int'l Arb (2009), 249.

Hulbert, R. — *Further Observations on Chromalloy: A Contract Misconstrued, a Law Misapplied, and an Oportunity Foregone* (1998) 13 ICSID Review – Foreign Investment Law Journal, 124.

Jarrosson, Ch. — Note sous *Hilmarton*, Rev. Arb. 1994, 164.

Kaufmann-Kohler, G. — *Globalization of Arbitral Procedure*, 36 Vanderbilt Journal of Transnational Law (2003), 1314.

Qui contrôle l'arbitrage? Autonomie des parties, pouvoir des arbitres et principe d'efficacité, Liber Amicorum Claude Reymond – Autour de l'arbitrage, Litec Paris, 2004, 153.

King, D. B. — *Enforcing Annulled Awards: U.S. Courts Chart Their Own Course*, 15 Mealey's Int. Arb. Rep. 2000, 15.

Koch, Ch. — *The Enforcement of Awards Annulled in their Place of Origin: The French and U.S. Experience*, 26 J Int'l Arb (2009), 291.

Kreindler, R. — *Arbitral Forum Shopping: Observations on Recent Developments in International Commercial and Investment Arbitration*, in *Parallel State and Arbitral Procedures in International Arbitration – Dossiers of the ICC Institute of World Business Law*, Cremades/Lew (eds), ICC Publishing, 2005.

Kröll, Stefan — *Antragsvoraussetzungen und Präklusion im Verfahren zur Vollstreckbarerklärung ausländischer Schiedssprüche*, IPRax 2002, 384.

OLG Rostock, 28 October 1999 – 1 Sch 3/1999; Add 8 zu BB 2000, 20.

Die schiedsrechtliche Rechtsprechung 2007 (part 2), SchiedsVZ 2007, 119.

Lalive, P. — *Les règles de conflit de lois appliquées au fond du litige par l'arbitre international siégant en Suisse,* in L'arbitrage international privé et la Suisse, Rev. Arb. 1972, 155.

Transnational (or Truly International) Public Policy and International Arbitration, in *Comparative Arbitration Practice and Public Policy in Arbitration*, 3 ICCA Congress Series 1998, 256.

Lastenouse, P. — *Why Setting Aside an Arbitral Awards is not Enough to Remove it from the International Scene*, 16 J Int'l Arb 1999, 25.

Lew, J.D.M. — *Achieving the Dream: Autonomous Arbitration*, 22 Arb. Int. 2006, 179.

Mallmann, R. — *Die Bedeutung der Schiedsvereinbarung im Verfahren zur Anerkennung und Vollstreckbarerklärung ausländischer Schiedssprüche*, SchiedsVZ 2004, 152.

Mann, F. A. — *Lex Facit Arbitrum*, in International Arbitration: Liber Amicorum for Martin Domke (1967), 157.

Mayer, P. — *L'Etat et le droit international privé,* 16 Droits 1993, 33.

Mezger, E.	*Das Europäische Übereinkommen über die Handelsschiedsgerichtsbarkeit*, RabelsZ 29 (1965), 231.
Michaels, Ralf	*Anerkennung internationaler Schiedssprüche und ordre public*, Anm. zu OGH 23.02.1998, 3 Ob 115/95 (OLG Wien 10.07.1995, 14 R 56/95; LG Wien 01.12.1994, 30 Nc 102/89), ZfRV 1999, 5.
Mourre, A. Radicati di Brozolo, L.	*Towards Finality of Arbitral Awards: Two Steps Forward and One Step Back,* 2 J. Int'l Arb 2006, 171.
Mustill, M. J.	*Arbitration: History and Background*, 6 J. Int'l Arb 1989, 43.
Neuteufel, K.	*Das Europäische Übereinkommen über die internationale Handelsschiedsgerichtsbarkeit*, Anwaltsblatt 2004, 547.
Oberhammer, P.	*Gemeinschaftsrecht und schiedsrechtlicher ordre public*, RdW 1999, 62.
Öhlberger, V.	*Vollstreckung ausländischer Schiedssprüche in Österreich und deren Formvoraussetzungen nach dem New Yorker Übereinkommen*, SchiedsVZ 2007, 78.
Oppetit, B.	Note sous Cass. 1st, 23 March 1994, *Hilmarton*, RCDIP 1995, 356.
Paulsson, J.	*Enforcing Arbitral Awards Notwithstanding a Local Standard Annulment (LSA)*, 9 ICC Bull. 1998, 14 .
	Ethics, Elitism, Eligibility, 14 J. Int'l Arb, 1997, 13.
	May or Must Under the New York Convention: An Exercise in Syntax and Linguistics, 14 Arb. Int. 1998, 227.
	Arbitration Unbound: Award Detached From the Law of its Country of Origin, ICLQ 1981, 358.
	Delocalisation of International Commercial Arbitration: When and Why it Matters, ICLQ 1983, 53.

The Case for Disregarding LSAS (Local Standard Annulments) under the New York Convention, Am. Rev. Int. Arb. 1996, 99.

Arbitre et juge en Suède: Exposé général et réflexions sur la délocalisation des sentences arbitrales, Rev. Arb. 1980, 476.

L'éxecution des sentences arbitrales en dépit d'une annulation en fonction d'un critère local (ACL), 1 ICC Bull. (1998), p. 14.

Sovereign Immunity from Execution in France, International Lawyer, 1977, 674.

Plaßmeier, H. *Vollstreckung nicht "endgültiger" Schiedssprüche – Zugleich eine Anmerkung zum Beschluss des BayObLG vom 22.11.2002* (SchiedsVZ 2003, 142), SchiedsVZ 2004, 234.

Posch, W. *Vergemeinschaftung des Kollisionsrechts und die Verordnung Rom II,* University of Graz, online publication available on: www.uni-graz.at/eurechtundpolitik/Rom_II_Prof.Posch.pdf.

Poudret, J.F. *Quelle Solution pour finir avec l'affaire Hilmarton? Reponse à Philipp Fouchard,* Rev. Arb. 1998, 7.

Pryles, M. *Reflections on Transnational Public Policy*, 24 J. Int'l Arb 2007, 1.

Radicati di Brozolo, L. *Antitrust: A Paradigm of the Relation between Arbitration and Mandatory Rules: A Fresh Look at the "Second Look"*, 23 Int. Arb. L. Rev. 2004, 28.

Reiner, A. *Zur Vollstreckung eines Schiedsspruchs nach dem Europäischen Übereinkommen von 1961 trotz Aufhebung im Ursprungsland und zum Umfang der ordre public – Kontrolle nach Art. 81, 82 EGV*, IPRax 2000, 323.

Sampliner, G. *Enforcement of Nullified Foreign Arbitral Awards – Chromalloy Revisited,* 14 J. Int'l Arb 1997, 141.

Enforcement of Foreign Arbitral Awards after Annullment in their Country of Origin, 11 Mealey's Int. Arb. Rep. 1996, 22.

Sanders, P. *A Twenty Years' Review of the Convention on the Recognition and Enforcement of Foreign Arbitral Awards*, 13 The International Lawyer 1979, 269.

Schwartz, E. *A Comment on Chromalloy Hilmarton, à l'américaine*, 14 J. Int'l Arb 1997, 125.

Smit, H. *The Internationalization of Law and Legal Practice: A-national Arbitration*, Tul. L. Rev. 1989, 629.

Söderlund, Ch. *Lis Pendens, Res Judicata and the Issue of Parallel Judicial Proceedings*, 22 J. Int'l Arb 2005, 301.

Tannock, Q. *Judging the Effectiveness of Arbitration through the Assess ment of Compliance with and Enforcement of International Arbitration Awards*, 21 Arb. Int. 2005, 71.

Thrope, Jessica *A Question of Intent: Choice of Law and the International Arbitration Agreement*, Disp. Resol. J. 1999, 16.

Turner, P. *Grounds for Refusal of Recognition and Enforcement Under the New York Convention: A Comparative Approach*, Experts Group Meeting on Dispute Resolution and Corporate Governance, 2003, available online: *http://www.oecd.org/dataoecd/2/62/3860479.pdf*

van den Berg, A. *New York Convention of 1958: Refusals of Enforcement*, 18 ICC Bull. 2007, 15.

Annulment of Awards in International Arbitration, in Lillich, R.B. and Browner, Ch.N. (eds), *International Arbitration in the 21st century: Towards 'Judicalization' and Uniformity?*, Twelfth Sokol Colloquium (1994), 135.

Enforcement of Annulled Awards, 9 ICC Bull. 1998, 15.

Hypothetical Draft Convention on the International Enforcement of Arbitration Agreements and Awards and *Explanatory Note,* available online on: *http://www.arbitration-icca.org/media/0/12133703697430/explanatory_note_ajb_rev06.pdf*

Verbist, H. *Reform des belgischen Rechts der Schiedsgerichtsbarkeit,* Add 42 to BB 1998, 5.

Webster, Th. *Evolving Principles in Enforcing Awards Subject to Annulment Proceedings*, 23 J. Int'l Arb 2006, 201.

Wetter, J. G. *The Present Status of the International Court of Arbitration of the ICC: An Appraisal*, 1 Am. Rev. Int. Arb. 1990, 91.

Case Law

Austrian Case Law

Supreme Court of Austria, 23 February 1998, 3 Ob 115/95, published on RIS, ZfRV 1999, 24; IPRax 2000, 314.

Supreme Court of Austria, 20 October 1993, 3 Ob 117/93, published on RIS, SZ 66, 131; EvBl 49, 513.

Supreme Court of Austria, 26 January 2005, 3 Ob 221/04b published on RIS.

Belgian Case Law

Brussels Court of First Instance. 6 December 1988, unreported, but excerpts in XV Y. B. Com. Arb., P. Sanders (ed.) (1990), 370.

Dutch Case Law

District Court of Amsterdam of July 12, 1984, translated in 24 I.L.M. (1985), p. 1040,

Court of Appeals of Paris of 12 July 1984;

French Supreme Court, 6 January 1987, 2 Mealey's Int. Arb. Rep. 1987, 17.

French Case Law

Berardi v. Clair

Court of Appeal of Paris, 20 June 1980, Unpublished Case No. 11542, excerpts in VII Y. B. Com. Arb., P. Sanders (ed.), (1982), 319.

Palbak Ticaret v. Norsolor

Award of 26 October 1984 in ICC Case No. 3131, IX Y. B. Com. Arb. (1984), 109-110

Cour de Cassation, 18 November 1982, in IX Y. B. Com. Arb., P. Sanders (ed.) (1984), 159.

Polish Ocean Line v. Jolasry

Court de Cassation, 10 March 1993, in 2 Rev. Arb. 1993, 276; XIX Y. B. Com. Arb., A. van den Berg (ed.) (1994), 662.

OTV v. Hilmarton

Award of 19 August 1988, ICC Case No. 5622, published in XIX Y. B. Com. Arb. (1994), 105 et seq.

Court of Appeal of Geneva, 17 November 1989, in Rev. Arb. 1993, 327; XIX Y. B. Com. Arb., A. van den Berg (ed.) (1994), 214 .

Supreme Court, 17 April 1990, in Rev. Arb. 1993, 322.

Court of Appeal of Paris, 19 December 1991, in XIX Y. B. Com. Arb., A. van den Berg (ed.) (1994), 655.

Tribunal de Grande Instance Nanterre, 22 September 1993, in XX Y. B. Com. Arb., A. van den Berg (ed.) (1995), 194.

Cour de Cassation, 23 March 1994, in 2 Rev. Arb. 1994, 327.

Court of Appeal of Versailles, 29 June 1995, 4 Rev. Arb. 1995, 630.

High Court of Justice, Queen's Bench Division, 24 May 1999, in XXIVa Y. B. Com. Arb., A. van den Berg (ed.) (1999), 777.

Lesbats v. Esterer (Dr. V. Gruber)

Court of Appeal of Paris, 18 January 2007, No. 05/10887, in XXXII Y. B. Com. Arb., A. van den Berg (ed.) (2007), 297.

Putrabali v. Rena Holding

Cour de Cassation, 29 June 2007, 3 Rev. Arb. 2007, 507; XXXII Y. B. Com. Arb., A. van den Berg (ed.) (2007), 299.

Court of Appeal Paris, 31 March 2005, 3 Rev. Arb. 2005, 792; 3 Rev. Arb. 2006, 665.

German Case Law

Higher Regional Court of Rostock, order of 28 October 1999 – 1 Sch 3/99, in Add 8 to BB 2000, 20.

Higher Regional Court of Berlin, order of 18 May 2006 – 20 Sch 13/04, in SchiedsVZ 2007, 100.

Higher Regional Court of Dresden, order of 31 January 2007 – 11 Sch 18/05, in SchiedsVZ 2007, 327.

Higher Regional Court of Thuringia, order 08 August 2007 – 4 Sch 03/06, in SchiedsVZ 2008, 44.

U. S. Case Law

Chromalloy v. Egypt

Court of Appeals of Cairo, 5 December 1995, in XXIVa Y. B. Com. Arb., A. van den Berg (ed.) (1999), 265.

District Court of Columbia, 31 July 1996, 939 F. Supp. 907, in XXII Y. B. Com. Arb., A. van den Berg (ed.) (1997), 1001.

Alghanim v. Toys "R" Us et al.

Court of Appeals for the Second Circuit, 126 F.3d 15, 19, (13) cert. denied, 522 U. S. 1111, 118 S. Ct. 1042, 140 L.Ed.2d 107 (1998) in XXIII Y. B. Com. Arb., A. van den Berg (ed.) (1998), 1058.

Baker Marine v. Chevron

Court of Appeals for the Second Circuit, 12 August 1999, Nos. 97-9615, 97-9617 in XXIVa Y. B. Com. Arb., A. van den Berg (ed.) (1999), 909.

Spier v. Calzaturificio

District Court of Southern New York, No. 86 Civ. 3447 (CHS), 22 October 1999, in XXV Y. B. Com. Arb., A. van den Berg (ed.) (2000), 641.

Petramina v. KBC

Court of Appeals for the Fifth Circuit, 18 June 2003, No. 02-20550, in XXVIII Y. B. Com. Arb., A. van den Berg (ed.) (2003), 908.

TermoRio v. Electrana

District Court of Columbia, 17 March 2006, No. Civ.A. 03-2587(PLF), XXXI Y. B. Com. Arb., A. van den Berg (ed.) (2006), 1457.

Columbia Court of Appeals, 25 May 2007, 487 F.3d 928, No. 06-7058, XXXIII Y. B. Com. Arb., A. van den Berg (ed.) (2008), 955.

European Court of Justice

Marc Rich u. Justice Co. AG/Societa Italiana Impianti PA

Decision of 25 July 1991 – Rs C-190/89 in NJW 1993, 189 – 190.

Dieter Krombach v. André Bamberski

Decision of 28 March 2000 – Rs. C – 7/98, in IPRax 2000, 406.

Eco Swiss ChinaTime Ltd./Benetton International NV, Hoge Raad der Nederlanden

Decision of 01 June 1999, Rs. C-126/97, in WBL 1999, 409.

Zusammenfassung

Die vorliegende Arbeit befasst sich mit der Frage, ob und unter welchen Voraussetzungen ein Schiedsspruch, der im Forumstaat aus Nichtigkeitsgründen aufgehoben wurde, anschließend im Ausland noch vollstreckt werden kann.

Um sich der Antwort auf diese Frage zu nähern, werden in der Arbeit zunächst die grundlegenden völkerrechtlichen Abkommen dargestellt, welche die Anerkennung und Vollstreckung von Schiedssprüchen regeln:

Das bedeutendste dieser Abkommen ist das Übereinkommen der Vereinten Nationen über die Anerkennung und Vollstreckung ausländischer Schiedssprüche von 1958. Während dieses Übereinkommen darauf gerichtet ist, die Anerkennung und Vollstreckung von Schiedssprüchen in anderen Staaten grundsätzlich zu erleichtern und zu fördern, sieht es aber auch Fälle vor, in welchen die Anerkennung und Vollstreckung ausnahmsweise versagt werden kann, beispielsweise wenn ein Schiedsspruch aufgehoben wurde. Fraglich ist dabei allerdings, ob es sich um ein "Versagen dürfen" oder „Versagen müssen" handelt.

Für die Vollstreckung in europäischen Staaten kann neben dem UN-Übereinkommen auch das Übereinkommen des Europarats über die Handelsschiedsgerichtsbarkeit von 1961 Anwendung finden, das sich in einem Artikel der Vollstreckung von im Forumstaat aufgehobenen Schiedssprüchen zuwendet.

In welchem Verhältnis diese beiden bedeutenden Abkommen zueinander stehen und nach welchem letztlich über die Vollstreckung eines aufgehobenen Schiedsspruchs zu entscheiden ist, ist Gegenstand der weiteren Ausführungen der Arbeit, ehe anschließend die entsprechende Vollstreckungspraxis nationaler Gerichte in ausgesuchten europäischen Staaten sowie in den USA untersucht wird.

Da sich aus dieser Vollstreckungspraxis jedoch keine einheitliche Anwort auf die Frage der Vollstreckbarkeit eines zuvor aufgehobenen Schiedsspruchs entwickeln lässt, wird im Weiteren untersucht, ob und inwiefern die EuGVVO bei der Anerkennung entweder des Schiedsspruchs oder des ihn aufhebenden Gerichtsurteils weiterzuhelfen vermag.

Im letzten Teil der Arbeit werden sodann verschiedene Ansätze zu einer Vereinheitlichung der Vollstreckungspraxis von im Ausland aufgehobenen Schiedssprüchen vorgeschlagen und ihre Tauglichkeit erörtert.

Völkerrecht, Europarecht und Internationales Wirtschaftsrecht

Herausgegeben von Peter Hilpold und August Reinisch

www.peterlang.de

www.ingramcontent.com/pod-product-compliance
Ingram Content Group UK Ltd.
Pitfield, Milton Keynes, MK11 3LW, UK
UKHW021832100926
8556IPUK00004B/296

9 783631 603789